SEMPER FI

STORIES OF THE UNITED STATES MARINES
FROM BOOT CAMP TO BATTLE

SEMPER FI

STORIES OF THE UNITED STATES MARINES FROM BOOT CAMP TO BATTLE

EDITED BY CLINT WILLIS

Thunder's Mouth Press
New York

SEMPER FI:
STORIES OF THE UNITED STATES MARINES FROM BOOT CAMP TO BATTLE

Compilation copyright © 2003 by Clint Willis
Introductions copyright © 2003 by Clint Willis

Adrenaline® and the Adrenaline® logo are trademarks of
Avalon Publishing Group Incorporated, New York, NY.

An Adrenaline Book®

Published by
Thunder's Mouth Press
An Imprint of Avalon Publishing Group Incorporated
161 William Street, 16th floor
New York, NY 10038

Book design: Sue Canavan

frontispiece photo: Attacking Marines, Vietnam, October 17, 1970; Copyright:
© Hulton-Deutsch Collection/Corbis

Library of Congress Cataloging-in-Publication Data is available.

ISBN 1-56025-504-8

Printed in the United States of America

Distributed by Publishers Group West

For Andrew "Duke" Stevens

c o n t e n t s

Introduction

Every good story is a story about love, and war stories are no exception. The Marine Corps sells itself to potential recruits as an institution whose members are bound together by mission and purpose. The institution's motto, *Semper Fi,* expresses a commitment to perpetual loyalty that is derived from love. And Marines are not always shy about owning up to this attachment, which arises in training and combat. For some Marines it becomes a feeling they cannot lose or do without; it sustains and comforts them in their affliction.

The Marine Corps lays the groundwork for this attachment in part by isolating its recruits from their fellow citizens. Some newly minted Marines, fresh from basic training, already find civilian life contemptibly lax. John Schaeffer wrote these lines in the days after he finished boot camp:

> This place makes
> No sense, people slouch,
> Doors close in front of
> Old women, people are fat!
> I hate the rudeness, the chaos . . .

Schaeffer is among many boot camp graduates dismayed to find that the friends they left on street corners a few weeks ago are still there. These young Marines already have found an identity and a home; shared values and a way to live; a community that offers them purpose. They think they have discovered a way to grow up and away from lives that may have offered little status or fulfillment. They are grateful; they are learning to love the Marine Corps.

This is just guesswork, of course; and every Marine experience is different. But these stories help us to imagine how some Marines experience their attachment to each other. Some stories suggest how that attachment evolves during combat. It becomes less innocent and more passionate; a coldness also seeps in; there is more anger and more pain associated with it. We are reminded that love is a feeling; that it does not abide within conceptual parameters; that it arises amid the most vile slaughter and hatred and then disappears.

Love has shapes and agendas; it assigns us roles that we don't choose or even notice. The attachment that Marines form for each other in training or combat may resurface later as something more familiar; as a memory like certain other memories associated with loss or awakening—abhorrent and precious at once; this memory belongs in us; it defines us; it *is* us.

Here is how William Manchester recalled his love for his fellow Marines on Okinawa during World War II:

> I had been, and after the war I would again be, a man who usually prefers his own company, finding contentment in solitude. But for the present I had taken others into my heart, and given of myself to theirs. This was especially true in combat . . . Like Saul on the Road to Damascus, I had entered the true fold by turning my previous customs on their heads. I had no inkling then of how vincible that made me, how terrible a price I might have to pay . . .

Some Marines who try to write or talk about it later can offer only a catalogue of loss; we are moved, but we know that something is missing; their pain is beyond us to imagine or share. It may strike those of us who aren't Marines or combat veterans that we have only two alternatives: turn away, or stand aghast—aghast that we can't protect each other from each other even now; aghast that we don't know what these Marines know.

Some Marines' stories are reminders that war is a far greater tragedy than we generally can bring ourselves to acknowledge and that it cannot be redeemed by nostalgia or even by love. Long after their combat experience is finished, Marines like William Manchester and Jim Johnston and Kenneth Sympson struggle to accept the suffering they have caused and experienced; they feel guilt and anger; they grieve. And they are among the lucky ones—they survived and found the strength to acknowledge and experience their pain, to bring it into the light and ultimately to share it with the rest of us.

Their stories often afflict us. It feels right to try to assume a small portion of their heavy burden. We may try to compensate them for their losses by telling them and each other that they killed and suffered for us—to defend our liberties and privileges. These stories suggest that these Marines' intentions are more complex; they killed and died to stay alive and to protect their fellow Marines; they killed out of rage and sorrow; they killed because they were frightened and because they had been taught to kill.

Some of these storytellers have been so afraid and so angry and so violent that they seem ashamed. They don't often talk of pride or honor, and when they do it sometimes feels like a mask for some kind of pain. We may feel that we should share some part of their shame as well. It is perhaps more useful to try to understand them in ways they cannot understand themselves; even to offer them the forgiveness that they cannot find in themselves. Our forgiveness is presumptuous only if it implies judgment. It is useful to these storytellers only if we ask them to forgive us as well—for not protecting them; for judging them; for being unconscious and unjust and otherwise fallible in all of the ways that cause war.

My father, a naval officer during World War II, is 81 years old. He participated in several of the war's bloodiest invasions, including Okinawa and Iwo Jima, where Marines died by the thousands. Once, aboard ship during an invasion, he opened a door to a room that was stacked almost to the ceiling with the bodies of newly dead Marines. He told me that story only recently, and I take the considerable liberty of repeating it here because it is the closest thing I have to a war story: I love my father, and my father was there; he saw those dead Marines; he remembered them and he told me; now I'm telling you.

Almost 50 years later, Anthony Swofford served as a Marine scout and sniper during the Gulf War. He writes that men who survive war "are spared for the single purpose of spreading the bad news when they return . . ." The Marines who tell their stories in this book have performed that difficult task with a healing passion that is our best hope for peace. For that, I honor them.

—Clint Willis
Series Editor, Adrenaline Books

from Making the Corps
by Thomas E. Ricks

Thomas E. Ricks tracked a platoon of Marine recruits through basic training in the spring of 1995.

It begins just like in the movies: A busload of recruits traverses a causeway across the tidal swamps of Archer Creek and arrives at the Marine Corps boot camp on Parris Island. It is 1:50 a.m., the middle of a chilly late-winter night on the coast of South Carolina, when the bus' air brakes sigh and the bus rolls to a halt outside the red-brick receiving station. Most of the thirty-six recruits on the bus already have been awake twenty hours or more, since they reported to military processing stations at dawn Wednesday. They won't sleep for another eighteen, until sunset Thursday. A haze of cigarette smoke hangs in the air of the silent bus. It is the last tobacco they will smell for eleven weeks.

Staff Sgt. Gregory Biehl, his face half-hidden by his big flat campaign hat—drill instructors hate it when tourists call it a Smokey the Bear hat—charges up the metal footsteps of the bus and faces the thirty-six faces, all male, most adolescent, many strained with fear.

"Now!" begins Staff Sergeant Biehl. It is the first word they hear on Parris Island, and it is entirely appropriate. For the next eleven weeks, every order they hear will carry a tacit insistence that it be executed immediately. That first word locks them into the present, and that is where they will remain. For nearly three months, no one in a position to know will tell them anything about their schedule. All they really have to go on are the movies they've seen on television, such as *Sands of Iwo Jima* and *Full Metal Jacket*, plus a few tall tales from older brothers and neighborhood kids who have come home wearing Marine uniforms. In their new lives here on the island, they simply will be ordered to march, and will find out what they are going to do next when ordered to stop marching.

At Parris Island, officers think about the weeks ahead, drill instructors think about the days ahead, and recruits think about the task at hand. The recruits don't know it and won't be told, but the Marines' theorists of boot camp indoctrination break the eleven-week process into five distinct phases. First is the initial receiving of recruits, which lasts about four disorienting days. Next is a period of similar length, the "Forming" of platoons, when the recruits are turned over to the drill instructors who will take them through the rest of boot camp. Then comes the main body of boot camp, "Training," which begins with basic drilling and rudimentary fighting, proceeds to riflery, and then puts it all together with basic combat training. Then, because Marine boot camp is three weeks longer than the other services', comes an odd ten-day period called "Advanced Training" in which nothing much appears to happen, but is significant because it puts on the recruits the final touches of indoctrination, polishing the best and sometimes reaching the recalcitrant. Finally comes the series of ceremonies and rituals that constitute graduation into the Marine Corps.

Many of the bewildered young men staring at Staff Sergeant Biehl will never make it that far. Some will be gone within a few days. But even for those who will make it the whole way, graduation at this moment is an unimaginably remote goal. Simply getting through each next moment of boot camp will consume all their mental and physical energies. And for most of the rest of their careers in the Marines, their officers will strive to keep them just as tightly focused: Not on whether they might eventually die, not on whether the mission will succeed, not on where their wife or girlfriend is and what she might be doing, but on the here and now.

"Now!" the sergeant repeats. "Sit up straight. Get your eyes on me. If you have anything in your mouth, get it out now." They stare at the sergeant, not knowing he is a passing figure in their lives, one who will move them along for exactly an hour and then never be seen again. The actual moment of shock will come three days later, at the "Forming," when they will meet the three drill instructors who will dominate every waking moment of their lives, and even some of their dreams, for the next eleven weeks. But right now, the Corps wants only to disorient the arriving recruits, not shatter them. The job now is to strip them of their old civilian identities before building new Marines.

"Now, get off my bus," shouts Staff Sergeant Biehl. They hadn't known it was his bus—but they soon will realize that they are on *his* island, in *his* Corps, and playing by *his* rules. Every drill instructor they meet will talk to them the same way. Nothing here is theirs, not even the right to be called "Marine." They are simply "recruits." They will have to earn the title "Marine"—and that is why most of them joined the Corps. Staff Sergeant Biehl pauses a moment, sufficient time for any attentive Marine to get going, and then raises the volume: "Let's go. Now. Move. Move! *Move!*"

They charge off the bus onto rows of yellow footprints painted on the asphalt: in their first moment on the ground of Parris Island, they also have stepped into the Marine Corps' powerful and distinctive culture. The footprints, four to a row, eighteen rows, are so closely packed that the newcomers can't been seen as individuals. Standing nearly heel to toe in the dark night their faces are hardly visible, and their bodies become one mass. The effect is intentional: Marine Corps culture is the culture of the group, made up of members who are anonymous. Later, Lt. Col. Michael Becker, commander of the Third Battalion, of which these men will soon become a part, will make the point by gesturing to the framed reprint on his office wall of perhaps the most famous photograph from World War II, that of the Marines raising the American flag at Iwo Jima. "Who are they? Just five Marines and a corpsman. It isn't Patton. It isn't Eisenhower. It's five Marines and a corpsman—you can't even see their faces." Indeed, two have their backs turned to the camera, two have their sides turned, and the fifth is hidden except for his arms and hands supporting the flag.

Who are these thirty-six recruits standing on the yellow footprints? Where are they from? How did they get here? Among them are an accountant fired by Ernst & Young because he flunked his CPA exam; a self-professed gang member from Washington, D.C.; the son of a Merrill Lynch bond trader; a Dutch-American who considers himself a pacifist; a former white-supremacist skinhead from Mobile, Alabama; a dozen former employees of Taco Bell and other fast food joints; and a handful of one-time workers at small, off-the-books construction firms.

They are mainly eighteen and nineteen years old, with a smattering of men in their twenties. The youngest is seventeen, the oldest twenty-seven. They come to Parris Island without strong prospects in the civilian economy. With a few exceptions, they are drawn from the 39 percent of young American males who don't attend college, and so live on the wrong side of the widening gap between the earnings of high school graduates and college graduates. To a surprising degree, they have been living part-time lives—working part time, going to community college part time (and getting failing grades), staying dazed on drugs and alcohol part time. They are, with a few exceptions, denizens of the bottom half of the American economy, or on the way there— poor kids with lousy educations, and a few wealthier ones sliding off the professional tracks their parents had taken. Consciously or not, they don't see much of a place open to them in postindustrial America. Most of them knew they were heading for mediocre jobs at wages that will always seem to lag behind inflation. They have come here from Shubuta, Mississippi, from Bayonne, New Jersey, from Destin, Florida, from Pittsburgh, Pennsylvania, and from forty other small towns and crumbling eastern cities to pursue one of the few rites of passage left in America. Here they can try to attain excellence.

In truth, society sees many of these kids more as threats than as contributing members. They are off the map—literally, in some cases. "You go into any high school in April, you'll see a map of the United States up on the wall showing where kids are going to college," says Staff Sgt. Michael Marti, a Marine recruiter in Boston who helped enlist Andrew Lee and Charles Lees III, two members of the group getting off this bus. "But that's only seventy-five percent or so. The other kids, the ones that are going the nontraditional route, they don't put them on the map at all. A kid who joins the military isn't honored, but the kid who goes to college is."

Spending their days in high schools, pool halls, and gyms, trolling for prospects, recruiters see a lot of adolescent America, probably more so than most parents of teenagers. Their reports are chilling. "I don't believe any of the statistics I see," says Sgt. Arthur Banester, who works the suburbs south of Boston. "I haven't seen one kid who hasn't used marijuana.

"It's rich down there," he continues. "It's midway between Providence and Boston, and there's a lot of nothing to do. So we get drugs, assault and batteries, breaking and entering. Alcohol's really bad."

Yes, echoes Staff Sergeant Marti, the chief of the recruiting station: "Alcohol's worse than anybody's nightmare."

The new recruits are propelled from home by fear of failure and drawn here by their desire to be Marines. That is very different from what attracts American youth to the other military services. One current recruiting pamphlet for the Navy carries the headline "What's in it for you." For years, the Army has advertised under the self-actualizing motto, "Be all you can be." The Marines, by contrast, take an ascetic, even forbidding approach: "Maybe you can be one of us," one of "a few good men," "the few, the proud."

For high-strung Andrew Lee, rippling with muscles and tension, there was never a question about where he wanted to be. He grew up just across the street from the Vietnam Veterans Memorial in South

Boston. The first such monument in the country, it displays the names of twenty-five dead. Some fifteen of those names are followed by the letters "USMC." He grew up with the brothers and cousins of those names.

Suffering from dyslexia, Lee never liked school much. But he loved the summers. As a teenager he began working as a lifeguard at South Boston's Farragut Beach. "I met this guy Herb Cavellas there," Lee will later recall. "He's the reason I joined the Marines. He was a quiet guy. He wore a 'Semper Fi' hat. He talked to me about Vietnam, where he was a scout/sniper. He talked to me about the Marines being a true brotherhood. Despite everything they went through—I wasn't there, but, you know, government lies, hypocrisy—they still hold true to the Marines."

One day late in 1994, Lee went downtown and signed up with the Marines on a delayed entry program. Then he caught a bus back to South Boston and told his parents. His mother, a social worker in a Boston school, was distraught. For months she tried to talk him out of it. "My mother, there's a real generation gap between she and I," Lee will later explain. "She's a good woman, an excellent mother, but she comes out of the Vietnam thing."

"She wouldn't hang up on me," recalled Sgt. Rodney Emery, Lee's recruiter, who would check up on Lee two or three times a month. "But every once in a while she'd voice her opinion." Lee's father, the principal of South Boston's middle school, wasn't much pleased either.

On the morning he was to "ship" to Parris Island, his mother got up early and made him a big breakfast. She cried the whole time.

Traveling with Lee from Boston is Charles Lees III, a big two hundred seventy-five-pound Samoan with a Band-Aid on his forehead. The wound on his head was sustained while trying to qualify for boot camp; just getting to this point has been a struggle for Lees. A graduate of Holy Cross, Lees was looking for something more in life than computer sales. He came into the recruiting office heavily overweight. The recruiters determined that he would need to drop forty-seven pounds simply to qualify to begin boot camp. They had him visit once a day, then twice, to exercise him into shape.

He reported as ordered the night before he was to ship, in mid-February. But he was still six pounds over the limit. The sergeants at the processing station dressed him in a heavy sweat suit and kept him running all night. To keep the weight off, he wasn't allowed to eat. When thirsty, he was given an ice cube to lick. Toward morning, he later recalls, "everything went yellow." He woke up on the floor, looking up at the master sergeant. In fainting he somehow cut his forehead. He was sent home to recuperate for two weeks.

So, by chance, Lee and Lees ship out the same day. The two Bostonians with similar names will become the heart of their platoon at Parris Island. Assigned by the alphabet to share a bunk bed, they become a team: Andrew Lee, the small, wiry, inarticulate leader by example, and Charles Lees, the hulking, reflective recruit who has the intelligence to teach his slower comrades, the maturity to know how to do it, and the physical strength to ensure that they listen.

Also part of the Boston shipment is Paul Bourassa, a graduate of the University of Massachusetts who enlisted after being fired by Ernst & Young. He broke the news to his parents over dinner at an Applebee's restaurant in Methuen, up near the New Hampshire border. "She began crying, made a scene. She said I was gonna die. My dad said I was crazy."

Parents' resistance to their sons' joining the Marines is common among this group. "My mother and uncles tried to talk to me. They didn't want me to go anywhere dangerous," James Andersen, one of five recruits shipped here today from Pittsburgh, says later. "I said, 'It's my choice, and I need it.'" The nineteen-year-old had been a shift manager at a Taco Bell in the Pittsburgh suburb of Bethel Park, "partying" every night; he "didn't give a shit about anything."

In eastern Pennsylvania, just outside Philadelphia, Nathan Weber, who had been sliding from one dead-end job to another, enlisted and then went to a friend's house for dinner. When his friend's father heard the news over the meal, he gave him a disgusted look and said, "Kids these days want to be so tough." Several other friends, and his parents, are puzzled by his decision.

Failing to persuade her son to renege on enlisting, the mother of another Pittsburgh recruit, Joshua Parise, decided to wrest from the recruiting sergeant a promise that her son would be safe at boot camp. Then at dawn she was shocked when a different sergeant appeared at the front door to collect her boy. She stood in her bathrobe hugging her son—and refused to let go. This went on for several minutes, until he finally lifted her arms and extracted himself. "She kind of wigged out," Parise later says.

If some parents try to bar the door, others actively open it. Craig Hoover's dad, a retired government cartographer, suggested that his son try something new in life. Hoover had just dropped out of Montgomery College, in the prosperous Maryland suburbs of Washington, D.C., and he'd quit his job as a waiter because he didn't like some of the other staff at the diner. "I needed a break, a change of scene," he says later.

At dawn on March 1, 1995, this wave of recruits reported to military processing stations across the eastern United States. Their recruiters already had given them physicals and vetted their names with local police for criminal records. Each was checked for open wounds and fresh scars. Then a recruiting sergeant interrogated them one last time. "Did you get in any trouble? Did you smoke some dope? We know you have going-away parties, drink a few beers, have some trouble." After a final paperwork check, each was driven to a local airport in a government minivan, usually with three or four other recruits. At Boston, the recruits left for Logan Airport at 12:30. On arrival at Charleston, South Carolina, they were met by a Marine and taken to a special room. They were told to sit with their hands flat on their knees, facing forward, and to remain silent. They waited for hours, stock still.

Finally, just after midnight, thirty-six recruits had accumulated. They were told to file onto a bus illuminated by the otherworldly orange lights of the airport parking lot. They immediately felt the humidity and relative warmth of the Deep South. The bus cut south and surprisingly soon left behind motels and automobile dealers on the outskirts of town. Route 17 narrowed to two lanes and plunged into the pitch darkness of the South Carolina sea marshes, a land of rice, cotton, alligators, and mud, one of the most remote areas east of the Mississippi. The recruits were permitted to talk, but no one did. They stared out the window trying to see something in the piney woods and marshes along the Edisto River basin. The blackwater stream itself was invisible in the night, just a negative strip of emptiness. They caught glimpses of Spanish moss hanging in great masses from the branches of live oaks. Some smoked. Charles Lees asked himself, *What have I done?*

Nearly ninety minutes later, the lights of the Parris Island guardpost looming out of the dark signal the beginning of the answer to that question. Symbolically, boot camp begins here as the bus slows, but doesn't stop at the gate at the mainland end of a causeway that leads out to the island. The Marine guard waves the bus through, and it takes the recruits across the border from the America they know into Marine territory, where they will remain until they graduate months from now, or until they are washed out and sent home.

The bus is again in darkness as it traverses the 2.3-mile-long causeway. *Good-bye, world*, Lees thinks, sensing the psychological remoteness of the place. This isolated atmosphere is somewhat artificial. In reality, the bright lights and yacht-set bistros of antebellum Beaufort, South Carolina, are just a few miles from the Marine camp. But to the recruits, the 7,000 flat, wet acres of sand that make up Parris Island might as well be a thousand miles out in the Atlantic Ocean.

The Devil's Island atmosphere of the place is no accident. In the late nineteenth century, after a naval station and dry dock were established on the island, the Navy used the installation as a "disciplinary barracks"—that is, a military jail. The Marines first began training recruits on the island in 1915, for service in World War I. Since then, the Marines are fond of saying, more than a million recruits have trained on the island, with about 20,000 coming through annually nowadays. At any given point, there are about 4,300 recruits training on Parris Island—fewer in mid-winter, more during the late summer and early fall, as the high school graduation bulge passes through. They are governed by just under 600 drill instructors.

This being the history-minded Marine Corps, the roads on Parris Island are named after the Corps' great battles and campaigns. The bus leaves the causeway and enters Boulevard de France, evoking World War I, the conflict that did more than any other to elevate the Corps from a naval police force into a legitimate fighting force that could stand as an alternative to the U.S. Army. The Marine base on the island is a haphazard, charmless collection of two- and three-story brick buildings with live oaks and pines growing in the grassy areas between them, but grass fights a losing battle in the salty, sandy soil; walk five minutes away from the main buildings, and the green thins and gives way to the sand that is the natural ground cover here. Beyond the sand ripples the deceptive waters of Atlantic Ocean inlets. As the tide recedes, it becomes clear that the water is just a few inches deep. The water peels back to reveal slick black mudflats, aromatic ooze that almost seems to have a pulse, and wafts hints of shrimp and crab toward shore. The locals call this rich tidal mud "pluff," for the sighing sound it makes when a foot plunges into it.

The bus heads toward the billboard-size sign that spans the boulevard, supported by four steel legs, proclaiming PARRIS ISLAND: WHERE THE DIFFERENCE BEGINS. Then it turns right toward the receiving building and disgorges the recruits onto those yellow footprints.

The thirty-six recruits stand dazed as Staff Sergeant Biehl initiates them by reading two articles of the Uniform Code of Military Justice: First, they may not strike a Marine. Second, if they run away, they are subject to military law. It is similar to a police officer's reading the Miranda rights to a suspect—except that here the rights are those of the institution, not the individual.

The sergeant ushers them into the processing station and sits them in a kind of classroom, a brick room filled with rows of stainless steel one-piece desk-chairs. The walls are decorated with photographs of boot camp training. Waiting in the chairs are eleven other recruits who had arrived earlier from points south, kids from northern Florida and the Carolinas who simply were driven to Parris Island from Marine recruiting stations. After the dark of the cloudy night outside, the fluorescent overhead lights blaze like spotlights on the shiny steel desktops.

"Now," says Staff Sergeant Biehl, "I'm going to 'splain something to you. You are not at home. You are not back on the block. Everything you do will be done quickly and loudly." This emphasis on behavior and language, not military training, will form the core of their boot camp experience. It may not be what the recruits expected, but it is central to the process of transformation they are about to experience. Marine Corps basic training is more a matter of cultural indoctrination than of teaching soldiering, which comes later, at combat training or, for the real grunts, at infantry school. Before they can learn to fight, they must learn to be Marines. "We're getting them from a society that is in many ways disintegrating," the commandant of the Marine Corps, Gen. Charles Krulak, says in his speeches. "Unless there is a change in this nation, this problem is going to manifest itself in larger proportion as we go along." That view is widely shared in the Marines. Sergeant Biehl, in a private moment, sums up the mission of Parris Island this way: "The Marine Corps is like a family, and we teach family values."

As if to underscore that they have entered a new world, Staff Sergeant Biehl begins to teach them a new language. Its peculiarly nautical tone grows out of the Marines' origins as a sea service. "We don't call it a floor, we call it a deck," he lectures, striding purposefully back and forth at the front of the desks. "We don't call it a door, we call it a hatch." For no apparent reason relating to the sea, writing pens are now to be called inksticks and sneakers are go-fasters.

Then he introduces them to another aspect of language on Parris Island: Orders generally are issued in the future imperative, the drill instructor's favorite verb tense. "You are going to write this number," Staff Sergeant Biehl says, perfectly confident that they will. "Three-zero-eight-six." They use Magic Markers to write the four numbers on their left hands. "This is now your platoon number," he says. "You are now part of Platoon Thirty Eighty-six." That number is now more important than their own names.

With a unit assigned, the recruits now have an address, which means they can mail a letter home and tell their families how to contact them. Then they are given the letter to mail: It is from Col. Humberto "Rod" Rodriguez, commanding officer of the Recruit Training Regiment. "Your Marine recruit has arrived safely at Parris Island," the letter states. "We have instructed him to write to you regularly."

Recruits alert enough to scan the letter get a hint of the pace that awaits them. "Please do not be alarmed if his first letters to you report that he has not received any mail yet," it continues. "Due to the rigorous training, recruits lose track of days."

The Colonel's letter then gets to the point of Parris Island: "Our responsibility in the Recruit Training Regiment is to transform your young man and thousands like him from a civilian into a basically trained Marine, capable of accepting full responsibility for his present and future roles in our Corps. . . . In the process, he must prove to himself, his comrades, and his officers and drill instructors that he is worthy of the respect and confidence which are part of our title and uniform."

Next, as if they were entering prison, the recruits inventory the civilian clothes they are about to place in a brown bag. (Lacking civilian clothes makes it much harder for recruits to flee the island.) "We don't call them pants, we call them trousers," the sergeant helpfully reminds the newcomers. Moving back to the future imperative, the sergeant says, "Right now, all jewelry will come off your body."

Johnny Thomas Jr., a skinny black recruit from Delray Beach, Florida, not destined to make it through Parris Island, finds this order somehow humorous or embarrassing, and looks up at the sergeant with a slight smile. Unfortunately, he has a gold tooth in the middle of the smile that catches the sergeant's eye. "On your feet," Sergeant Biehl shouts, charging at him and waving a finger a few inches in front of his mouth. "I guarantee you that in the next couple of hours I'll wipe that smile off your face."

It is a very credible threat. Recruit Thomas's smile is gone in seconds. The sergeant resumes the in-processing. "Now, this is your last chance to cough up anything that shouldn't be on your body." Without explanation, he orders them to turn over any weapons, knives, cigarettes, matches, lighters, candy, food, gum, soda, drugs of any kind, liquids of any kind, dice, playing cards, subversive material, "pornographic material, naked pictures of your girlfriend or mother, rubbers, prophylactics, or any of that trash, put them in that orange crate right now, 'cause you ain't got any need of that now."

At 2:50 a.m., precisely one hour after meeting the bus, he ushers them into the next room and turns them over to Sgt. Ansil Lewis, a fine-boned infantry scout from the Virgin Islands who will run Platoon 3086 for the next three days.

Sergeant Lewis begins with the next big step in the disorientation process: He withdraws from the recruits the right to use the first person. Their first names also are banished. "From now on, you are no longer he, she, it, or whatever you was," he says in a clear, quiet voice. "You are now 'Recruit-and-your-last-name,' understand?" Coming from a society that elevates the individual, they are now in a world where the group is supreme. Using "I" raises suspicions: Why would you care more about your self than about your unit? You are 3086.

Sergeant Lewis's second move is to emphasize that no matter what they are doing, they are not doing it fast enough. He moves them in a single file toward the barber's stand in the back of the receiving station. "Let's go. Hurry up. Hurry. Tighter."

Buzz cuts begin at 3:30 a.m. and take twenty-five seconds per recruit. For some, six months' growth of hair flutters to the floor with each stroke of the barber's shaver. The barber is a broken-down looking civilian wearing a black T-shirt inscribed, in red letters, with the words PAIN FEAR IRONY DESPAIR DEATH. It is an unusual job, shaving the heads of terrified young men in the middle of the night. He doesn't speak as he does it. The recruits emerge from the barber's cubbyhole in the back of the receiving station and are made to line up in unnatural proximity, each recruit's toes almost touching the heel of the one before him, crotches within a foot of the buttocks of the recruit in front. This is far closer than the "comfort zone" of most Americans, especially adolescent males. But they already know enough to remain absolutely silent. As the last of the platoon is being shorn, Sergeant Lewis, in keeping with the drill instructor's ethic of using every available moment, begins teaching the shaveheads. "Whenever a drill instructor says 'Ears,' you say, 'Open.' Whenever a drill instructor says 'Eyeballs,' you say, 'Snap.' "

He plucks out two recruits to sweep the hair. He hurries them along, as DIs always do, by irritatedly saying, "Any day."

Then they are marched through a supply room and issued all the clothes they will wear and everything else they will need for eleven weeks, including such unique items as "rifle towels," which carry printed outlines showing where to place each piece of the M-16 as it is cleaned. The issuing clerk, an old man in casual civilian clothes, says the Marines used to do this in a roughshod way, having a sergeant distribute the gear and screaming at the recruits as they ran through, but found that caused so much trouble with confusion over equipment that they civilianized the task.

They carry their gear upstairs to the receiving barracks, a big unsympathetic chamber where identities evaporate. With its empty white cinderblock walls and bare floor, furnished only with sheetless mattresses on bunk beds, it may be the world's most anonymous room. The regular barracks on Parris Island at least display Marine Corps signs and instructive material on their walls; this lacks even the graffiti of a drunk tank. It offers absolutely no clues. It is 4:00 a.m., an empty hour. A recruit chancing on a mirror might not even recognize his own pasty-white hairless head.

The beds are inviting. But Platoon 3086 has long to go before it will sleep. Instead, at 4:50 a.m., Sergeant Lewis begins teaching it to toe the line. Literally. He assembles them along the two white lines painted the length of the spartan barracks. "Right in front of you is a little line," he says. "I want you to put your toe on it."

The sergeant then teaches them a few basic elements of how to walk

in formation—"Left foot strikes the deck"—and marches them to the
3rd Battalion's mess hall. "When we go to the chow hall, nobody's
going to run their mouth, understand?" he orders. The platoon moves
through the windswept trees, a flashlight in each of their forty-seven
hands, with forty-seven beams of light swinging and catching spooky
glimpses of Spanish moss hanging from live oaks. Steam swirls around
the platoon from the island's overground heating pipes. A fat raccoon
squats and watches the group move by, its eyes flashing red in the
swinging beams. It is an exotic and unsettling environment to the
recruits from the cities and farms of the north, where palm trees and
sea breezes signify vacation luxury, not boot camp.

The scene outside the mess hall in the predawn darkness is bewil-
dering to outsiders. Young men appear in formation and move quickly
amid great shouting, ranks of four peeling off at a time, but it isn't
apparent how this high-energy system works, or why it requires continual yelling and stomping. Amidst this inexplicable whirl, 3086
stands in ragged formation on the veranda of the mess hall, a small
rock in a rushing rapid. No one explains anything to it. "The disorientation is part" of the receiving process, says Master Sgt. Wilbert Altman,
a receiving sergeant. "They never know what's going to happen next."

Some members of 3086 bite their lips. On the chins of others, baby
fat quivers. Of the fifty-nine people who soon will make up the platoon, fourteen will be classified as overweight. They look like a mess,
but they are typical of the platoons created at this time of year. There
is an old Parris Island saying, "Summer from the school halls, winter
from the pool halls." Most of this crew has more in common with
Minnesota Fats than with Rambo. "Most of the kids got out of school
last summer and then sat around playing Nintendo, eating potato
chips, maybe working part time at McDonald's, or doing some construction work for a friend," says 1st Sgt. Charles Tucker, an eighteen-
year-veteran of the Corps who is the senior sergeant for 3086's Kilo
Company. "You sit around idle for eight or nine months, you can lose
a lot psychologically."

Opposite 3086 on the cement veranda stands a seasoned platoon a day away from graduation. It is lean, cocky, and rock-band loud as it stands at crisp attention, chanting: "Three-zero-five-six/We don't need no stinkin' chicks'." It stomps into the mess hall, driving its boot heels into the cement and shaking the floor.

At 5:20 in the morning the platoon sits down to a good breakfast—French toast, cereals, two apples, and orange juice. They remain stock still until Sergeant Lewis, standing over them, shouts an order: "Drink some water!" The drill instructors don't eat with the platoon, or even in front of them: It would make them appear human. The platoon's first meal on the island is over in eleven minutes, which is easy, because recruits in this battalion are forbidden to speak at meals, except to address their superiors. Swirling around them, more experienced recruits shout, "Morning, gentlemen," at a civilian standing with a drill instructor. The Third Battalion, of which they are a part, even though they don't yet know it, is known on Parris Island as the "Heavy D" unit, for its emphasis on discipline, a priority that seems to have been quietly decided by its drill instructors. "They're kind of strict in the Third Battalion," Sergeant Lewis later explains. The 2nd Battalion, by contrast, located across Boulevard de France, is known for its emphasis on weapons training: "All kill, no drill."

They march back outside, where dawn brings light but no more warmth. The pale sun rises on a group shorn of its past. "Everything is taken away—hair, clothes, food, and friends," says Navy Lt. James Osendorf, a Catholic priest for the 3rd Battalion. "It's a total cutoff from previous life. That's why you get so much loneliness, and so many suicidal tendencies." Religion will become important to many for the first time, he says, because it will be the only window they have back into their old lives.

"The sign on the road as you come into Parris Island says, WHERE THE DIFFERENCE BEGINS," adds Father Osendorf. "But to me it's more than that, it's where the transformation begins."

Over the next eleven weeks, the recruits will receive a value system transfusion, as they learn the Marine Corps way of walking, talking, and thinking. They will endure a pace of as many as fifteen orders per minute, every one a reminder that they have left a culture of self-gratification and entered a culture of self-discipline. Here, pleasure is suspect, and pain and sacrifice are good. The recruits will be denied all the basic diversions of the typical American youth—television, cigarettes, cars, cards, candy, soft drinks, video games, music, alcohol, drugs, and sex. Unlike in the other military services, they won't train alongside women. Here on Parris Island, women train separately, over in the 4th Battalion, in a citadel-like two-story barracks that shelters its own drill deck, gymnasium, mess hall, and beauty shop. "We don't have to go out of our own little world," says Lt. Mary Cogdill, the 4th Battalion's operations officer. But the atmosphere within the female battalion is very much that of Parris Island. A sign posted flat on the ceiling of one of its squad bays reads: PAIN IS GOOD, EXTREME PAIN IS EXTREMELY GOOD. It is located on the ceiling so recruits can contemplate it while doing punishment sit-ups. The only times the recruits of 3086 will encounter these female recruits will be on Sundays, at recruit chapel. Even then the females sit in their own assigned section of pews at the far side of the building.

Filling the vacuum in the recruits' lives will be their drill instructors. Many of these recruits have come here seeking a new identity. It is striking how little influence parents and family have had on most of the recruits. They don't define themselves through their families or work, as do many American adults. Asked about their pasts, many of these recruits talk about their leisure activities—"Drinking the forty ounce on the corner," as one Pittsburgh recruit puts it. They have come to boot camp to try the straightforward and simple definition of manhood offered by the Marines. To many, their drill instructors will become among the most important people they will ever meet, and these eleven weeks will become the central experience in their entire lives. Any Marine veteran can reach back thirty or forty years and summon the names of his drill instructors. Flying in a Marine jet over Parris Island, Brig. Gen. Randy West looks down on the swampy land and simply says, "I was born there."

The next step in the separation is "Recruitment Liaison," a process informally known as "the moment of truth." Mandatory one-on-one meetings with receiving sergeants, which take up the entire morning, give recruits a last chance to confess to previously undisclosed drug use or criminal convictions. This is also a way for the Corps to screen out unqualified or ineligible recruits that hard-pressed recruiters, trying to meet their quotas, might have tried to sneak by the authorities. Platoon 3086 and its companion platoon, 3085, move through together. The interviews reveal a cross section of the minor trouble that American youth can make. "I got into an argument with my mother, and this small-town cop, he didn't like me, and he took me out on a back road and beat me up," says a member of 3085 from Perry, New York, explaining a charge of assaulting an officer. One of his comrades has a record of burglary, aggravated assault, and breaking into cars in Fort Lauderdale, Florida, in 1992. But he told the recruiter about that, and he insists that nothing else will show up on his record when the Marines check.

For many members of 3086, marijuana use has been routine. Some tell Gunnery Sgt. Timothy Gulledge that they have dabbled in cocaine, LSD, and PCP. After each confession, Sergeant Gulledge asks, "Do you know the Marine Corps position on illegal drugs?" Each recruit is required to state that he understands the Corps doesn't tolerate drug use.

"You've used marijuana twenty-five times?" Sergeant Gulledge says to one recruit.

"Yes, sir," the uneasy recruit says. Both he and his interrogator know the number is probably far higher. But the point of the exchange is to underscore that, whatever the actual figure, it won't increase.

"You got a waiver for that. You understand you get no more chances?"

"Yes, sir." In fact, nearly half of all Marine Corps recruits enlist under some sort of "waiver" for crimes, drug use, and medical and psychological problems.

After a hurried lunch, Sergeant Lewis begins to teach them to march as a unit, beginning with how to stand erect like a Marine, how to lift a foot, how to stand in line. He repeats each step with a quiet, crisp tolerance.

By 5:30 that afternoon, the platoon, still without sleep since arriving the previous night, is dragging. But it already is looking more like a group of recruits, and less like a frazzled crowd of civilians. As the platoon enters its temporary barracks in the receiving building, most of its members remove their "utility hats"—the enlisted Marines' everyday headgear. Several say, "Good afternoon, sir," to a passing civilian. They also are learning to work as a group, rather than as individuals. They march to the mess hall for an early dinner, then back to the barracks, where Sergeant Lewis gives them twenty seconds to remove and hang up all their gear—hats, canteens, canteen web belts. The more astute members realize that the only way to do it within that limit is to aid one another. When Daniel Armstrong, a gangling, storklike road construction worker from Florida, gets tangled trying to remove his canteen belt, Christopher Anderson, a smart, short black recruit who plans to study criminology at the University of Maryland, leans over and helps him. Sergeant Lewis watches in silent approval: They are getting the message.

But that is a moment of clarity in a world of chaos. For the most part, the platoon learns by error. They live in a blur of anonymous drill instructors sweeping by them and yelling at them for committing sins they didn't know existed. One recruit gazes for a moment at a sergeant watching the platoon. "Get your eyeballs off me, recruit," the sergeant snarls. The platoon doesn't know it, but in a few weeks that small man will take on a godlike status for them. He is Staff Sgt. Ronny Rowland, who will become their senior drill instructor. He has come to quietly observe the material he will be inheriting from the receiving station.

By the approach of evening at the end of their first full day on Parris Island, the recruits' identities have been hollowed out. They know very little about anything, except toeing the line, which they are getting good at doing. The entire platoon can now be on line in just three seconds, down from twenty last night, and five this morning. Their heads are shaved. They are wearing anonymous military camouflage uniforms that don't yet have their names stenciled on them. The recruits around them are still strangers. They live in the disorienting, empty world of the receiving barracks. The sole clue to their identity is the black ink on their left hands: "3086."

They only want one thing: to lie down and go to sleep as soon as possible. They haven't slept for thirty-six hours, since they hugged their mothers and reported to the processing stations. But first they must learn how to make a bed in proper Marine style, with the sheets tucked at each corner with a forty-five-degree fold.

And they must do this through a haze of fatigue and dislocation, asking questions and making requests in the new language they are learning. Jonathan Prish, the self-declared former skinhead from Mobile, Alabama, is so tired that it takes him seven agonizing attempts before he is able to correctly formulate a simple question in proper Marine style.

"I need to . . ."

"No."

"Sir, I need to . . ."

"No."

"Sir, can I go to . . ."

"No."

Finally, after four more tries, he puts it all together, dropping the first person and including a "sir": "Recruit Prish requests permission to make a head call, sir."

The platoon never will be left alone at night on Parris Island, but on their first night here they are watched with special attention. Many members of 3086 are so disoriented that they seem incapable of considering where they are, and why. Sergeant Lewis keeps a close eye on them. "After a full day of this, everyone yelling at them, tired, scared, that's when they knock on my hatch and say, 'I don't want to stay here.'" Usually, he says, two or three do so on the first night.

Sure enough, at 7:00 p.m., the first recruit cracks—and hard. Recruit Campbell's tone is almost conversational, an eerie contrast to the hoarse shouts of most recruits' utterances, as he seeks to control himself. He quietly approaches Sergeant Lewis. "Is it possible I could go to the doctor tonight, if you don't mind?" he asks in a voice that strains to be casual, but clearly isn't.

Sergeant Lewis goes on full mental alert. This one won't be just a matter of sitting him down with a senior sergeant for a fatherly talk. This one could go sour fast. At the drill instructors' school on Parris Island, every drill instructor has pounded into him the fact that abuse of recruits has given the Marines a black eye in the past. In the most notorious incident, the Ribbon Creek "death march" of April 1956, Staff Sgt. Matthew McKeon, a DI from the Third Battalion, decided, after drinking heavily one night, to march a platoon into the tidal stream behind the rifle range. Six recruits drowned in the deep "trout holes" in the swirling tide. Later, during the demoralized post-Vietnam days of the 1970s, when the Corps was at a low point, poorly trained drill instructors, frustrated by the low quality of the recruits of that era, fell into a pattern of harassment and even maltreatment. Two recruits died during training, one after being beaten into unconsciousness in pugil stick training. "In the seventies, the process [of abuse] became institutionalized," concluded a report by Marine Lt. Gen. Bernard Trainor. These days, when a recruit hints that he feels bad, the Marines listen. They don't want recruits killing themselves on Parris Island, and the congressional inquiries that would provoke.

Partly to ensure that he has a witness, Sergeant Lewis leads the recruit downstairs to where Sergeant Biehl is doing paperwork. Recruit Campbell explains himself to the two men: "Sir, I feel real bad about something I did, sir. I feel kind of depressed about it."

"Do you feel suicidal?" Sergeant Lewis asks. It is the key question. The answer will determine whether Recruit Campbell will be off the island tomorrow morning.

"A little bit, sir." That alone is probably enough to win him a bus ticket home. His subsequent confession that he wasn't completely candid in his enlistment, that there was information he should have told the recruiter but didn't, ensures that his career in the Marines will end before it begins. Because all the doctors have left the island for the day, Sergeant Lewis assigns shifts of two recruits each to stay up and watch Recruit Campbell as he sleeps. "Two shadows will be put on him all night."

So ends 3086's first long day in the Marines. At 8:00 p.m. they tumble into their bunks and sleep.

But not for long. Less than seven hours later, at 2:50 a.m. Friday, March 3rd, Sergeant Lewis strides into the receiving barracks, flips on the fluorescent overhead lights, and shouts, "Get on line NOW! Get on line! Get! On! Line!" The forty-eight recruits wake up, scared, sleepy, and bald. If they had a moment to think, they might ask where they were. But there is no time to ponder. They are being berated in the middle of the night by a black man demanding immediate and unquestioning obedience. It is a novel experience for most white Americans. The membership of the platoon will change as some recruits drop out and others, who have overcome injuries or other problems, are "picked up" from preceding platoons. But 3086's racial and ethnic composition will remain throughout about three quarters white and one quarter black and Hispanic.

What's more, there is the matter Sergeant Lewis is yelling about: drugs. Yesterday they were told the Corps won't tolerate drug abuse. Now it is going to prove it is serious. The sergeant has them get on line, count off one through forty-eight, and then get dressed as a unit. First, everyone dons a T-shirt. Then socks and trousers. Then right sneaker. But when one recruit goes ahead and puts on his left sneaker as well, the sergeant has them take off the right sneaker and start again. Then each member of the platoon is told to open his canteen, chug the entire quart, and then hold the empty container upside down over his head. Recruit Armstrong, the storklike Floridian, nearly overwhelmed by the barrage of orders, looks near tears. At 3:30 a.m., Sergeant Lewis lines them up and marches them into the latrine to provide samples for urinalysis. Anyone testing positive for heroin, cocaine, or opium will be ejected from the Corps.

Morning chow is wolfed down in silence and finished by 5:00 a.m. Next are two long bureaucratic processes, as much a part of military life as taking orders and doing exercise. First, starting at 6:30 a.m., their rifles are issued, with serial numbers duly logged in duplicate. Their M-16s will be constant companions, carried on marches, hung on the ends of their bunk beds at night. But they will never be given bullets, except at the rifle range, when each round will be tracked with laser-like precision. The rest of the morning is taken up by the dental check. Several members of the platoon have cavities and abscesses. The naval dentists issue them military fillings and a few false teeth.

The overcast afternoon brings the "initial strength test." The Corps wants to know if the recruits are even in sufficiently mediocre condition to *begin* getting in shape. Recruits whose bodies—especially their feet and legs—aren't able to absorb the impact of physical training constitute the leading cause of dismissal from Parris Island. "The kids I trained in '78, '80 were distinctly different" from today's recruits, says Brig. Gen. Jack Klimp, the island's commanding general. "A lot of them back then were tough, hard kids—a lot more physically tough, less fragile than today's kids. A lot of today's kids are the Nintendo generation, spending their lives looking into computers. They're the highest quality recruits we've ever had [in terms of education], but we've had to change our physical training to adjust to them. They are more fragile than recruits were ten years ago. A lot of them have never hit someone, or been hit."

For the entire afternoon the platoon is put through rounds of pull-ups, sit-ups, and running on a big field near the receiving building. The drill instructors of the Third Battalion make the five-minute walk over to the receiving area to watch these recruits and assess the material with which they will work for the next eleven weeks. One DI looks at Dana Patrick, struggling along, and calls him "a bowl of jelly." Five of the forty-seven recruits fail the strength tests, including Recruit Patrick, who doesn't complete the run. Judged unready to begin training, three will be sent to the Physical Conditioning Platoon to get them into sufficient shape to begin. The "PCP"—which inevitably becomes known as the "Pork Chop Platoon"—is Parris Island's purgatory. On average it is peopled by ninety recruits, most of them Initial Strength failures who can't do two pull-ups or run a mile in ten minutes and thirty seconds. For about thirty days, the PCPers are put through a regime of exercise, diet, and drill. Most are then "picked up" by a new platoon. But about one in five never is able to get in shape, and washes out of boot camp before really beginning it.

Staff Sergeant Rowland exercises his discretion to keep two border-line test failures. One of them is Shane Logan, a big, thoughtful kid from Oneonta, New York, who wants to be a social worker. "The kid only did one pull-up—the minimum is three—but he had such huge desire to be a Marine," Rowland explains. (His assessment is correct: By the time Logan graduates from boot camp, he will be doing fifteen pull-ups.) The platoon averages nine and a half pull-ups, fifty-two sit-ups, and twenty-four minutes for the three-mile run. By graduation it will be doing twice as many pull-ups, half again as many sit-ups, and will have cut three minutes from the run. As a new platoon, "I'd say they're about average," Staff Sergeant Rowland concludes.

They also look to be typical mentally, adds Staff Sgt. Ivan Pabon, the acting gunnery sergeant for this "series," or group, of platoons. "The biggest problem we have with these kids is that everybody in America thinks they know everything, and their way is the right way," he says as he watches the platoons stream in from the three-mile run, the first of many they will perform in the coming weeks. Parris Island is the first place many of them ever encounter absolute and impersonal standards of right and wrong, of success and failure, says Sergeant Pabon, a native of Puerto Rico who learned to speak English in boot camp. "When they mess up at home, they don't get punished, they get 'explained.' The parents, the media, want to 'explain' everything. Here, you screw up, we stop you and penalize you immediately, before you forget it."

"The broken family kids are one of the bigger problems we have here," adds 1st Sgt. Charles Tucker, the senior NCO for 3086's Kilo Company. "A lot of them have never had anyone get on them. It's a big shock when they come down here and get told, 'No, you are doing it wrong.' A lot of them, if they came from a single-parent household, and their mother's working, they've pretty much had free rein."

For Platoon 3086, the shock of the absolute looms just over the horizon. Here, the absolute actually has a body, title, and name: Sgt. Darren Carey, USMC, the "heavy hat" drill instructor who will land on them tomorrow morning. But they don't know that as they march to Friday night chow. They move almost as a unit. They are beginning to look like recruits. A few may even think they have this place figured out. They will soon find out they are wrong. Friday is their last day in the "low-stress environment" of receiving. On Saturday morning they will move to the real world of Parris Island.

from Over There

by Carl Andrew Brannen

Carl Andrew Brannen joined the Marines on February 11, 1918. He arrived in Europe in time to participate in the bloody battle of Belleau Wood, where Marines helped turn back a German advance. These selections are from Brannen's war journals.

When America declared war in 1917, I was a few months past eighteen years of age and just finishing my first year in college. By the time I was to reenter in the fall for the second year, war activities were [proceeding] on a large scale. Men were going into some branch of the service on all sides. I felt that my family should do their bit in uniform, and my age designated me as the most appropriate one. With this decision behind, the next was selecting a branch of service. The aviation corps was the first choice, but in my mind there was the danger of never qualifying as a pilot, so I took second choice, the Marine Corps. The "First to Fight" recruiting posters were appealing. Accordingly, I joined the exodus from Texas A&M College, as cadets went into different branches of service. My resignation was January 27, 1918, at midterm.

I was sworn into service at Parris Island, South Carolina, February

11, 1918. The camp, out on an island, was uninhabited except by soldiers and a few Negroes, and since a "boot" had no privileges, contact with the outside world was broken, except for mail.

The system used in drilling recruits was for an expert drill master to take about forty men and train them in close order drill. Expert rifle and pistol shots helped instruct on the range in the latter part of the training, but the drill sergeant had charge until we left this camp at the end of about two and one-half months. The drill sergeant bore down in order to show us what little we knew of military affairs, and in my case he succeeded admirably. My military training in college helped me over many rough places in one way and was a hindrance in others. Any movement which had been slighted before had to be done with precision now. Sergeant Boynton, my drill master, was satisfied with nothing short of perfection. He flew into a rage at one time and broke his swagger stick into several pieces because we were not doing as well on the drill as we should. Many times the air almost turned blue with the things he said. There was an order which kept a recruit from being cursed directly, but he caught it indirectly. A young fellow such as I was made to feel that he was no earthly good to his nation and the sooner he got cut down on the front line the better off the country would be.

We did all of our own housekeeping. Each one helped at the kitchen periodically except when he was punished by doing extra duty. We washed our own clothes and sewed them when necessary. Among my washing one day was a pair of socks which my brown shoes had stained. I scrubbed and scrubbed, but the stain remained. When our washing was inspected, Sergeant Boynton's helper, a corporal from Massachusetts, knocked my wash in the dirt because he thought the socks were not clean and ordered me to wash them over. He took the attitude that I had not tried to wash them good. I almost forgot the ordeal of a court-martial and waded into him, but a breach of discipline in training camp would have carried a severe penalty. I was conscious of the necessity of this training, but it was much worse than [I had] expected.

When orders came that we were to be moved to make way for a new group of recruits, the boys got together and by each contributing about fifty cents, a nice little cash present was made up for Sergeant Boynton and his helper. I regretted the part of mine which went to the helper.

The sergeant lined us up before our barracks the last time and told us that we were well-drilled marines and would have spoken further, but stopped and turned his back. We understood and saw him through blurred eyes as we moved off to catch the train and he sadly took up another bunch of boots. I heard that he finally succeeded in getting transferred to France and never survived the war. We stopped some time in Florence, South Carolina, and I'm sure that if our recent instructor could have seen us swinging through the streets on parade in perfect time to the music, he would have been proud of his work. We were sent to the Marine Camp at Quantico, Virginia, near Washington, where a battalion was assembled for overseas. Some of the battalion came from the battleship *Tennessee.* In a few more days we arrived at Philadelphia, marched through to the strains of "Over There," and embarked on the transport *Henderson.* Five hundred sailors were aboard, going to France to man the big naval guns to be used for bombarding purposes. We were stuffed in like sardines, but I happened to get a hammock hung from the ceiling out on deck. I got seasick the first day by the time we were out of sight of land down Delaware Bay, and remained sick and miserable the entire thirteen days crossing. The ship was kept in complete darkness at night, as a light would have betrayed us to any submarine nearby. Each fellow wore a life preserver at all times, and they were somewhat uncomfortable to work and sleep in. One night one of the cannons fired, and we were immediately ordered out on deck. They thought a submarine was trying to torpedo us and we would have to leave the ship if it started sinking.

There were five or six ships in our convoy, all painted in the striped camouflage color. I don't see how they kept from running into each other at night, but each morning they would be about the same distance apart. My job on the ship was to stand watch in the steering room certain hours each day so we could keep the ship on its course by hand if the electrical apparatus went wrong.

No one was allowed to throw anything over in the water because it would get the whales or fish to following the ship and a submarine might pick up the trail from them. The garbage was collected and thrown over at one time. When [we arrived] in the real submarine zone near Europe, orders went out that if anyone fell overboard, the ship would not stop to pick them up. I watched my step around the rail. In one of the storms the waves were rolling so high that they came over my deck spraying everything, creating the danger of my being washed overboard.

As soon as our boat docked, we were put to work unloading it. The sailors and marines worked in relays. From among the boxes of canned goods being loaded for the crane, I picked up an odd-shaped box which I set out on the dock with the rest. Imagine my astonishment a few minutes later when a big naval officer dashed down in the hold where we were and wanted to know who sent that box up. He said that it contained enough nitroglycerine to blow up Brest Harbor. No one said a word, but I had a mental picture of its being thrown around up there with the other boxes.

When the ship was unloaded, we struck out for the Napoleon barracks five miles away. The barracks were some old stone buildings which the emperor had used to house his soldiers, but we used our tents. It was warm during the day and cold and disagreeable at night, but anything was better than the unbearable crowded condition of the boat. The hike after being cooped up caused the soles of my feet to become so sore I could scarcely bear to put them to the ground. But it was up early and work or drill all day while we were there and drag off dog-tired to bed at night to shiver in the cold, even though it was the first part of May. We evidently were the first troops to begin this camp. A year and a half later when I returned, it was scarcely recognizable. The camp then had the capacity for handling several thousand soldiers comfortably at one time.

At the end of a week, we received our first ride on a French troop train. The capacity of these cattle cars were forty men or eight horses. It would be horses one trip and maybe men the next. There was room for the forty to sit in the boxcar, provided each one drew his legs up under his chin and slept by leaning over on someone else. Usually there was a layer of straw on the floor, which helped some. It was hard to choose which was worse, the ship or the boxcar. The advantages with the latter were that a stop was made two or three times a day and the men were allowed to stretch their legs, and no train ride lasted over two or three days. Besides the discomfort of both modes of travel, there was the danger of being torpedoed out of the water in one case and bombed from the air in the other.

During this ride, our train stopped in a railroad yard alongside a flat car with a big barrel of wine on it. Some of the men pried around the big peg in the barrel until it came out, and along with it came a stream of wine. There was a mad scramble out of the cattle cars, all with cups and canteens ready. Soon the wine was ankle deep on the ground, so that some of the men began getting it there. The officers, riding comfortably and uncrowded in the better cars apart from the men, soon found out what was going on back down the line, but most of us got back in our cars by the time they arrived. Those men who were so far gone on the wine that they could not make it back to the cars, and did not care either, were court-martialed. They did time under guard and had part of their pay deducted. Another time, at a stop a soldier bought a quart of wine from a Frenchman, but an officer saw him and took the bottle and broke it on the track. Discipline was strict, and nothing was to interfere with the Americans' training. After the newness of being in France wore off, there were not so many restrictions about drinking when off-duty and back from the line.

From Brest we went diagonally across France to an obscure place in the southeastern part near the Swiss border. At Dijon we ate a meal of white bread, the last for many of us. Because of America's unprepared condition, we were now eating French rations of brown bread and the so-called monkey meat from South America.

Those among us designated as machine gunners were issued French Chau Chau's. The riflemen still had the good old American-made

Springfields. These Springfields were not only excellent shooting irons, but good for close quarters and bayonet fighting.

In this mountain camp, the final touches were put on for the front lines. Most commands were executed at the double, meaning it was executed at a run. The drill ground was the flat top of a high hill. It was up before daylight, a hurried breakfast, a little while to police up quarters, and then the man-killing ascent to the top of the hill. We reached the drill ground exhausted, but there were only a few minutes to blow, followed by hours of hard training. In addition to the other drill, I found out all about my machine gun. I could take it apart and reassemble it blindfolded. This was necessary in order to be able to repair the machine gun in the dark if it should jam on the front line.

We were in a peaceful little village eight miles from a railroad. One day when it was my time to work in the village at camp instead of drilling, we were digging a ditch and, in order to get through a rock, a grenade was touched off. After the explosion, the French nearby began running around in circles scanning the sky and saying *Boche*, their name for a German. They thought at first that a plane was bombing us.

On the Western Front, the Germans, having brought their troops from the Eastern Front, who had been used against Russia, were steadily advancing. They were shelling Paris with the Big Bertha. Some American Regulars, two or three divisions of National Guard, and a brigade of marines had been in France for several months and had been on the line in sections where no active fighting was being done during late winter and early spring. The brigade of marines, with two brigades of Regulars, made up the 2nd Division, which was a unit of 28,000 men commanded by Major General Harbord. My battalion of a thousand men was used as replacements for the Marine Brigade of the 2nd Division.

The German drive had been on since March 21. General Haig had issued his famous "Back to the Wall" order for the British, and the

French were exhausted. Conditions became so critical in the face of the enemy advance that the Allies laid aside all differences and united under one commander, the French General Foch, for the first time in the war. The French and English did not expect the Americans to be of much help at the front, as they felt that inexperienced troops could not hold where veterans had failed. However, the news came into our camp from British wounded that the Americans should be put in, to see what they could do.

One night about nine o'clock, sometime after the first of June, we were ordered to pack and be ready to leave right away. None of us knew where we were going, but at the appointed time every man was on the road with his pack containing everything he possessed and with his rifle in his hand. We swung off into the black night, headed for our railroad station. We reached it near daybreak, tired but glad for any kind of change. We had come to accept the condition of being tired and hungry as an almost continual feeling. Our train traveled all day in a northern direction, and that night when it stopped we could hear a distant rumble, which was the bombardment at the front. The next day we passed villages where the houses showed effects of shell and machine-gun fire. That evening we passed through the suburbs of a large city which we recognized as Paris, from the Eiffel Tower which reached over nine hundred feet into the air. Next came St. Denis and Meaux. At the latter place, we left the train, since that was as close as a train dared go to the front, and got on trucks.

Our trucks traveled toward Metz, a German city at that time, on the Paris-Metz Highway, which crosses the Marne River at the city of Château-Thierry. We were going toward the hottest part of the front, where the Germans had whipped all opposition to the spearhead of their drive for Paris. This great French highway was crowded with the American troops going toward the front and the civilian population fleeing in the opposite direction. A few civilians would remain with their homes and take chances with the German occupation, but most of them fled. There was danger of being killed when much fighting took place right at one's home. That evening we viewed many a sad face, with tragedy written in every line, going in the opposite direction. They kept well over on the side or completely off the road so as not to impede our progress. There were old people and children traveling by different conveyances. Only the crippled and very young children would be riding on household goods and valuables which were not to be left for the enemy.

We rode fifteen or twenty men per truck and had standing room only. There were about sixty trucks, for our battalion stretched out for over half a mile. The only French soldiers I saw were some on the ridges around Meaux who were feverishly digging a network of trenches out across the wheat fields. Of course the young wheat, about half knee high, was suffering from the depredations. I was told later that the American commander was ordered to contact the enemy and retreat [in] as orderly [a manner] as possible back to the trenches, where both forces would try to make the last stand that side of Paris. His reply was, "Retreat, hell! We just got here!"

We were unloaded near the front and lay down beside the road with our packs on. By this time we were used to keeping on our clothes all the time and eating when there was anything to eat. The clothes kept off the cold at night, and you were always ready to move at a moment's notice. During the night, a train of trucks with provisions for the front stopped along beside us, and some men were able to get a few loaves of bread before being stopped. After daylight, a number of ambulances sped by, each one loaded down, going to the hospitals in Paris. The Americans had met the Germans with a deadly machine-gun fire at Château-Thierry, while the marines made a stand northwest of the city outside of Belleau Wood. On June 6 they attacked the strong Belleau Wood position. It was now the day after that and the wounded were being evacuated.

My battalion was scattered out among the two marine regiments which were on the front to take the place of the killed and wounded. On June 8 about fifteen of us were attached to the 80th Co., 6 Reg. This company had only about eighty men left out of the two hundred and fifty that made the attack. Captain Coffenberg had been wounded and

Captain Lloyd, who had commanded me since we left Virginia, became captain. The first day, while we were lying in support just back of the front, one of the new men near me shot the trigger finger off his right hand. I never had anything make me jump any worse than when his gun went off right behind me.

We lay in our foxholes for protection against the shrapnel for a few days, being careful to stay hidden when German planes flew over looking for targets for their shells. We then took over a company's place on the line, while they lay in support for us. If the enemy captured the first line position, he would be against another right behind it, while still further back there was another line of reserve troops. The shifting of the men from position to position, or from the front, depended on how badly they had fared. A narrow tongue of a rocky wooded ridge about thirty feet wide and a hundred yards long jutted out into a wheat field. Across the field a short ways on either side and in front was another rocky wooded ridge or ravine. This tongue of timber was my first front line position. Belleau Wood was probably a mile square, with irregular patches of land here and there in cultivation.

By this time we had thrown away all of our pack, including extra underwear, a shirt, toothbrush, razor, etc. Crossing an open space must be done at full speed in order to make as poor a target as possible. There might be bayonet fighting at close quarters when there was no more time to load, and one could not afford to be hampered with excess weight. The only thing one should carry was food, if any, and ammunition. They were firing on us from three sides with one-pounders, rifles, and machine guns—some initiation for an inexperienced front-line man. They made a raid on us the first night, and I pumped so many bullets through my rifle that the barrel was too hot to hold. We sent up flares which showed them to us like we had been shown the night before while making relief.

I had been so horrified at the death, destruction, and danger on all sides that I had forgotten about my stomach. During the lull in watching the next day, I thought of my last meal behind the lines, when the cook told us to take some extra steaks which were cooked and save them for a later need. Mine had a greenish look to it, but was eaten with relish. Then I realized how thirsty I was.

A half-mile off and just inside our lines was the village of Bouresches, the only water supply in that vicinity. Lieutenant Robbinson [sic] with twenty-five men of the 96th Co. had charged through the streets and captured it in the general attack. Since it was uncertain when water could be gotten, I gathered up the canteens from my nearest companions and wormed my way down just behind the lines toward the well. There were woods of shattered trees for protection until I was within two hundred yards of the well.

As I went this route, the realities of war were exposed at their worst. Bodies of men, most of them killed three or four days before, were scattered in all directions, lying as they fell. One could not have recognized his own brother, since their faces had turned black. Possibly their knapsacks had been searched by the men nearest them for any food they might have had. Since I was so thirsty, the thought struck me, why not carry two canteens. All Americans carried the same size canteens, but the German officer carried a larger one than the common soldier, with a cloth fitting skintight around it and a strap to carry it around your shoulder. I selected one of that kind on a dead officer and carried it with me.

At the edge of the wood, I paused to speak to a group holding a position. "Get your head down, Greeny," one said in a low quick voice. I obeyed instantly and missed a volley. At the edge of the opening, I got on my stomach and crawled through the young wheat to the village.

The houses were razed, but when shelling began, I would run in a cellar. They were trying to hit our well and cave it in, apparently, for I had to run two or three times before getting all the water I wanted and filling my canteens. The wool cloth had closed back over a bullet hole through the German officer's canteen, and it was useless.

The return trip was made the same way. When we were relieved, I had been on the front three days without batting an eye. Troops left the front line with a haggard, worn look on their faces.

One night not very long after this, we were lying in our foxholes near the front and a runner brought word that help was needed at the front line. The Germans were breaking through. The night was inky black, and I had taken off my wrapped leggins [*sic*] and had to crawl around feeling for them under the heels of some artillery horses tied right by me and almost got my brains kicked out. I decided right then that I would never pull off anything at night again. I just had time to get my leggins in my pocket and move off with the line.

The guide moved off with a man right behind holding onto his pack with one hand, another held onto the second, and so on through the woods in single file. The guide was supposed to know the best route for the least shelling. It did not matter if it was across ravines, over boulders, and across timber felled by the shells and machine-gun fire.

We had gone just a short ways when there was a terrific gas shelling. It does not take long to tell the difference in the sound of the explosion of a gas, shrapnel, or high explosive shell. Every man immediately stopped, put on his gas mask, and then continued the journey. The mask is uncomfortable at any time and especially when you are perspiring from exertion, with the rubber mask air tight over your face. If it is daytime, the lens clouds up on the inside and you can't see. We got out of the gas area with plenty of stumbling along and found things not quite as critical at the front as was expected.

At other times we lay for hours in our foxholes with masks on. There was no breeze on the hot June nights to carry the gas away through the foliage. One day my nearest companion, Becker, brought his canteen to his mouth, brushing it against some foliage where the gas had settled, burning his tongue and lips. The inside of my nostrils stayed raw for several days from breathing the gas from the high-explosive shells. Scratches on your body were kept irritated by the gas, and where the pack rubbed your shoulders it would burn. The Germans could not retake our part of the woods by attacking, so they were trying to gas us out. Whenever a shell hit directly under a man, he would be hurled into the air and rain down in pieces. Slivers of flesh would go some distance.

The most optimistic person I ever saw was Lieutenant Gates of the

96th Company in our battalion. In one of the gas attacks his entire command was wiped out, and he was attached to my group until more men could be brought for him to command. With his winning personality, he was able to cheer us when everything looked as dark as it possibly could. His lion courage in the face of any danger was enough to bolster one's morale. I hated to see him leave us.

The lieutenant in command of my platoon, Johnny Overton, had a slender athletic body. In the spring of 1917, he was captain of Yale University's track team and held the American record for the mile run. Johnny was a he-man through and through. Our casualties were so heavy in going to or from the lines in large groups that the plan was hit upon to come off in small groups and reassemble at some appointed place. This plan was all right when you had been on one front long enough to know the territory well. It did my heart good to follow Overton. His torrid pace didn't seem bad going away from the front.

During the nights on the front, we stood in our trench watching without ever sleeping. Some sleepyheads would dose off now and then, while in the daytime most of us would catnap. I never slept at night and for only a few minutes at a time during the day. The times I carried a rifle with the bayonet on it instead of a machine gun, I could set the butt on the ground and the end of the bayonet reached to my chin. When I was so sleepy that I would start to sink down from a standing position the bayonet would pierce my chin and arouse me. During the long hours of night at "stand to," you would think of everything in the world.

At one time my trench faced a young peach orchard out in no man's land. The trees were spaced evenly to resemble men in attack formation; more than once while it was breaking day and light enough to show their forms, I would get over my gun with fingers on the trigger and ready to begin mowing down men when it would dawn on me about the orchard. The attack was always made at daylight by either side, and that was about the most nervous time of the day. When we captured a new position, the first thing was to fortify it as much as possible against attack. One night a number of four-foot stakes sharpened at one end were brought us with a spool of barbed wire. I was sent out with the detail to put up the wire in front of our trench. The fellow holding the stake while another drove it in the hard ground with the maul was in danger of having his hands hit or maybe even hit across his tin hat. This had to be done at night when the enemy could not see to shoot at you. When a flare was shot into the air, we hid as quickly as possible, but even at that there were always some being hit. After the stakes were set, we twisted the wire around among them, making a mass for our enemy to cross before getting on us. Some of our men back in the trenches thought the wire detail had returned to the trenches when we had not. Hearing us out there in the dark moving around, they thought it was a raiding party and opened fire. We only saved ourselves by dropping to the ground until they found out who we were.

A raid would be made now and then to get prisoners for questioning. This was to try and find out if there was anything out of the ordinary being planned by the opposite side. Another way to find out if preparations were being made under cover of darkness on the other side was for two or three men to slip over near the enemy trench and hide behind something and listen. If you made any noise like stepping on a stick and breaking it, you had better hide quickly or run like everything, because they would send up a flare, making things as light as day for a minute.

Food and water were brought to the front line once in twenty-four hours, at night, if the shelling didn't stop them. One morning the detail was so late that they arrived after daylight. Part of my company was out in a very exposed position. However, rather than see his men go without nourishment, Sergeant Willie went out with the food and water himself. Just as he reached the hole where they were, a bullet dropped him in with them. Word came back to where I was by the grapevine route that he was bleeding badly and something should be done to save him. Lieutenant Overton asked for volunteers. A fellow named Walker and I procured a stretcher and went out. We stood there in full view of the enemy trench for what seemed like an hour, when in reality it was only a minute, while he was passed up to us. We put him on the stretcher and walked off without being fired at directly, it seemed. The Dutchmen could have taken aim and got both of us. As we went back through the woods, a shell hit close, but we jumped behind a tree with our stretcher, and no one was hurt badly. Walker received a gash across the back of one hand from the flying shrapnel but kept carrying his end of the stretcher. We reached a deep ravine behind the lines, where a first-aid station had been set up, and left our cargo. On the return to my place in line, I ran into an Austrian 88 Whizz Bang barrage. I jumped into the nearest hole, landing next to a fellow who had been dead several days. The scent was stifling, but I stayed with him until the firing settled down above me.

Belleau Wood was captured a piece at a time, and by the first of July it was all in the Americans' possession. The Prussian Guards, the pick of Germany's troops, had been pushed back. They had us outnumbered in this forty days of fighting about three to five. We could tell from the numbers on the uniforms of the prisoners and dead and by talking with them what troops they were. The first prisoners, upon asking and being told we were Americans, refused to believe it, saying we were Canadians. They said that the Americans could not get through their submarines. Newspapers taken on the prisoners or in their trenches emphasized the German success considerably.

My last position on that front was facing the present American cemetery for that section of the country, where the American soldiers were taken from their first hurried burial places and placed in orderly rows. While occupying this position, a companion and I were operating a machine gun down in advance of the remainder of the company. We sneaked down the wooded hill to this place in the edge of the woods at night, so our gun could cover the open level space in front if an attack was made on us. We laid our gun down and set to work digging a hole to be in when daylight came, intending to put our gun on the edge in front, pointing out through the brush. When we were almost through, we realized day would soon come and we had not gotten any food or water since the night before. My companion went back to see about it, while I finished the job. Just as it was light enough to see some little ways, I suddenly saw a German soldier walking diagonally toward me along a path which went out in the open about six or seven feet from me. He was carrying his rifle in his right hand at the balance, with the bayonet, of course. My absent companion had the only Colt .45 between the two of us, and the German was too close for me to make a dive for my machine gun. I stood there still as a mouse, with shovel in hand, and looked at every feature on this young man's face as he walked by without seeing me.

He had an athletic build, [was] nearly six feet tall, and weighed about one hundred and seventy pounds. I never told of this incident for fear of being reprimanded for not shooting him in the back as he walked away. I should have gotten my machine gun after he passed and tried to take him prisoner. I had instructions to keep this machine-gun nest well hidden, which made me reluctant about firing when the game was so small. Out in the open, he was shot at three or four times, fell once, and lost his rifle but got away apparently unhurt. I heard a sergeant later chiding his men for missing such a good shot.

A few days before the 4th of July, orders came that some of the men (except machine gunners) would go back to Paris and parade. That left me out. Upon their return they reported that they were almost mobbed by a thankful people, and the Americans were being given credit for saving Paris. This battle of Belleau Wood was not large, as far as numbers of men engaged was concerned, but it was a great moral victory for the Allied side. The Germans named the American marines "Devil Dogs." The French government changed the name of Belleau Wood to American Marine Wood.

We were relieved from the front by the 26th (Yankee Division) from the New England states, but remained at the Marne River in reserve until the night of the 16th of July. A long-range shell came our way occasionally at this place, ten or fifteen miles from the front, but otherwise it was peaceful.

We stayed in the French houses, as practically all of the inhabitants were gone. We washed our clothes in the river without soap and swam around while they dried. We also fished with hand grenades until the officers stopped us.

On the fifteenth, we stood by our guns ready, as the Germans were launching an attack trying to break through.

On the night of July 16, we gathered near the Marne River and ate supper. Soon after dark, trucks arrived to carry us back to a rest camp (we hoped) after five weeks in Belleau Wood, and everyone seemed in good spirits. There were not enough trucks, and my company had to wait until near day for some more to arrive. We rode nearly all day toward our unknown destination. By evening hopes of not going back to the front had about vanished. A straggler out of the First Division of Regulars caught my truck and rode a piece.

In the evening rather late, we were unloaded on the edge of Villers-Cotterêts forest and started toward the front about seven miles away. There seemed to be a general convergence of troops toward this forest, and the narrow graded road was inadequate for the traffic. To make matters worse, a rain had just fallen. In one place a tank had gotten ditched and caused a temporary holdup. We had to leave the road several times, all of which seemed to throw us behind some prearranged schedule. Delays caused worried looks to appear on the officers' countenances. Traveling through the dark forest at night was extremely difficult, and the fact that we had not eaten in twenty-four hours made it worse. We reached the front line exhausted but, without slowing up, immediately went into battle at daybreak. We reached the line just in time to go over the top at the zero hour.

Our troops were playing the role of Stonewall Jackson's men (foot cavalry) in the Civil War. After forced marching and riding, a sudden, unexpected attack was being made. The prisoners captured, on being told we were American marines, said "No, the Marines are at Belleau Woods." Sometime during the day, I got about a spoonful of corned beef, which several of us divided. One of the men had gotten hold of a can somewhere and opened it with his bayonet.

The French cavalry with their long spears were back of us. A division of Americans was on the right flank and a division on the left flank in the drive, while a division of Moroccans was attacking in the center. Much airplane fighting was going on, and several [planes] got shot down. A battle in the air is interesting, and we always watched them if we were not too closely occupied. We must have gained seven or eight miles that day, driving toward Rheims on the left flank of the Marne salient. That night we stood by our guns to hold the gain, but we were tired and hungry.

The morning of July 19, the second day of the battle and the third day without food, we formed our lines in a road through a cut or ravine and came out for a charge across a sugar beet field. The tanks were leading, with our lines right behind them. In trying to stop the charge, the Germans turned loose everything they had. It seemed to rain shells. One hit between me and the man on my left, Red Williams. It knocked a hole in the ground, half covered me with dirt, and left my hands and face powder-burned, but the shrapnel had missed. Red was not quite so lucky and received his death wound. I left him writhing and groaning on the ground to continue the attack.

The last glance I had of Lieutenant Overton, he was walking backward and trying to shout something back to us. He carried his cane in the left hand and a .45 [pistol] in the right. The din and roar was so terrific that I didn't have any idea what he was saying, but interpreted it from his expression to be some words of encouragement. He was soon down, killed. The gunnery sergeant was killed.

Just ahead of me, a few men grouped and started down a ditch. My training told me to keep out of groups, for a shell could kill several at one time. I leaped some barbed wire to the right of them as a shell hit, making a clean sweep. One of the men near me was shot through the shoulder; another had a finger shot off his hand. I opened our first-aid package and applied the gauze to the wound. They both left for the rear, hoping to make the hospital. By this time, all of the tanks had been crippled or stopped and all the men around me shot down. I was now nearing the woods across the field in front of our attack zone. Realizing this, I began to look for a stopping place and found it in an old sunken road less than a foot deep. A volley from a machine gun missed me by inches, and, falling where I stood in the road, I drew fire which barely cleared my body for the rest of the day.

In thirty or forty minutes, our regiment had been almost annihilated. The field which had been recently crossed was strewn with dead and dying. Their cries for water and help got weaker as the hot July day wore on.

There I was, under the enemy gun and almost in his lines by myself. I will never know how I went through that curtain of shells untouched. I was black from the powder of the exploding shells. Most of my trousers was left in the barbed-wire entanglements. At first I expected a counterattack and was prepared to come to my feet and sell myself as dearly as possible. The slaughter of my comrades had left a bad taste. The attack never came, but enemy planes flew low over the battlefield during the day and, as the pilot leaned his head over the side looking through his glasses, I lay feigning death. The hot sun made my thirst almost unbearable. A slug of shrapnel hit my foot, but the hobnails saved [me from] a serious wound.

Late in the evening, while I was wondering if I could get away after dark and contact any of my forces which were left, I saw an American uniform crawl across the road some hundred yards away. Laboriously crawling to where he disappeared, I found my old friend Lieutenant Cates of the 96th Company holding a trench with about twelve or fifteen men. He asked me where the rest of the 80th Company was, and I told him that I didn't know, but thought most of them were hit. A dead German soldier was lying across the barbed wire in front of the trench. He was shot as he slowed up to cross. One of the men sneaked out and found a piece of black rye bread in his pack. I had a spoonful of sugar in my condiment can and with the sugar to sprinkle on the bread we got a bite around.

After midnight a force of Algerian troops came to relieve us, and gathering as many of our wounded as we could carry, we started back. Three of us were carrying Cooper of my company in a blanket. I was at the feet with the other two going ahead with the other end. Cooper was shot through the leg, arm, and head. We lost our hold on the blanket several times, letting him slip to the ground. Each time he greeted us with a groan. Finally we got back to a well, and I'm sure that I drank near a gallon of water within twenty minutes' time. We went back a mile or two behind the lines and lay down.

The surviving marines who left the battle line were a terrible looking bunch of people. They looked more like animals. They had almost a week's growth of beard and were dirty and ragged. Their eyes were sunk back in their heads. There had been very little sleep or rest for four days and no food. Late in the evening of July 20, we survivors got a meal of slum gullion.

One of our group related that while he was near an Algerian he smelled a very offensive odor and upon investigation found him carrying a pouch with human ears in it. Some of the ears were pretty old. It was their custom to take the ears from the enemy they killed.

There were so many wounded in the attack that the ambulance service broke down. Many were piled in trucks and jolted back over shell-torn roads, causing wounds which had become quite sore several hours after their infliction to start bleeding again. Gangrene caused other deaths when an early evacuation would have saved lives.

The stretcher bearers all wore a Red Cross band around one arm to distinguish them from combatants, so they could go out in the open without being shot at. They never carried any arms. However, that branch of service suffered heavy casualties and had to keep giving first aid to the wounded and being subject to shell fire after the fighters dug in.

The battalion of four compnaies was put together, but that did not make one good-sized company. We laid down to rest near a battery of our artillery while food was being gotten ready. Soon sleep was interrupted by the boom of the battery sending a few shells over to Heinie. I was awakened suddenly by a fellow near me becoming a raving maniac. The strain had been too much and something had slipped in his head. Cases like this were called shell shock. We tried to reassure him that he was among friends away from the front, but he evidently thought he was in the middle of a terrible battle and surrounded by enemies. I dropped back down to sleep while he was being carried away.

An observation balloon was near the place where we were. A German plane dived and shot it down. The machine-gun bullets set fire to the balloon, but the observer came out in a parachute, landing in a tree.

The boys were more despondent than I ever saw them after this last battle, and no wonder. As far as I know, I was the only survivor of Overton's platoon of about fifty men. There were eight able to walk away from the front, out of 212 on the company roster at the time. However, there were some fifteen or twenty men who claimed they got lost off during the night and were not in the terrible slaughter in the sugar beet field.

from Helmet for My Pillow
by Robert Leckie

Robert Leckie, a machine gunner and scout for the First
Marine Division in the South Pacific during World War II,
saw his first combat on Guadalcanal.

t was the day our liquor ran out. I was among those who joined the
other men from our company and marched away from the beach,
through the coconut grove, into the kunai, and so to the point we
would defend outside Henderson Field.

In front of me marched No-Behind. He was a tall, slender, noisy
fellow from Michigan who was oddly capable of exasperating anyone
in H Company merely by marching in front of him. It was an odd
affliction in that it was no affliction: No-Behind actually seemed not
to have a behind. So long and flat were his hips that his cartridge belt
seemed always in danger of slipping to his ankles. No curve of bone or
flare of flesh was there to arrest it. He seemed to walk without bending
the knees of his long thin legs, and, most maddening, where his
trousers should have bulged with the familiar bulk of a behind, they
seemed to sag inward! When to this was added a girlish voice that

seemed forever raised in high-pitched profanity, there emerged an epicene quality which enraged those unlucky enough to march behind No-Behind. Often I quivered to draw my bayonet and skewer No-Behind where his behind was not.

This day, as we passed with fixed bayonets through the kunai toward the line of wood beyond which a round red sun had fallen, Corporal Smoothface marched behind No-Behind. Smoothface was drunk on the last of the sake. He seemed to be babbling happily enough, when, suddenly, with a crazy yell, he lowered his rifle and drove the bayonet at No-Behind.

We thought Smoothface had killed him, for No-Behind's scream had been that of a dying man. But, fortunately for No-Behind, his very insufficiency in the target area had saved him; the bayonet passed through his trousers without even breaking the flesh, and it had not been the cutting edge of the bayonet but the hard round feel of the rifle muzzle that had provoked his expiring shout.

Smoothface found it so funny he had to sit down to contain his laughter. Then, as he arose, a battery of artillery concealed in the wood gave nerve-jangling voice. They were our seventy-five-millimeter howitzers, shooting at what we did not know, for they shot frequently and we never knew if they were merely registering terrain or actually blasting the enemy. But the sudden crash of field pieces is always a disturbing thing, even if the guns turn out to be friendly.

Smoothface bared his small, even teeth in an animal snarl. He unlimbered his rifle again, and returned the fire. That was the end of the Guadalcanal Campaign for Corporal Smoothface. He was led away under guard.

But he had one last glorious round remaining. Placed in the rear of a captain's jeep, he rose to his feet, abusing him.

"Ah'll never ride with Captain Headlines," he swore, and as he swore it, the jeep leapt forward. Smoothface was ejected in a slow somersault into the air, came down on his ankle, broke it and was taken to the hospital, where, that very night, a rare transport landed on our airfield. He was evacuated to New Zealand, was cured, given a light brig

sentence, and finally turned loose to browse among the fleshpots of
Auckland. His broken ankle, although perhaps not honorably suffered,
was the very first of the "beer wounds," which all veterans covet so
mightily—those merely superficial holes or cuts or breaks which take
a man out of battle and into the admiring glances and free drinks of
civilization.

It was still light over the airfield when we left it and stepped into the
gloom of the jungle. It was as though one had walked from a lighted,
busy street into the murk and silence of a church, except that here was
no reverence or smell of candle-grease, but the beginning of dread and
the odor of corruption.

We were told off at staggered intervals of about ten yards. I have no
idea how many men were on the patrol, perhaps slightly more than a
hundred of us, of which some thirty would have been from H Company. We never knew these things. All that we knew was that in front
of us lay the dark and moving jungle and quite probably the enemy,
behind us the airfield in which reposed absolutely all of Guadalcanal's
military value.

Our entrenching tools made muffled noises while we scooped foxholes out of the jungle floor. It was like digging into a compost heap
ten thousand years old. Beneath this perfection of corruption lay a
dark rich loam. We had barely finished when night fell, abruptly,
blackly, like a shade drawn swiftly down from jungle roof to jungle
floor. We slipped into the foxholes. We lay down and waited.

It was a darkness without time. It was an impenetrable darkness. To
the right and the left of me rose up those terrible formless things of my
imagination, which I could not see because there was no light. I could
not see, but I dared not close my eyes lest the darkness crawl beneath
my eyelids and suffocate me. I could only hear. My ears became my
being and I could hear the specks of life that crawled beneath my
clothing, the rotting of the great tree which rose from its three-cornered
trunk above me. I could hear the darknesses gathering against me and
the silences that lay between the moving things.

I could hear the enemy everywhere about me, whispering to each other and calling my name. I lay open-mouthed and half-mad beneath that giant tree. I had not looked into its foliage before the darkness and now I fancied it infested with Japanese. Everything and all the world became my enemy, and soon my very body betrayed me and became my foe. My leg became a creeping Japanese, and then the other leg. My arms, too, and then my head.

My heart was alone. It was me. I was my heart.

It lay quivering, I lay quivering, in that rotten hole while the darknesses gathered and all creation conspired for my heart.

How long? I lay for an eternity. There was no time. Time had disintegrated in that black void. There was only emptiness, and that is Something; there was only being; there was only consciousness.

Like the light that comes up suddenly in a darkened theatre, daylight came quickly. Dawn came, and so myself came back to myself. I could see the pale outlines of my comrades to right and left, and I marveled to see how tame my tree could be, how unforbidding could be its branches.

I know now why men light fires.

Urgency and a certain air of injury and reproach characterized the manner of the Major as he drove his jeep through the coconuts, stopping at each squad mess along the line to commandeer the provender. Except for the urgency, he might have been a scoutmaster scolding his charges for having eaten their lunch by midmorning.

The Major's tour marked the death of the squad messes. Our brief escape from battalion authority was ended, and a battalion galley was being set up. But the Major found precious little food to cart off to a pyramidal tent which was set up about two hundred yards in from the beach. This was where we ate, and this was where we were introduced to our new diet of rice. The food had belonged to the enemy, and so had the wooden bowls from which we ate it. We preferred these to our own mess gear with its maddening capacity for making all food taste like metal. We ate a bowl of rice for breakfast and had the same for supper. Once a marine complained of worms in the rice to one of our two doctors.

"They're dead," he laughed. "They can't hurt you. Eat them, and be glad you have fresh meat."

He was joking, but he was serious. No one resented it. Everyone thought the doctor had a good sense of humor.

The day after our diet of rice began, the Major's unwonted urgency became clear to us. We were ordered up from the beach to new positions on the west bank of the Tenaru River. Our orders commanded us to urgency.

The enemy was expected.

The Tenaru River lay green and evil, like a serpent, across the palmy coastal plain. It was called a river, but it was not a river; like most of the streams of Oceania, it was a creek—not thirty yards wide.

Perhaps it was not even a creek, for it did not always flow and it seldom reached its destination, the sea. Where it might have emptied into Iron Bottom Bay, a spit of sand, some forty feet wide, penned it up. The width of the sandspit varied with the tides, and sometimes the tide or the wind might cause the Tenaru to rise, when, slipping over the spit, it would fall into the bosom of the sea, its mother.

Normally, the Tenaru stood stagnant, its surface crested with scum and fungus; evil, I said, and green. If there are river gods, the Tenaru was inhabited by a baleful spirit.

Our section—two squads, one with the Gentleman as gunner, the other with Chuckler as gunner and me as assistant—took up position approximately three hundred yards upstream from the sandspit. As we dug, we had it partially in view; that is, what would be called the enemy side of the sandspit. For the Tenaru marked our lines. On our side, the west bank, was the extremity of the marine position; on the other, a no man's land of coconuts through which an attack against us would have to pass.

The Japanese would have to force the river to our front; or come over the narrow sandspit to our left, which was well defended by riflemen and a number of machine gun posts and barbed wire; or else try our right flank, which extended only about a hundred yards south of us, before curving back north to the Tenaru's narrowest point, spanned by a wooden bridge.

The emplacement for the Gentleman's gun was excellently located to rake the coconut grove opposite. We dug it first, leaving Chuckler's and my gun standing some twenty yards downstream, above the ground, protected by a single strand of barbed wire strung midway down the steeply sloping river bank. We would emplace it next day.

We dug the Gentleman's gun pit wide and deep—some ten feet square and five feet down—for we wanted the gunner to be able to stand while firing, and we wanted the pit to serve as a bomb shelter as well, for the bombs were falling fiercer.

But furiously as we worked, naked to the waist, sweat streaming so steadily our belts were turned sodden, we were unable to finish the pit on the first day. When night fell, only the excavation was done, plus a dirt shelf where the gun was placed. We would have to wait for the next day to roof it over with coconut logs.

We felt exposed in our half-finished fortifications, unsure. The dark made sinister humpbacks of the piles of soft red earth we had excavated, and on which we sat.

But, because we did not know real battle—its squallish trick of suddenness—we could not feel foreboding as we sat atop the soft mounds, concealing the telltale coals of our bitter Japanese cigarettes in cupped hands, softly smoking, softly talking. We were only uneasy in that shiftiness that came each night and disappeared each dawn.

No one went to bed. The stars were out, and this was enough to keep everyone up, unwilling to waste a bright night.

Suddenly in the river, upstream to our right, there appeared a widening, rippling V. It seemed to be moving steadily downstream. At the point of the V were two greenish lights, small, round, close together.

Jawgia whooped and fired his rifle at it.

To our right came a fusillade of shots. It was from G Company riflemen, shooting also at the V. More bullets hit the water. The V disappeared.

The stars vanished. The night darkened. Like our voices, the men began to trail off to bed, wrapping themselves in their ponchos and lying on the ground a few yards behind the pit. Only the Chuckler and myself were left, to stand watch.

Lights—swinging, bumping lights, like lanterns or headlights—glittered across the river in the grove. It was fantastic, a truck there, as though we might awake next morning and find a railroad station confronting us across that stagnant stream. The coconut grove was no man's land. The enemy had a right to be there, but, by all the experience of jungle warfare, it was inviting death to mark himself with lights, to let his truck wheels shout, "Here we are!"

"Who goes there?" the Chuckler bellowed.

The lights bumped and swung serenely on.

"Who goes there? Answer, or I'll let you have it!"

The lights went out.

This was too much. Everyone was awake. The mysterious V in the river and now these ghostly lights—it was too much! We jabbered excitedly, and once again warmed our souls in the heat of our voices.

Shattering machine gun fire broke out far to the left. As far down as the sandspit, perhaps. There came another burst. Again. Another. The sharply individual report of the rifle punctuated the uproar. There followed the "plop" of heavy mortars being launched behind us, then the crunching roar of their detonation across the Tenaru. The conflagration was sweeping toward us up the river, like a train of powder.

It was upon us in an instant, and then we were firing. We were so disorganized we had not the sense to disperse, clustering around that open pit as though we were born of it. Falsetto screeching rose directly opposite us and we were blasting away at it, sure that human intruders had provoked the cry of the birds. I helped the Gentleman fire his gun, although I was not his assistant. He concentrated on the river bank, firing burst after burst there, convinced that the Japs were preparing to swim the river. The screeching stopped.

The Gentleman spoke softly. "Tell those clucks to quit firing. Tell them to wait until they hear the birds making a clatter, 'cause a smart man'd try to move under cover of it. That's when they'll be moving."

I was glad he gave me this little order to execute. I was having no fun standing in the pit, watching the Gentleman fire. I crawled out and told everyone what he had said. They ignored it and kept banging away. There came a lull, and in that silent space, I, who had had no chance to fire my own weapon, blasted away with my pistol. I leaned over the mound and shoved my pistol-clenching hand into the dark and emptied the clip. There came a roar of anger from the Hoosier.

"Dammit, Lucky, ain't you got no-better sense'n to go firing past a fellow's ear? You like to blow my head off, you Jersey jerk!"

I laughed at him, and the Chuckler crawled back from the bank and whispered, "C'mon, let's get our gun."

We snaked up the bank on our bellies, for the night was alive with the angry hum of bullets. The Chuckler took the gunner's spot and I crouched alongside in the position to keep the gun fed. We had plenty of ammunition, the long two-hundred-and-fifty-round belts coiled wickedly in the light green boxes, those same sturdy boxes which you now see slung on the shoulders of shoe-shine boys.

The Chuckler fired and the gun slumped forward out of his hands, digging its snout into the dirt, knocking off the flash hider with a disturbing clatter, spraying our own area with bullets.

"That yellow-belly!" the Chuckler cursed.

He cursed a certain corporal who was not then distinguishing himself for bravery, and who had set up the gun and done it so sloppily that the tripod had collapsed at the first recoil.

I crawled down the slope and straightened it. I leaned hard on the clamps.

"She's tight," I told the Chuckler.

His answer was a searing burst that streaked past my nose.

A man says of the eruption of battle: "All hell broke loose." The first time he says it, it is true—wonderfully descriptive. The millionth time it is said, it has been worn into meaninglessness: it has gone the way of all good phrasing, it has become cliché.

But within five minutes of that first machine gun burst, of the appearance of that first enemy flare that suffused the battlefield in unearthly greenish light—and by its dying accentuated the reenveloping night—within five minutes of this, all hell broke loose. Everyone was firing, every weapon was sounding voice; but this was no orchestration, no terribly beautiful symphony of death, as decadent rear-echelon observers write. Here was cacophony; here was dissonance; here was wildness; here was the absence of rhythm, the loss of limit, for everyone fires what, when and where he chooses; here was booming, sounding, shrieking, wailing, hissing, crashing, shaking, gibbering noise. Here was hell.

Yet each weapon has its own sound, and it is odd with what clarity the trained ear distinguishes each one and catalogues it, plucks it out of the general din, even though it be intermingled or coincidental with the voice of a dozen others, even though one's own machine gun spits and coughs and dances and shakes in choleric fury. The plop of the outgoing mortar with the crunch of its fall, the clatter of the machine guns and the lighter, faster rasp of the Browning Automatic Rifles, the hammering of fifty-caliber machine guns, the crash of seventy-five-millimeter howitzer shells, the crackling of rifle fire, the *wham* of thirty-seven-millimeter antitank guns firing point-blank canister at the charging enemy—each of these conveys a definite message, and sometimes meaning, to the understanding ear, even though that ear be filled with the total wail of battle.

So it was that our ears prickled at strange new sounds: the lighter, shingle-snapping crack of the Japanese rifle, the gargle of their extremely fast machine guns, the hiccup of their light mortars.

To our left, a stream of red tracers arched over to the enemy bank. Distance and the cacophony being raised around us seemed to invest them with silence, as though they were bullets fired in a deaf man's world.

"It's the Indian's gun," I whispered.

"Yeah. But those tracers are bad stuff. I'm glad we took 'em out of our belts. He keeps up that tracer stuff, and they'll spot him, sure."

They did.

They set up heavy machine guns in an abandoned amtrack on their side of the river and they killed the Indian.

Their slugs slammed through the sandbags. They ate their way up the water-jacket of his gun and they ate their way into his heart. They killed him, killed the Indian kid, the flat-faced, anonymous prize fighter from Pittsburgh. He froze on the trigger with their lead in his heart; he was dead, but he killed more of them. He wasn't anonymous, then; he wasn't a prelim boy, then.

They wounded his assistant. They blinded him. But he fought on. The Marines gave him the Navy Cross and Hollywood made a picture about him and the Tenaru Battle. I guess America wanted a hero fast, a live one; and the Indian was dead.

The other guy was a hero, make no mistake about it; but some of us felt sad that the poor Indian got nothing.

It was the first organized Japanese attack on Guadalcanal, the American fighting man's first challenge to the Japanese "superman." The "supermen" put bullets into the breast of the Indian, but he fired two hundred more rounds at them.

How could the Marines forget the Indian?

Now we had tracer trouble of a different kind. We had begun to take turns firing, and I was on the gun. The tracers came toward me, alongside me. Out of the river dark they came. You do not see them coming. They are not there; then, there they are, dancing around you on tiptoe; sparkles gay with the mirth of hell.

They came toward me, and time stretched out. There were but a few bursts, I am sure, but time was frozen while I leaned away from them.

"Chuckler," I whispered. "We'd better move. It looks like they've got the range. Maybe we ought to keep moving. They won't be able to get the range that way. And maybe they'll think we've got more guns than we really have."

Chuckler nodded. He unclamped the gun and I slipped it free of its socket in the tripod. Chuckler lay back and pulled the tripod over him. I lay back and supported the gun on my chest. We moved backward, like backstroke swimmers, almost as we had moved when we stole the case of beer out of the North Carolina shanty, trying, meanwhile, to avoid making noise that might occur during one of those odd and suspenseful times of silence that befall battles —noise which might attract fire from the opposite bank—if anyone was there.

For, you see, we never knew if there really was anyone there. We heard noises; we fired at them. We felt shells explode on our side and heard enemy bullets; but we could not be sure of their point of origin.

But, now, there was no enemy fire while we squirmed to our new position. We set up the gun once more and resumed firing, tripping our bursts at sounds of activity as before. We remained here fifteen minutes, then sought a new position. Thus we passed the remainder of the battle; moving and firing, moving and firing.

Dawn seemed to burst from a mortar tube. The two coincided; the rising bombardment of our mortars and the arrival of light. We could see, now, that the coconut grove directly opposite us had no life in it. There were bodies, but no living enemy.

But to the left, toward the ocean and across the Tenaru, the remnant of this defeated Japanese attacking force was being annihilated. We could see them, running. Our mortars had got behind them. We were walking our fire in; that is, dropping shells to the enemy's rear, then lobbing the projectile steadily closer to our own lines, so that the unfortunate foe was forced to abandon cover after cover, being drawn inexorably toward our front, where he was at last flushed and destroyed.

We could see them flitting from tree to tree. The Gentleman's gun was in excellent position to enfilade. He did. He fired long bursts at them. Some of us fired our rifles. But we were out of the fight, now; way off on the extreme right flank. We could add nothing to a situation so obviously under control.

"Hold your fire," someone from G Company shouted at the Gentleman. "First Battalion coming through."

Infantry had crossed the Tenaru at the bridge to our right and were fanning out in the coconut grove. They would sweep toward the ocean.

Light tanks were crossing the sandspit far to the left, leading a counterattack.

The Japanese were being nailed into a coffin.

Everyone had forgotten the fight and was watching the carnage, when shouting swept up the line. A group of Japanese dashed along the opposite river edge, racing in our direction. Their appearance so surprised everyone that there were no shots.

We dived for our holes and gun positions. I jumped to the gun which the Chuckler and I had left standing on the bank. I unclamped the gun and fired, spraying my shots as though I were handling a hose.

All but one fell. The first fell as though his underpart had been cut from him by a scythe, and the others fell tumbling, screaming.

Once again our gun collapsed and I grabbed a rifle—I remember it had no sling—which had been left near the gun. The Jap who had survived was deep into the coconuts by the time I found him in the rifle sights. There was his back, bobbing large, and he seemed to be throwing his pack away. Then I had fired and he wasn't there any more.

Perhaps it was not I who shot him, for everyone had found their senses and their weapons by then. But I boasted that I had. Perhaps, too, it was a merciful bullet that pounded him between the shoulder blades; for he was fleeing to a certain and horrible end: black nights, hunger and slow dissolution in the rain forest. But I had not thought of mercy then.

Modern war went forward in the jungle.

Men of the First Battalion were cleaning up. Sometimes they drove a Japanese toward us. He would cower on the river bank, hiding; unaware that opposite him were we, already the victors, numerous, heavily armed, lusting for more blood. We killed a few more this way. The Fever was on us.

Down on the sandspit the last nail was being driven into the coffin.

Some of the Japanese threw themselves into the channel and swam away from that grove of horror. They were like lemmings. They could not come back. Their heads bobbed like corks on the horizon. The marines killed them from the prone position; the marines lay on their bellies in the sand and shot them through the head.

The battle was over.

Beneath a bright moon that night, the V reappeared in the river. The green lights gleamed malevolently. Someone shot at it. Rifle fire crackled along the line. The V vanished. We waited, tense. No one came.

Lieutenant Ivy-League strode up to our pits in the morning. He sat on a coconut log and told us what had happened. He smoked desperately and stared into the river as he talked. The skin around his eyes was drawn tight with strain and with shock. His eyes had already taken on that aspect peculiar to Guadalcanal, that constant stare of pupils that seemed darker, larger, rounder, more absolute. It was particularly noticeable in the brown-eyed men. Their eyes seemed to get auburn, like the color of an Irish setter.

"They tried to come over the sandspit," the lieutenant said. "There must have been a thousand of them. We had only that one strand of wire and the guns. You should see them stacked up in front of Bitenail's gun. Must be three deep. They were crazy. They didn't even fire their rifles." He looked at us. "We heard firing up here. What happened?"

We told him. He nodded, but he was not listening; he was still intent on that yelling horde sweeping over the sandspit. When he spoke again it was to tell us who had been killed. There were more than a dozen from H Company, besides more than a score of wounded. Four or five of the dead were from our platoon. Two of them had been hacked to death. A Japanese scouting party had found them asleep in their hole on the river bank and sliced them in pieces.

It is not always or immediately saddening to hear "who got it." Except for one's close buddies, it is difficult to feel deep, wracking grief for the dead, and now, hearing the lieutenant tolling off the names, I had to force my face into a mask of mourning, deliberately adorn my heart with black, as it were, for I was shocked to gaze inward and see no sorrow there. Rather than permit myself to know myself a monster (as I seemed, then) I deliberately deluded myself by feigning bereavement. So did we all.

Only when I heard the name of the doctor who had joked about the wormy rice did a real pang pierce my heart.

Lieutenant Ivy-League arose, still staring into the river, and said, "I've got to get going. I've got to write those letters." He turned and left.

We got the second gun emplaced that morning. Then, the Hoosier and I sneaked off to the beach.

Our regiment had killed something like nine hundred of them. Most of them lay in clusters or heaps before the gun pits commanding the sandspit, as though they had not died singly but in groups. Moving among them were the souvenir hunters, picking their way delicately as though fearful of booby traps, while stripping the bodies of their possessions.

Only the trappings of war change. Only these distinguish the Marine souvenir hunter, bending over the fallen Jap, from Hector denuding slain Patroclus of the borrowed armor of Achilles.

One of the marines went methodically among the dead armed with a pair of pliers. He had observed that the Japanese have a penchant for gold fillings in their teeth, often for solid gold teeth. He was looting their very mouths. He would kick their jaws agape, peer into the mouth with all the solicitude of a Park Avenue dentist—careful, always careful not to contaminate himself by touch—and yank out all that glittered. He kept the gold teeth in an empty Bull Durham tobacco sack, which he wore around his neck in the manner of an amulet. Souvenirs, we called him.

The thought of him and of the other trophy-takers suggested to me, as I returned from the pits, that across the river lay an unworked mine of souvenirs to which I might rightfully stake a claim.

When I had shot the Japanese fleeing down the river bank, something silver had flashed when the first one fell. I imagined it to be the sun's reflection off an officer's insignia. If he had been an officer, he must have been armed with a saber. This most precious prize of all the war I was determined to get.

I slipped through the barbed wire and clambered down the bank. I left my clothes at the water's edge, like a schoolboy on a summer's day, and slipped into the water. I had a bayonet between my teeth; still the schoolboy, fancying myself a bristling pirate.

I swam breast stroke. Not even the fire of the enemy would induce me to put my face into that putrid stream. The water was thick with scum. My flesh crept while I swam, neck stiff and head erect like a swan's, the cold feel of the bayonet between my teeth, and my saliva running fast around it so that it threatened to slip out at any moment.

I paddled carefully around the body of a big Japanese soldier, lying in the water with one foot caught in the underbrush. He swayed gently, like a beached rowboat. He seemed unusually bloated, until I perceived that his blouse was stuffed with cooked rice and that his pants were likewise loaded to the knees, where he had tied leather thongs to keep the rice from falling out. "Chow hound," I thought, and felt an odd affection for him. My feet touched the slime of the river bottom. I had to advance about three yards up the bank. My feet sank so deep in the soft mud I feared momentarily that I was in a bog. The mud came up to my calves and made greedy sucking sounds with every step, while surrendering little swarms of fiddler crabs that scuttled away in sideways flight.

Dead bodies were strewn about the grove. The tropics had got at them already, and they were beginning to spill open. I was horrified at the swarms of flies; black, circling funnels that seemed to emerge from every orifice: from the mouth, the eyes, the ears. The beating of their myriad tiny wings made a dreadful low hum.

The flies were in possession of the field; the tropics had won; her minions were everywhere, smacking their lips over this bounty of rotting flesh. All of my elation at the victory, all of my fanciful cockiness fled before the horror of what my eyes beheld. It could be my corrupting body the white maggots were moving over; perhaps one day it might be.

Holding myself stiffly, as though fending off panic with a straight arm, I returned to the river bank and slipped into the water. But not before I had stripped one of my victims of his bayonet and field glasses, both of which I slung across my chest, crisscross like a grenadier. I had found no saber. None of the dead men was an officer.

I swam back, eager to be away from that horrid grove. My comrades, who had covered my excursion with our guns, mistook my grimace of loathing for a grin of triumph, when, streaked with slime, I emerged from the Tenaru. They crowded around to examine my loot. Then, I went to chow.

Coming back, I noticed a knot of marines, many from G Company, gathered in excitement on the river bank. Runner rushed up to them with my new field glasses.

He had them to his eyes, as I came up. I thought he was squinting overhard, then I saw that he was actually grimacing. I took the glasses from him and focused on the opposite shore, where I saw a crocodile eating the fat "chow-hound" Japanese. I watched in debased fascination, but when the crocodile began to tug at the intestines, I recalled my own presence in that very river hardly an hour ago, and my knees went weak and I relinquished the glasses.

That night the V reappeared in the river. Everyone whooped and hollered. No one fired. We knew what it was. It was the crocodile.

Three smaller V's trailed afterward.

They kept us awake, crunching. The smell kept us awake. Even though we lay with our heads swathed in a blanket—which was how we kept off the mosquitoes—the smell overpowered us. Smell, the sense which somehow seems a joke, is the one most susceptible to outrage. It will give you no rest. One can close one's eyes to ugliness or shield the ears from sound; but from a powerful smell there is no recourse but flight. And since we could not flee, we could not escape this smell; and we could not sleep.

We never fired at the crocodiles, though they returned to their repast day after day until the remains were removed to the mass burning and burial which served as funeral pyre for the enemy we had annihilated.

We never shot at the crocs because we considered them a sort of "river patrol." Their appetite for flesh aroused, they seemed to promenade the Tenaru daily. No enemy, we thought, would dare to swim the river with them in it; nor would he succeed if he dared. We relied upon our imperfect knowledge of the habits of crocodiles ("If they chase you, run zigzag: they can't change direction.") and a thick network of barbed wire to forestall their tearing us to pieces. Sometimes on black nights, in a spasm of fear, it might be imagined that the big croc was after us, like the crocodile with the clock inside of him who pursues Captain Hook in *Peter Pan.*

So the crocodiles became our darlings; we never molested them. Nor did any of us ever swim the Tenaru again.

from Semper Fi, Mac
by Henry Berry

Henry Berry for his 1982 oral history conducted more than 100 interviews with Marines who survived the Pacific war. The book included a conversation with Prate Stack, who served in campaigns on Peleliu and Okinawa.

LEE P. (PRATE) STACK, JR.
1st Lieutenant, 1st Tank Battalion
1st Marine Division

I was probably one of the last to hear about the Pearl Harbor attack. I was a member of the Yale Dramatic Club at the time. We never received as much publicity as Harvard's Hasty Pudding, but we always felt we were as good if not better than they.

Anyway, we were about to go on tour for the first time over the 1941 Christmas holiday. We had locked ourselves in one of the Yale halls on December 7 for a hard-working rehearsal on a show called *Waterbury Tales*. It was a takeoff on Chaucer's *Canterbury Tales*, I guess. That evening, maybe around eight or so, some guy came running into the hall.

"Jesus Christ," he yelled, "haven't you heard the news? The god-damn Japs have bombed Pearl Harbor. I don't know where the hell that is, but we're at war."

Do you know, not a one of us could tell him where Pearl Harbor was. Can you believe that? Here is a group of young so-called scholars, attending one of the great universities in this country, and none of us knew the location of our country's main naval base in the Pacific. The East Coast just wasn't oriented toward the Pacific.

The next day things started to really hop at New Haven. Everyone was talking about the same thing—what the hell each guy was going to do. I was in my junior year and already a member of the Naval ROTC. But my brother Steve, a year behind me at Yale, decided to join the Marine Corps and so did my roommate, a guy named Jack Tilliey. The two of them talked me into switching over to the Corps. Besides, the Marine program allowed you to finish college before going on active duty. I figured there'd be plenty of war left by the spring of '43—it wasn't going anywhere in a hurry—and I was right.

Yale, I may add, was a tremendous place to be that first year of the war. You know, weekends in New York City, meeting some lovely under the clock at the Biltmore, those great jazz bands on Fifty-second Street and, of course, the football games at New Haven. I was a member of Chi Psi Fraternity and we had great times. I don't think the country really got drab until the first part of 1943. By that time casualty reports were beginning to show up and you really knew you were at war.

One other thing that made New Haven great then was the Glenn Miller Band. We had a large Army Air Corps group at Yale so they based Miller's Air Corps Band there. Can you imagine being at college and listening to those great musicians all the time? "Chattanooga Choo Choo," "Tuxedo Junction," "In the Mood," "American Patrol." It was tremendous.

It all ended in June 1943 when both my brother and I got the word to report to Parris Island on July 14, which happens to be both my birthday and Bastille Day. I was lucky my parents didn't name me Napoleon or something crazy like that.

Well, you know the old expression, "Be sure and get off on the right foot." Unfortunately that's exactly what Steve and I didn't do.

Here's what happened. My father had loved railroads all his life, he knew all about them. He was even on the boards of directors of a couple of them. He felt that riding on a government ticket could get pretty crummy south of Washington, D.C., and he was right. All the college guys headed for the officers' candidate platoon that we were going to be in found this out the hard way—all of them except the Stack boys, that is.

Dad insisted we have private accommodations on a Pullman train that would get us down there a little ahead of the regular group. He even wired ahead saying when we would arrive. The only problem was the other train was on time and we were late.

Oh Christ, we stepped off the train, dressed in seersucker jackets, button-down shirts, striped ties and, of course, white shoes. The rest of our bunch, the ones who had been on the cattle cars, and a very irate Marine sergeant were waiting for us. We both felt about two feet high.

Our crushed feelings did not impress the sergeant one bit. He was fuming.

"I've already got what is undoubtedly the dumbest bunch of college bastards who will ever come to Parris Island," he snarled, "and now I have a couple of big-time clowns like you two. You college guys are a swift pain in the ass."

Naturally he's got the whole crew very concerned and Stack and Stack are about as popular as Billy Graham in a cathouse. Then the old sarge let go a beauty that relaxed everyone.

"Besides," he yells, "you know what college does to you morons; it makes you more stupider, that's what!"

Well, you didn't have to be an English major to know this guy was something else.

So we started our training and one of the first things we had to learn was to use nautical terms. Most of us knew what they were, but we'd never called the ground in an open field a deck or the wall in a wooden barracks a bulkhead. It could get confusing as hell at first and sometimes hilarious.

Take the new platoon in the barracks next to ours. Similar to our own setup, their back door had wooden stairs leading up to the second floor. I can't remember if we had to call the doors latches or not, but I don't think it became that absurd.

Anyway, we did call the stairs ladders. One morning their DI was standing right outside the barracks. He yelled for the platoon to hit the ladder. You know the old routine: "Assholes and heels and I don't want to see them very long."

Now, they did have a fire ladder, I mean a real ladder, leading to the roof inside the barracks and the predictable happened. Before the DI could stop them, half his platoon is out on the roof trying to stand at attention. The DI was livid. He made those poor bastards go up and down the ladder/stairs for the next hour. I will say one thing, those men knew what he meant the next time the DI told them to hit the ladder.

Back to my own platoon. I still don't know what one of our DIs was trying to prove, but he seemed to get huge joy out of pitting me and my brother against each other. The first time he did this I was amazed. I was coming out of the head when he collared me.

"Stack," he whispered, "your brother just told me you were chicken shit. Tomorrow I'm going to match you two up against each other for some hand-to-hand stuff."

Well, damn it, my brother and I have always been rather close, even for brothers. Naturally I went over to Steve and asked him what was going on.

"Prate," he laughed, "I was going to ask you the same thing. That idiot just told me you said I was a big yellow baboon."

So now we knew what our DI was up to even if we didn't know why. We gave our platoon a good show the next day, but we would have done that anyway. See that scar on my lip? Steve gave me that a week or so later in bayonet drill. We weren't going to learn anything by playing games so we really went at it. But whenever it was one-on-one, it was always Stack against Stack.

There is one more thing I'd like to say about Parris Island and that concerns a great football player from Georgia named Frank Sinkowitz. I say this because I think he got a bum rap. Okay, he wasn't very modest, but why should he be? He was just about the best football player in the country at the time.

All American or not, the guy had flat feet—hell, they were flat as a board. Maybe that helped him with his balance when he was running. Maybe he could easily put all his cleats on the ground at the same time, I don't know. But I do know his feet were pure misery after an all-day hike with full marching gear on his back. He was eventually surveyed out of the Corps. The scuttlebutt was that the Corps wanted to get rid of him but that was baloney. The poor guy had real flat feet, that's all.

Another guy in my platoon was James Whitmore, the actor. I knew him from school days. I'd played football against him when he was at Choate and I was at Pomfret. He's got a peculiar kind of build; I think he's bowlegged. We called him "Alley Oop" after that prehistoric cartoon character who used to be in the funnies. I never did hear what happened to him after boot camp.

Our platoon's next move after Parris Island was to Quantico, Virginia, where we were to have three more months of training as PFCs. It was during this time that several of the men did flunk out. After all, it wasn't cast in stone that we had to get commissions. It was no snap course, I'll tell you that.

One thing above all that they pushed at Quantico was decision-making. They'd try and set up as many situations as possible where you'd be forced to act under extreme tension. I guess they wanted to see how each guy would react. If you couldn't take pressure when you got into combat, it would be too late to do anything about it. Your mistakes could not only cost your life but those of the men serving under you.

After three months of OCS we got our commissions, which also meant a new life. We still worked just as hard but had about every weekend off. This meant some great liberty in Washington, D.C., for the next three months.

So on my first trip to the nation's capital I reserved a double room each weekend for the next three months. I told the hotel my wife would be joining me each weekend. Of course I was a bachelor at the time, but I didn't want any nosy clerk poking into my affairs. My room was always registered under Mr. and Mrs.

Do you have any idea how many unescorted young damsels were floating around Washington at that time? Why, a one-legged man with BO and bad breath could have made out there. And I mean there were some real good-looking dolls, not dogs. It was a bachelor's dream.

One of my favorites was a real stylish lady who worked for American Airlines. Her job was handling the priorities for the flights. If you put in for a flight, you'd get a rating from one to four, depending on how important they felt your trip was—the higher the rating the better your shot at getting aboard.

At any rate, my friend let me in on a little trade secret. They also had a fifth rating, which was unofficial. It was called PF, meaning personal friend.

Here's what it meant. If you had some clout, you could usually get someone a PF rating, which meant they were almost certain of getting into Washington. That's how they kept a supply of exciting young beauties coming into town. After all, we had to keep our hard-working politicians relaxed, didn't we? They liked variety.

Well, these great weekends ended, or at least had a change of scenery late in February 1944, when I was ordered to report to Camp Elliott. I was assigned to, of all things, a tank battalion. This really surprised me as I'm not exactly the most mechanically minded man in the world. I did a little nosing around and found out why they put me in tanks. The reason was really something.

It seemed that when I enlisted, I had filled out a rather lengthy questionnaire. One of the questions concerning experience asked you to put a check mark next to each of the following vehicles you had driven. One of the listed vehicles was a tractor. Hell, I'd driven one at a summer camp when I was about fifteen years old, so I checked tractor. And that's why I ended up a tank man.

At any rate I soon turned to and tried to do the best job I could. It wasn't that I had much trouble in the mechanical end; it was just that such things bored me.

Bored or not, I reported to the tank farm, as they called it, near Camp Elliott, which is over by San Diego. We were situated back in a rock canyon. The Sherman medium tanks were just beginning to arrive, but we trained on nothing but light tanks. I didn't get a chance to work with any of the Shermans until I got overseas. Come to think of it, I never could figure out why they called the Shermans medium tanks; I never saw any bigger one while I was in the service.

In any case, we had three tanks to a platoon and five men to a tank. Then you also had servicemen attached to each platoon. We had the G.M. diesels, which were damn good motors.

Of course, you were cramped as hell in the tanks. I wouldn't recommend this duty to anyone who suffers from claustrophobia. And could it get hot! Jesus, there was one time later on, at Peleliu, when the thermometer reached well over a hundred degrees outside the tank. Then our blower went out of kilter. God knows what the temperature became inside. I knew we'd soon start passing out so I stopped the tank and had us all crap out until we could get things straightened out. Oh, it could be miserable all right.

I spent about three months in California and managed once again to pull some great liberty. My family knew a retired admiral who lived nearby in La Jolla. He had two new Buicks but very little gas, while I had no car but the tank farm had plenty of gas. I used to borrow one of his cars each weekend, always returning it on Sunday night with a full tank. Can you imagine what it was like driving up and down that West Coast in 1944 in a new Buick? I was not exactly the loneliest guy in California. I knew it couldn't last forever, but I was in no hurry to take off for the Pacific.

Sometime in the spring of 1944 it all ended when I received my orders for the Pacific. I ended up in charge of a replacement battalion and that's a story in itself. They placed me in command of what was called a casual company. I thought this was a little odd, what the hell, I was only a second lieutenant. Command of a company called for a captain and there were plenty of them around.

Remembering that great rule for a good officer—get to know your men—I started to ask these guys where they'd come from.

The first four or five had the same answer.

"They pulled me out of the brig to put me on board."

One of them even tried to pull my leg. "Didn't you see me come aboard with leg irons and handcuffs on? I was the guy who had the guard with the carbine walking behind me."

He was giving me a load of crap, a real wiseass, but it did seem to be true about my men having been in the stockade. Hell, here was Lee Prather Stack, an officer and a gentleman, by act of Congress, setting forth to fight for his country and I'm in command of a company of brig rats. Do you know something, I got along famously with them, particularly with a group that had come from Michigan, which was a story in itself.

A whole crew of men had joined up together in Hamtramck, a Polish-American district outside of Detroit. Somehow they'd ended up in a big hassle in San Diego and most of them landed in the brig. They had a natural leader with them named Bogard and once you had his trust, you were all set with the rest of them. They were one tough bunch of cookies. More about them later.

Well, the ship we were on was a newly commissioned Army transport manned by the Coast Guard. Among the crowded troops were Marines, soldiers and sailors, and what a mess it was, particularly the chow lines.

Fortunately for everyone, we had a no-nonsense Marine colonel aboard who knew what was going on. He went to the ship's captain with a proposition.

"Look," he told him, "we've got some great cooks in our group. We'll put them to work in your galley if we can also put some Marine MPs on guard at the chow lines."

Okay. The captain went along with the deal and the whole situation cleared up at once. There were complaints from some of the wise guys in the line who ended up with a club stuck up their rear ends, but it sure as hell worked.

We did have one more problem on our trip. Somewhere out in the Pacific our engines just plain stopped. I mean they stopped producing any power at all. This was around the middle of May, 1944, and there were plenty of Japanese submarines in operation. We just sat there dead in the water for about twenty-four hours. I can assure you every guy on that ship was on pins and needles.

We finally got under way to the relief of everyone and a day or two later pulled into Noumea on New Caledonia. We stayed here a few days after which the Marines boarded another ship for transport to our staging area on Guadalcanal.

While I never did get to see any of New Caledonia, I heard a great story about the famous Pink House, renowned throughout the Pacific. You see, there was very little chance for contact with any women in the Pacific, particularly if you were an enlisted guy. The Pink House was an exception. Of course you had to pay; the Pink House was a bordello, or in plainer words, a cathouse.

It never lacked for customers. As a matter of fact, you had to stand in line. When you reached the head of the line, a very corpulent madam would be waiting. You had to whip it out and if it wasn't already standing at attention, you had to go to the back of the line. It seemed that many of the men had been whacking off just before getting in line so they could last longer when it was their turn. The madam wanted no part of this foolishness.

So be it. It seemed we no sooner reached New Caledonia when we were off again. I can't remember when we reached Guadalcanal, but I'd say around the first part of June. Here I still had my company of brig rats and they really came through for me.

In such a situation you are supposed to keep all hands busy, you know, idle hands mischief makes and all that crap. So I took my stalwarts out on some kind of foolish exercise. Jesus, every officer who drove by us had his own jeep. This finally got to me.

"Christ, every officer on this goddamn island has his own jeep but me," I shouted, more or less to myself.

About two o'clock the next morning I was awakened by a gentle voice. Remember, an enlisted man cannot lay his hands on an officer, so this bird can't shake me.

"Lieutenant, lieutenant," I heard, "we have a present for you."

I looked up and it was my friend from Hamtramck.

"Bogard, what in the hell do you want?"

"Would the lieutenant please step outside with me? You don't have to dress."

So I stuck on my boondockers and, still in my skivvy drawers, walked out of my tent.

"Your jeep, sir," said Bogard as he saluted. "We found it."

That was it. There were no marks on it. My orders had arrived, so I drove it for the few days I had left on the Canal. Then I left it for a fellow officer and never heard of it again.

My new designation was Pavuvu, some 60 miles away on the Russell Islands. The time had come to start paying the price for wearing the green uniform. I was now an officer in the 1st Tank Battalion of the 1st Marine Division. My new outfit was getting ready for its third island invasion of the war. We were to hit a place about 600 miles east of the Philippines. The Japanese had heavily fortified this island and we had to take the place to support MacArthur's coming invasion. That's what we were later told, anyway. The island was Peleliu.

In the meantime, the 1st Division had left New Britain in April '44 to come to this island of Pavuvu, first for R&R and then to build up for their next fight. I don't think they could have picked a worse spot for rest. But by the time I joined the outfit, I had no time to worry about the location or the next invasion. I had to get to know all I could about the Sherman tanks and the men of my platoon. They had the 1st Tank Battalion on a perimeter where we worked our butts off for tank-infantry team training. Our tank operation was slated to play a big part in the coming invasion.

The landing on Peleliu was set for September 15, which turned out to be a month or so before MacArthur's invasion of Leyte. I went in on D-Day along with my platoon but no tanks. As you can imagine, this had the scuttlebutt running wild. My men were convinced that the brass figured all the men who had their tanks ashore on D-Day were going to be casualties and we would replace them. It didn't quite turn out that way even though the tank battalion had its share of casualties on Peleliu, but then so did everyone else.

Anyway, I spent the first night ashore in a foxhole. I'm sure the thought of an easy campaign promised by Major General Rupertus went out the window that very day. Not only did the Japanese artillery knock the hell out of our beachhead but we weren't ashore very long before the Nips started their counterattacks. I know they hit us with one shortly before dawn on the 16th.

Now, as I said, my platoon did not have our Shermans as yet but other tankers did. And it's a good thing, because on the first afternoon, the Nips sent down their own tanks toward our lines. They even had Japanese infantry riding on the tops of those tanks.

As I recall, the Marine tanks showed up in the nick of time and blasted the hell out of the Nip machines. We had noticeably heavier firepower than the Japs and it really was no contest. You could see their tanks burning all over the beachhead.

My platoon's tanks became available on the third day, and that's when I found out just how bloody hot it was on Peleliu. Even when the blower was going on inside the tank, it was torrid as hell, but when that conked out, you just couldn't exist in the tank. Peleliu is just not that far from the equator. I don't think the Marines ever fought on any other island where the heat was worse than on Peleliu.

Well, the big stumbling block was a place we called Bloody Nose Ridge. We had shelled the devil out of it but it seemed as formidable as ever. We later found out that it had something like six different stories of tunnels. You can imagine what a problem that place was, especially as the coral made it real tough for the Marine riflemen to dig in.

Anyway, they decided to temporarily bypass Bloody Nose and move us north. My platoon was then in support of the 5th Marines, who succeeded in taking the Jap radio station on the northern end of the line.

So as we were moving north, there was one night when we had to change tactics. Plans called for armor to pull behind the lines each night to rearm, refuel and have any needed maintenance work done.

But one night as we were moving north, we were told to stay right on the lines. It seemed a certainty that the Nips would counterattack and the colonel wanted all the firepower he could get.

The colonel was right. The Nips did hit us and our guns seemed to be going all night. You always had spare barrels and when one got too hot, you just put on your spare barrel.

There was another time when our tanks really piled those Japs up in stacks. Our riflemen had bottled up a large crew of them in one of those caves. It would have been madness to try and go in after them so the Marines saturated the place with flamethrowers.

In the meantime, we had our tanks lined up where we figured the rear entrance to the cave was located. Naturally the tremendous concentration of the flamethrowers screwed up the oxygen in the cave. So the Japs came running out the back side, which turned out to be just where we figured it would be.

My God, it was like shooting fish in a barrel. And remember, this was daylight; we could see our machine guns turning those poor guys into mincemeat. It wasn't a pretty sight. Then again, what was the alternative? With that damn code of theirs, they weren't going to surrender. The Germans were tough soldiers, but when they knew it was hopeless, they'd call it quits. The Nips weren't like that. Most of the time they'd blow themselves up before surrendering.

It was this type of action that used to really concern the tankers. We knew all about the kamikaze satchel chargers long before they had the suicide pilots. We had to be constantly on the lookout for them. They'd load themselves with dynamite and wait in some kind of a spider hole. When the tanks would appear, these nuts would jump out of the ground and run against the tanks. Someone had to plug them before they reached the tanks or the Sherman and everyone in it would blow sky high.

The closest call I had on Peleliu, though, didn't come from a satchel charger even though on two different occasions Marine riflemen shot down those suicide nuts coming at my platoon. It came from a split-second shootout where the alertness of my gunner saved our hide.

It all happened over near Bloody Nose Ridge. As I opened up one of our ports to get some air in, I saw this Marine field piece go sky high. I didn't know where the Japanese fire had come from, but my gunner had spotted this Japanese gun going in and out of one of those tunnels they had set up on a ridge. It was maneuvered on a railroad track.

"Lieutenant," he said, "when that baby comes out again, it is going to take a crack at us. Permission to fire to, sir."

"Hell yes," I answered. I'd say their gun was about a hundred yards away.

Sure enough, a minute or two later, out comes the Jap gun. I could see it now and so could my gunner.

Wham! he lets go with our 75 and blows the hell out of the Jap gun. It was like a shootout in one of those western movies we used to see. Thank God our gunner was a crack shot.

Well, sometime around the first part of October, they started taking my tank outfit off Peleliu and I think the rest of the 1st Division was off there toward the end of the month. The Army then had complete control. The Marines had done the job they were supposed to do in spite of suffering over seven thousand casualties. But just because we left, that didn't mean the Army didn't have plenty to do. The 81st Division had been landing piecemeal since late September. They did their share.

One more thing before leaving Peleliu. Shortly after my tank had knocked out that railroad gun, I had occasion to make a report to the colonel of the 5th Marines. While I was at regimental headquarters, Chesty Puller showed up. He was in command of the 1st Marines at the time.

"How many second lieutenants have you had killed so far?" he asked.

He was told the number—I can't remember what it was—and he sure as hell wasn't satisfied.

"What the hell are you doing, having a Sunday School picnic?" he bellowed.

Chesty was a real charismatic leader and he just didn't know what fear was all about. However, there were several Marines who thought he was a little off his rocker. You know, you can hear too many guns go off.

So they pulled us off Peleliu and much to everyone's disappointment took us back to Pavuvu. I will say, however, they had made a lot of improvements on that island since we took off for Peleliu. Regular showers, movies, even a few Red Cross ladies; the greatest improvement was a regular beer ration for the men. It was limited, of course—hell, you couldn't have the division falling down drunk—but it was there.

There was also a sadness, as far as I was concerned anyway. We had several suicides on Pavuvu, which was really a crying shame. I guess you had to expect this. The traumatic experiences the men had gone through on Peleliu were enough to affect anyone's mind. But to have a young guy go through all that misery and then take his own life after it was over was a real pity.

There was one officer I met at Pavuvu whom I should mention because he was such an unusual man. His name was Paul Douglas, the same Paul Douglas who was a senator from Illinois after the war. It wasn't unusual to have a regular officer as old as Paul, but Douglas was a reserve and not one who'd spent many years as a reserve between the wars. His reasons for being there were unique.

As it turned out, these reasons went back to World War I. It seemed Douglas had either been just a shade too young to go into the service in 1918 or else he'd stayed in college at the time. Anyway, he felt he owed his country a war and when this one came along, he enlisted as a private. He didn't end up with some cushy job back in the States either. He was right there in the Pacific. I think he came out a major when the war was over. He was quite a guy.

Well, we overhauled the division to get ready for the next move. It turned out to be the biggest campaign the Marines fought in divisional strength. Our 1st Division and the newly formed 6th Marine Division were to land on the island of Okinawa with the 2nd Marine Division in reserve. Why the hell they kept the 2nd in reserve as long as they did, I'll never know. We kept hearing about their landing on small islands near Okinawa with no Japs on them but never the main event. The 8th Marines of the 2nd Division did come into some nasty stuff toward the end of the campaign, but the 2nd and 6th Marines never came to the main island. We could have used them.

At any rate, Okinawa was the largest island any Marine division fought on. We felt it would be the closest thing to a land mass type of area we would run into and therefore ideal for tanks. I was switched into intelligence with our tank battalion so I had a general idea of what we did with our tanks on the island.

But, as I look back, the first thing I can recall is the old saying that no matter what goes on, someone will always figure a way to make a buck. I guess it's just a plain old American custom. Things were pretty quiet in the north when we first went in and the agile mind of one of our battalion officers quickly went to work.

It seems that we had taken over what appeared to be the headquarters for the Japanese Imperial Marines. The place was loaded with hundreds, maybe thousands, of the Nip Marine insignia.

So this enterprising officer dug up some sewing machines, got some cloth and put everyone he could find to work making Japanese Imperial Marine battle flags. I must confess they were a hell of a lot better than the ones from the Nip army.

Then he took the flags out to some of the hundreds of U.S. Navy ships off Okinawa. My God, did he clean up! But he was generous to a fault. Somehow he managed to buy a tremendous amount of beer for all hands, enough to last until we moved south. Tragically, it was going to be the last beer many of these Marines would ever have.

After we did move south, we ran into some of the roughest stuff of the entire Pacific war, particularly the Shuri Castle area where the 1st Division had it so rough. My job as intelligence officer took me back and forth between the command posts and the front lines and one of my trips to a CP allowed me to witness something the Corps believes in.

You see, there was this hill near Shuri—I can't remember its name—that had to be taken. But it was turning into a real tough nut to crack.

So the lieutenant colonel in command of the battalion that was really getting the hell knocked out of it was at the CP as was the ADC (assistant divisional commander). As you might imagine, the battalion commander was a walking basket case, he shouldn't even have been on the lines. Unfortunately, the ADC couldn't, or wouldn't, take this into consideration even though he never raised his voice when giving orders to the lieutenant colonel.

"Colonel," he said, "General del Valley [the 1st Division commanding officer on Okinawa] says we have to have that hill tonight."

"But my men are all used up," replied the battalion commander. "Half of them belong in sick bay."

"Colonel, you have your orders. If you don't take the hill, heads will roll."

"Yes, sir."

The battalion commander saluted and walked out. I knew the lieutenant colonel, so I walked over to try and offer some consolation. He turned toward me as I approached him. There were tears in his eyes.

"We'll take the fuckin' hill, but I don't care if I come off it or not."

The battalion did suffer more casualties but they took the hill. I don't believe the commander was hit even though I think he was wounded later on.

But that was the Marine way of thinking and you can argue for or against it. Who the hell knows if they're right or not?

The Corps says if you keep moving against the enemy, flanking them if possible, you lose fewer men than if you stay in a hole and let the enemy work you over with artillery and mortars. Brutal as it sounds, it usually works.

As we continued to move south, we were on the right, with the 6th Marine Division on our left. I think the Japanese had more artillery on Okinawa than on any other island the Marines fought on and they gave our tanks hell. One of the reasons for this was the goddamn rice fields. I mean, you just can't move a Sherman tank through a rice field.

Here's how they'd work. The Nips knew we'd have to keep our tanks on the roads between those rice fields and that's the area they'd zero in on. They'd wait until you had reached that point, then they'd open up.

And it wasn't only our tanks that suffered from those guns. Remember, each tank usually has a supply of riflemen and other troops moving along with it.

Another thing on Okinawa that was a real bastard was those tombs. If you take a look at a picture of them, you'll see a little wall surrounding each one. It was supposed to be shaped like a woman's womb, the reasoning behind this being that you come from a woman's womb and when you die, you return to one.

The Japs would frequently use these tombs as fortresses. You'd never know which ones they might be in. I guess they wanted to put as many of us back in our mothers' wombs as possible.

But, you know, as rough as things could get, you always had these funny stories floating around. Some were true, others half-true and a lot of them just plain fantasies. Take the one about the lieutenant coming across a young Marine in a foxhole. The lieutenant looks down and he sees the young lad is beating his meat.

"Hey, Marine," the officer yells, "what in hell are you doing?"

"Just a little something to keep my mind off the shelling," comes the reply.

And it was always added that the kid didn't miss a beat.

Back to Shuri Castle. Now, you know all about the great picture of the flag raising on Suribachi. What you may not know is that the Marines seemed always to raise a flag wherever they went.

There was this rifleman from Georgia in the 7th Marines who was one of those professional rebel types. You know, always fighting the Civil War over and over. Come to think of it, I guess we had more of that type around forty years ago than we do now—you never see that kind anymore.

Anyway, he'd had a Confederate flag sent to him when we were on Pavuvu and when we finally did take Shuri, the first thing that goes up is the Stars and Bars. He even had a guy with a harmonica playing "Dixie." Most of the Marines, no matter where they were from, got a huge kick out of the whole act, but I heard some stuffed shirt Army general got really pissed off. So what!

Now, I've already told you how that Jap artillery fire had been taking a big toll on the tanks. To be precise, the Jap fire, plus normal maintenance problems, had reduced our battalion to just six tanks ready for duty. We'd gone in with sixty. We had to do something about the Jap artillery or we'd have no tanks left at all.

So as we continued to move south, we ran into one of those real big guns—it might have even been dismounted from a naval vessel—that we couldn't locate. All we could figure out was its general direction; we just couldn't pinpoint it. As intelligence officer I was supposed to know all about the Jap artillery fire on our tanks, so the colonel figured I was the guy to go up in an observation plane and radio back to our artillery the exact location of the Jap gun. I agreed.

The plane was a Stinson LS. It certainly wasn't built for combat, but it was ideal for observing. So they got a pilot, I grabbed some powerful binoculars and we were off.

Christ, try as I did, I just couldn't pinpoint the goddamn Jap gun. But I did narrow it down to what we called an acceptable target.

Then came the big blast. We lined up every available gun for miles around for TOT (time on target). The idea was for all the guns to shell the target at the same time. In other words, a gun three miles away would fire a short time after another gun maybe five miles away. That way shells would come in from every direction at the same time.

Unfortunately for us, no one bothered to tell us what time the big blast was set for and when it did come, the concussion to our plane was tremendous. It literally sent us upward as if we'd been shot out of a cannon. I'm happy to say my pilot kept control of the Stinson and none of our shells hit the plane. Apparently, they did blast the big Jap gun to kingdom come, which made our colonel happy as hell. He greeted us when we got back to our airstrip.

"Stack," he said, "you did such a great job, would you try it again tomorrow? We're having trouble with another one of their big bastards five or ten miles south of where you were this morning."

I've got to tell you I was in no hurry to go up into that mess again so soon, but you know the Corps. I answered the colonel in the affirmative, which turned out to be a very questionable decision on my part.

The next morning turned out to be absolutely crystal clear in all directions. And when you're up in that beautiful setting in a small plane like the Stinson, it seems like the war is on another continent.

But it wasn't and I soon found this out in spades.

The gun we were after was on a reverse slope placed in such a way that it was extremely hard to spot. Once again we had a general location but not enough accuracy to call in a strike.

Then I got lucky.

One of the Nip gunners threw an empty shell case out from underneath the camouflage. Why he did this I'll never know, but I caught the case's reflection from the bright sun. I guess with all their devotion to duty the Japs could fuck up just as badly as we could.

We radioed back the position of the Jap gun, both to our artillery and to several warships which were ringing the southern end of the island. They followed up immediately and blasted the area where I had spotted the reflection to pieces. We later found out that not only did we get the gun but also a large Nip command post in the same area. It was quite a show but it almost cost us our lives.

We were so busy watching the results of the shelling, we forgot how exposed we were to our own shells, particularly the fire from the ships in the bay. One of our naval shells—I think it was an eight-incher—passed about ten feet in front of our plane. Holy Christ, if it had hit us, parts of our plane would have been blown back to San Francisco. It was close enough to scare the wits out of us so we moved out of range. But, petrified as we were, it didn't improve our intelligence any. Looking back over the years, it's hard to fathom why we made our next move. Hell, we just plain decided to challenge the whole Jap Army. Can you believe that?

I guess the best explanation was that we just got too cocky. We'd been up two days in a row and both times we'd been successful as hell. The war had turned into a hide and seek game for us. Find the Japs, tell our people, and presto, no more Japs.

Anyway, we both had Colt automatics. We felt it would be a lark if we strafed the Japs at ground level with our pistols. We made some kind of a bet on who could hit the first Nip. What we forgot was they'd be firing at us with much more accurate weapons than pistols.

So down we went and opened up on them. The Japanese returned our fire with a vengeance. One of the Nips succeeded in putting a slug through our plane that also ripped through my right leg just below the knee.

Now, if you ever shoot a bullet through a piece of wood, you'll note a neat hole going in but a gaping hole where it comes out. That's what my leg looked like. My pilot got me back to a field hospital and my long fight to save my leg began.

From Okinawa I went to Guam and then to an amputation hospital on Mare Island, California. Both these trips were via a hospital plane. At Mare Island they told me that the damage to my bone meant my leg would have to come off.

"The hell with that," I told them, "get me back to the East Coast. My leg can be saved."

Of course, I really didn't know what the hell I was talking about, but I didn't want to lose my leg—who the hell would. I'd really gotten used to having it.

So I ended up at the Chelsea Naval Hospital outside of Boston. Here I ran into two great orthopedic surgeons who went to work on me. Among other things I had to keep my leg in traction for three months. It appeared that my leg could be saved but would it be any good?

In the meantime the war had ended and I had no trouble getting separated from active duty. Then I went into phase two of my rehabilitation, which was to find out if I could use my leg at all.

Now, as I look back, I have no bitterness at all. What the hell, I could have easily been killed at either Peleliu or Okinawa. I have quite a limp, but I can walk and for long distances. I think I'm pretty lucky.

But what about all the men who did lose a limb? Was such a devastating operation always necessary?

At the hospital they frequently would wake a man up at two in the morning and tell him they were sorry but an arm or a leg had to come off. They were probably right most of the time, but there must have been times when the doctors were wrong. Oh well, I guess that's how it goes.

One more thing. During my stay on either Guadalcanal or Pavuvu, can't remember which, I went out on a training exercise. There were no Japs anywhere near us but the exercise was under strict combat conditions, and under the command of one Major McIlhenny. I had a question so I looked up the major.

"Major," I started, but that's all I got out before he stopped me.

"Don't use rank out here. Use my code name, Tabasco Mac. What's your code name?"

Lieutenants didn't have code names, not that I knew of, but I thought fast.

"Ketchup Stack," I answered.

"Good, good. Now, what is it?"

So I told him and that was that. When I got back to camp, I asked another officer what the hell was going on.

"What's all this crap about Tabasco Mac?" I said.

"Oh, don't you know? McIlhenny's family produces Tabasco sauce; he's big as hell on that stuff!"

Well, many years after the war a buddy of mine married a girl down in New Iberia, Louisiana. I went to the wedding and it turned out the bride was my old major's niece, and there he was in all his glory.

"Hello there, Tabasco Mac, how are things?" I asked him.

The major looked at me carefully and then smiled.

"Just great, Ketchup Stack, just great!"

from The Good War
by Studs Terkel

Studs Terkel's 1984 oral history of World War II was a forerunner to more recent books about "the Greatest Generation." Terkel's interview subjects included E. B. Sledge, who served in the Pacific.

There was nothing macho about the war at all. We were a bunch of scared kids who had to do a job. People tell me I don't act like an ex-marine. How is an ex-marine supposed to act? They have some Hollywood stereoptype in mind. No, I don't look like John Wayne. We were in it to get it over with, so we could go back home and do what we wanted to do with our lives.

I was nineteen, a replacement in June of 1944. Eighty percent of the division in the Guadalcanal campaign was less than twenty-one years of age. We were much younger than the general army units.

To me, there were two different wars. There was the war of the guy on the front lines. You don't come off until you are wounded or killed. Or, if lucky, relieved. Then there was the support personnel. In the Pacific, for every rifleman on the front lines there were nineteen people in the back. Their view of the war was different than mine. The man up front puts his life on the line day after day after day to the point of utter hopelessness.

The only thing that kept you going was your faith in your buddies. It wasn't just a case of friendship. I never heard of self-inflicted wounds out there. Fellows from other services said they saw this in Europe. Oh, there were plenty of times when I wished I had a million-dollar wound. (Laughs softly.) Like maybe shootin' a toe off. What was worse than death was the indignation of your buddies. You couldn't let 'em down. It was stronger than flag and country.

With the Japanese, the battle was all night long. Infiltratin' the lines, slippin' up and throwin' in grenades. Or runnin' in with a bayonet or saber. They were active all night. Your buddy would try to get a little catnap and you'd stay on watch. Then you'd switch off. It went on, day in and day out. A matter of simple survival. The only way you could get it over with was to kill them off before they killed you. The war I knew was totally savage.

The Japanese fought by a code they thought was right: *bushido*. The code of the warrior: no surrender. You don't really comprehend it until you get out there and fight people who are faced with an absolutely hopeless situation and will not give up. If you tried to help one of the Japanese, he'd usually detonate a grenade and kill himself as well as you. To be captured was a disgrace. To us, it was impossible, too, because we knew what happened in Bataan.

Toward the end of the Okinawa campaign, we found this emaciated Japanese in the bunk of what may have been a field hospital. We were on a patrol. There had been torrential rains for two weeks. The foxholes were filled with water. This Jap didn't have but a G-string on him. About ninety pounds. Pitiful. This buddy of mine picked him up and carried him out. Laid him out in the mud. There was no other place to put him.

We were sittin' on our helmets waitin' for the medical corpsman to check him out. He was very docile. We figured he couldn't get up. Suddenly he pulled a Japanese grenade out of his G-string. He jerked the pin out and hit it on his fist to pop open the cap. He was gonna make hamburger of me and my buddy and himself. I yelled, "Look out!" So my buddy said, "You son of a bitch, if that's how you feel about it—" He pulled out his .45 and shot him right between the eyes.

This is what we were up against. I don't like violence, but there are times when you can't help it. I don't like to watch television shows with violence in them. I hate to see anything afraid. But I was afraid so much, day after day, that I got tired of being scared. I've seen guys go through three campaigns and get killed on Okinawa on the last day. You knew all you had was that particular moment you were living.

I got so tired of seein' guys get hit and banged up, the more I felt like takin' it out on the Japanese. The feeling grew and grew, and you became more callous. Have you ever read the poem by Wilfred Owen? The World War One poet? "Insensibility." (He shuts his eyes as he recalls snatches of the poem and interpolates) "Happy are the men who yet before they are killed/Can let their veins run cold. . . . And some cease feeling/Even themselves or for themselves. Dullness best solves/The tease and doubt of shelling." You see, the man who can go through combat and not be bothered by the deaths of others and escape what Owen calls Chance's strange arithmetic—he's the fortunate one. He doesn't suffer as much as the one who is sensitive to the deaths of his comrades. Owen says you can't compare this man to the old man at home, who is just callous and hardened to everything and has no compassion. The young man on the front line develops this insensitivity because it is the only way he can cope.

You developed an attitude of no mercy because they had no mercy on us. It was a no-quarter, savage kind of thing. At Peleliu, it was the first time I was close enough to see one of their faces. This Jap had been hit. One of my buddies was field-stripping him for souvenirs. I must admit it really bothered me, the guys dragging him around like a carcass. I was just horrified. This guy had been a human being. It didn't take me long to overcome that feeling. A lot of my buddies hit, the fatigue, the stress. After a while, the veneer of civilization wore pretty thin.

This hatred toward the Japanese was just a natural feeling that developed elementally. Our attitude toward the Japanese was different than the one we had toward the Germans. My brother who was with the Second Infantry Division in the Battle of the Bulge, wounded three times, said when things were hopeless for the Germans, they surrendered. I have heard many guys who fought in Europe who said the Germans were damn good soldiers. We hated the hell of having to fight 'em. When they surrendered, they were guys just like us. With the Japanese, it was not that way. At Peleliu, my company took two prisoners. At Okinawa, we took about five. We had orders not to kill the wounded, to try to take prisoners. If they surrendered, they'd give you information. But the feeling was strong . . . Some guys you meet say they didn't kill any wounded. They weren't up there living like animals, savages.

Our drill instructor at boot camp would tell us, "You're not going to Europe, you're going to the Pacific. Don't hesitate to fight the Japs dirty. Most Americans, from the time they're kids, are taught not to hit below the belt. It's not sportsmanlike. Well, nobody has taught the Japs that, and war ain't sport. Kick him in the balls before he kicks you in yours."

I've seen guys shoot Japanese wounded when it really was not necessary and knock gold teeth out of their mouths. Most of them had gold teeth. I remember one time at Peleliu, I thought I'd collect gold teeth. One of my buddies carried a bunch of 'em in a sock. What you did is you took your K-bar (he displays a seven-inch knife), a fighting knife. We all had one because they'd creep into your foxhole at night. We were on Half Moon Hill in Okinawa about ten days. It happened every night.

The way you extracted gold teeth was by putting the tip of the blade on the tooth of the dead Japanese—I've seen guys do it to wounded ones—and hit the hilt of the knife to knock the tooth loose. How could American boys do this? If you're reduced to savagery by a situation, anything's possible. When Lindbergh made a trip to the Philippines, he was horrified at the way American GIs talked about the Japanese. It was so savage. We *were* savages.

When I leaned to make the extraction, as the troops used to say, this navy medic, Doc Caswell, God bless his soul, said, "Sledgehammer, what are you doing?" I says, "Doc, I'm gonna get me some gold teeth." He said, (very softly) "You don't want to do that." I said, "All the other guys are doin' it." He says, "What would your folks think?" I said, "Gosh, my dad is a medical doctor back in Mobile, he might think it's interesting." He said, "Well, you might get germs." I said, "I hadn't thought of that, doc." In retrospect, I realized Ken Caswell wasn't worried about germs. He just didn't want me to take another step toward abandoning all concepts of decency.

I saw this Jap machine-gunner squattin' on the ground. One of our Browning automatic riflemen had killed him. Took the top of his skull off. It rained all that night. This Jap gunner didn't fall over for some reason. He was just sitting upright in front of the machine gun. His arms were down at his sides. His eyes were wide open. It had rained all night and the rain had collected inside of his skull. We were just sittin' around on our helmets, waiting to be relieved. I noticed this buddy of mine just flippin' chunks of coral into the skull about three feet away. Every time he'd get one in there, it'd splash. It reminded me of a child throwin' pebbles into a puddle. It was just so unreal. There was nothing malicious in his action. This was just a mild-mannered kid who was now a twentieth-century savage.

Once on another patrol, on Okinawa, I saw Mac take great pains to position himself and his carbine near a Japanese corpse. After getting just the right angle, Mac took careful aim and squeezed off a couple of rounds. The dead Japanese lay on his back with his trousers pulled down to his knees. Mac was trying very carefully to blast off the head of the corpse's penis. He succeeded. As he exulted over his aim, I turned away in disgust. Mac was a decent, clean-cut man.

We had broken through the Japanese lines at Okinawa. I had a Thompson submachine gun and went in to check this little grass-thatched hut. An old woman was sitting just inside the door. She held out her hands. There was an hourglass figure tattooed on it to show she was Okinawan. She said, "No Nipponese." She opened her kimono and pointed to this terrible wound in her lower abdomen. You could see gangrene had set in. She didn't have a chance to survive and was obviously in great pain. She probably had caught it in an exchange of artillery fire or an air strike.

She very gently reached around, got the muzzle of my tommy gun, and moved it around to her forehead. She motioned with her other hand for me to pull the trigger. I jerked it away and called the medical corpsman: "There's an old gook woman, got a bad wound." This is what we called the natives in the Pacific. "Hey, doc, can you do anything?"

He put a dressing on it and called someone in the rear to evacuate the old woman. We started moving out when we heard a rifle shot ring out. The corpsman and I went into a crouch. That was an M-l, wasn't it? We knew it was an American rifle. We looked back toward the hut and thought maybe there was a sniper in there and the old woman was acting as a front for him. Well, here comes one of the guys in the company, walking out, checking the safety on his rifle. I said, "Was there a Nip in that hut?" He said, "Naw, it was just an old gook woman. She wanted to be put out of her misery and join her ancestors, I guess. So I obliged her."

I just blew my top: "You son of bitch. They didn't send us out here to kill old women." He started all these excuses. By that time, a sergeant came over and we told him. We moved on. I don't know what was ever done about it. He was a nice guy, like the boy next door. He wasn't just a hot-headed crazy kid. He wanted to join the best. Why one individual would act differently from another, I'll never know.

We had all become hardened. We were out there, human beings, the most highly developed form of life on earth, fighting each other like wild animals. We were under constant mortar fire. Our wounded had to be carried two miles through the mud. The dead couldn't be removed. Dead Japs all around. We'd throw mud over 'em and shells would come, blow it off, and blow them apart. The maggots were in the mud like in some corruption or compost pile.

Did you ever get to know a Japanese soldier?

One of the few we captured at Okinawa was a Yale graduate. He spoke perfect English, but we never said anything to him. I must be perfectly honest with you, I still have a great deal of feeling about them. The way they fought. The Germans are constantly getting thrown in their face the horrors of Nazism. But who reminds the Japanese of what they did to China or what they did to the Filipinos? Periodically, we remember Bataan.

It always struck me as ironic, the Japanese code of behavior. Flower arranging, music, striving for perfection. And the art of the warrior. Very often, we'd get a photograph off a dead Japanese. Here would be this soldier, sitting in a studio, with a screen behind and a table with a little flower on it. Often he'd be holding a rifle, yet there was always that little vase of flowers.

We all had different kinds of mania. To me, the most horrible thing was to be under shellfire. You're absolutely helpless. The damn thing comes in like a freight train and there's a terrific crash. The ground shakes and all this shrapnel rippin' through the air.

I remember one afternoon on Half Moon Hill. The foxhole next to me had two boys in it. The next one to that had three. It was fairly quiet. We heard the shell come screeching over. They were firing it at us like a rifle. The shell passed no more than a foot over my head. Two foxholes down, a guy was sitting on his helmet drinking C-ration hot chocolate. It exploded in his foxhole. I saw this guy, Bill Leyden, go straight up in the air. The other two kids fell over backwards. Dead, of course. The two in the hole next to me were killed instantly.

Leyden was the only one who survived. Would you believe he gets only partial disability for shrapnel wounds? His record says nothing about concussion. He has seizures regularly. He was blown up in the air! If you don't call that concussion . . . The medics were too busy saving lives to fill out records.

Another kid got his leg blown off. He had been a lumberjack, about twenty-one. He was always telling me how good spruce Christmas trees smelled. He said, "Sledgehammer, you think I'm gonna lose my leg?" If you don't think that just tore my guts out . . . My God, there was his field shoe on the stretcher with this stump of his ankle stickin' out. The stretcher bearers just looked at each other and covered him with his poncho. He was dead.

It was raining like hell. We were knee-deep in mud. And I thought, What in the hell are we doin' on this nasty, stinkin' muddy ridge? What is this all about? You know what I mean? Wasted lives on a muddy slope.

People talk about Iwo Jima as the most glorious amphibious operation in history. I've had Iwo veterans tell me it was more similar to Peleliu than any other battle they read about. What in the hell was glorious about it?

from Flags of Our Fathers
by James Bradley
with Ron Powers

James Bradley's father, John, was one of the six flag-raisers on Iwo Jima in World War II's most famous photograph. The younger Bradley's book, written with Ron Powers, traced the lives of John and his fellow soldiers before, during and after the battle.

One of my dad's finer qualities was simplicity.

He lived by simple values, values his children could understand and emulate.

He had no hidden agendas; he expressed himself directly. He had a knack for breaking things down into quiet, irreducible truths.

"It's as simple as that," he'd say. "Simple as that."

But a flagraiser's existence wasn't always so simple.

In 1979, the *Chicago Tribune* writer Mary Elson was following up on Rene's death and surprised John Bradley at his desk at the McCandless, Zobel & Bradley Funeral Home.

He gave her about "ten agitated minutes of his time," puffing "nervously on a cigarette . . . sitting on the edge of his chair in the electric pose of a runner ready to bolt from a starting block."

He spent most of those ten minutes downplaying the perceived heroics of the flagraising. But in two of his sentences he revealed his thinking about that eternal 1/400th of a second. "You think of that pipe. If it was being put in the ground for any other reason . . . Just because there was a flag on it, that made the difference."

Here my father captured the two competing realities of The Photograph. It was an action of common virtue, not uncommon valor, as plain as a pipe.

But because of a fluke photo—a stiff wind, a rippling flag—this common action represents valor in the eyes of millions, maybe billions of people.

The reporter Mary Elson grasped none of this and wrote in the *Chicago Tribune* that John's pole comment was "an oddly irrelevant afterthought."

Odd? Irrelevant? A casual afterthought? I don't think so.

My dad had given Mary Elson the key to everything. *"Just because there was a flag on it, that made the difference . . ."* But just as the inquiring reporter in *Citizen Kane* had missed the significance of "Rosebud," Mary Elson remained oblivious to the revelation John had handed her.

By the early 1980's, the men of Easy Company were in their sixties. Their families grown, their work lives nearing an end, many of them felt an urge, long dormant, to reconnect with one another; to remember with their buddies.

Dave Severance became the catalyst for these reconnections. A career Marine, he had left the infantry to become a fighter pilot after World War II. He flew sixty-two missions in the Korean War, and won the Distinguished Flying Cross and four Air Medals before retiring with the rank of colonel in 1968. But as with anyone who had walked in the black sands, Iwo Jima would remain the defining event of his life. With the instincts of a company captain, Dave compiled a list of Easy Company veterans, searched for their addresses around the country, and began a newsletter round-robin that soon prompted several reunions.

Dave invited my father to all the reunions, but he never went. The burden of being an "immortal hero" and the press attention he'd attract made it impossible.

"I'd love to go," he told my brother Steve once, "but I couldn't just go and be myself and visit with the guys I wanted to. I couldn't just be one of the guys."

Perhaps there were other considerations as well. Perhaps they were similar to those revealed to me, through tears, by John Overmayer, a corpsman who had gone through medic training with John and was with him on Iwo.

"I stayed away from reunions at first; I didn't want to remember, but I'm glad now that I've been to a few," Overmayer told me. "I went through life wondering how I could be so proud of something that was so bad. I had twenty out of thirty of my guys killed within ten or fifteen minutes. I couldn't get them out. I was their nineteen-year-old doctor, priest, and mother. But I couldn't save them. It took two buddies to get me through that night. But the next morning, when someone cried 'Corpsman!' I got out of my foxhole and went to help him. I did it. I kept going.

"The number-one motivation on Iwo Jima was to stand with your buddies and not let them down. And all my life I was proud of that, but I couldn't talk about it. But after going to a reunion I found others who felt the same way. And now I feel better."

My father probably felt that need to seek out comrades for an affirmation of feelings. But his fame as a figure in The Photograph would not let him go.

Or maybe it was something else. Something too painful to reopen. In 1964, when he was forty and I was nine, my father hinted at why he couldn't talk about Iwo Jima. But I was too young to really understand.

My third-grade class was studying American history. When we got to World War II, there, on page 98 of our textbook, was The Photograph.

My teacher told the class that my father was a hero. I was proud as only a young son can be.

That afternoon I sat near the back door of our house with my history book open to page 98, waiting for Dad to come home from work. When he finally walked through the door, I jumped toward him before he'd even had a chance to take off his coat.

"Dad!" I exclaimed. "Look! There's your picture! My teacher says you're a hero and she wants you to speak to my class. Will you give a speech?"

My father didn't answer me right away. He closed the door and walked me gently over to the kitchen table. He sat down across from me. He took my textbook and looked at The Photograph. Then he gently closed the book.

After a moment he said, "I can't talk to your class. I've forgotten everything."

That was often his excuse, that he couldn't remember.

But then he went on: "Jim, your teacher said something about heroes . . ."

I shifted expectantly in my chair. I thought now I would hear some juicy stories of valor. Instead, he looked me directly in my nine-year-old eyes signaling that he'd like to embed an idea in my brain for the rest of my life.

Then he said: "I want you to always remember something. The heroes of Iwo Jima are the guys who didn't come back."

Simple as that.

Six years went by before I discussed the subject with him again. And for some reason, on one ordinary night—it was 1970—it all bubbled up to the surface. I asked him about Iwo Jima. And persisted through the initial silence.

And that was how I learned about one special hero of Iwo Jima. And about why he didn't come back.

It was just a normal evening in the Bradley household. Everyone else was asleep, except for Dad and me. He was forty-six then. I was sixteen, a high-schooler with pimples. The two of us were sitting up late, as we often did, watching Johnny Carson. For some reason that I've since forgotten, I brought up the subject that I knew by then was practically taboo. Iwo Jima.

Any information would have satisfied me. A couple of sentences. He'd never told me anything substantial. But as usual, on this night my father kept his silence, at least at first. I remember how he gave a half smile at me, then looked back at the TV—the blue screen reflecting in his glasses—then shook his head, sighed, glanced at me again.

On this night I decided not to let it go. After a long silence, I said: "Well, Dad, you were there. The Battle of Iwo Jima is a historical fact. It happened. You must remember *something*."

Again he listened to my question, then looked back at the TV. His mind was working, he heard me, but there was only silence.

I persisted. Finally he closed his eyes and dropped his head back against the headrest of his easy chair. Then he rubbed his forehead and said, "Geez." It sounded more like an anguished expulsion of air: *Sheeesh!!*

And then my father broke a long silence.

He said: "I have tried so hard to black this out. To forget it. We could choose a buddy to go in with. My buddy was a guy from Milwaukee. We were pinned down in one area. Someone elsewhere fell injured and I ran to help out, and when I came back my buddy was gone. I couldn't figure out where he was. I could see all around, but he wasn't there. And nobody knew where he was.

"A few days later someone yelled that they'd found him. They called me over because I was a corpsman. The Japanese had pulled him underground and tortured him. His fingernails . . . his tongue . . . It was terrible. I've tried so hard to forget all this.

"And then I visited his parents after the war and just lied to them. 'He didn't suffer at all,' I told them. 'He didn't feel a thing, didn't know what hit him,' I said. I just lied to them."

I didn't know what to say. I was young, unable to fathom the depths of emotion he had just revealed. And so we sat there for a few minutes in silence letting Johnny Carson's next guest change the subject.

Many years later, in researching my father's life, I asked Cliff Langley, Doc's co-corpsman, about the discovery of Iggy's body. Langley told me it looked to him as though Ralph Ignatowski had endured just about every variety of physical cruelty imaginable.

"Both his arms were fractured," Langley said. "They just hung there like arms on a broken doll. He had been bayoneted repeatedly. The back of his head had been smashed in."

Those were the relatively benign wounds. But they were not the worst of what had happened to Iggy, who had faked his urine sample to get into the Marines; Iggy, the proud Marine, the small, fresh-faced boy who had endured "Polack" ribbing with a good-natured smile.

My father remembered the worst thing. He kept the image alive under his many protective layers of silence and solitude. He never disclosed the worst thing to me, not on that night in front of the TV, not ever. But he mentioned it to my brother once, while I was in Japan.

Japan. How amazing it is that I found my way to that country— lived there—grew to love it—learned its history and studied its religious traditions—and did all of this without consciously connecting Japan to my father's past. Perhaps the currents of thought and motivation run deeper than we sometimes think.

I was hypnotically drawn into this old land, into what struck me as an almost mystically refined, cultured society. I'd arrived from a country where people joked about Japanese robot-workers building cheap cars, living in boxes, and eating rice and fish heads. What I found instead was an infinite lacing of social refinements that had evolved over centuries.

Here was a crowded island country smaller than California, but with 160 million people living on it. Eighty percent of that terrain was mountainous, compacting the available living space to an even greater density. Centuries of close living had distilled an elaborate system of courtesies designed to make this dense cohabitation enjoyable.

I grew more and more attuned to these rituals of humility and politeness. I didn't reflect on it at the time—indeed, not until many years later—but what I was experiencing was the irreducibly real Japan: the Japan that had existed before the militaristic epoch that culminated in the Pacific War, and that will continue into the next millennium. It was a Japan my father could never imagine.

Only now, years later, do I realize that the values of the Japanese and John Bradley were so similar. Quietness, politeness, integrity, honor, simplicity, devotion to family. Silent contemplation, looking inward for answers rather than prattling on.

I wanted my parents to come visit me in this Japan that I loved. I was sure they would see what fascinated me. I couldn't imagine any other reaction. I wrote them a letter of invitation. My mother responded that they couldn't make it. I never knew why or what my father's reaction had been—that is, until I spoke with my brother Steve in May of 1997, after Dad had died. He told me exactly what my father had said back in 1974 when he received my letter of invitation.

"It was at the funeral home," Steve told me. "Dad was agitated. He was jingling the change in his pockets like he did when he was upset.

"He said you had invited Mom and him to visit you in Tokyo. He didn't say anything for a long while. Then he blurted out, 'Jim wants us to come visit him. They tortured my buddy. The Japanese stuffed his penis in his mouth. I'm not too interested in going to Japan.' "

Memories of Iggy seemed to be always just under the surface. Maybe this accounts for my father's remarkable silence about the Battle of Iwo Jima and the flagraising. Maybe.

For many of the veterans, their memories of combat receded; supplanted by happy peacetime experiences. But there were others for whom the memories did not die, but were somehow contained. And for a few, the memories were howling demons that ruled their nights.

Among these last, a disproportionate number, I believe, are corpsmen.

It was the corpsmen, after all, who saw the worst of the worst. A Marine rifleman might see his buddy shot down beside him, and regret the loss for the rest of his life. But in the moment, he kept going. That was his training, his mission.

But the corpsman saw *only* the results. His entire mission on Iwo was to hop from blown face to severed arm, doing what he could under heavy fire to minimize the damage, stanch the flow, ease the agony.

The corpsmen remembered. And their memories ruled the night.

Danny Thomas, whose hypnotism in 1947 had ultimately proved ineffectual in blotting out the dreams, could never stop seeing the bodies at the edge of the water. "That's the thing I see in my dreams the most," he told me once. "How the tide and the motion of the waves would rock them.

"Just last night I woke up covered with sweat. I saw the shifting of the bodies on the Iwo Jima beach. My pajamas were drenched. I had to change. I still have to wring the sweat from my T-shirt on some nights.

"There's one body rocking on the sand that really grabs me. He's partially buried. His right shoulder and part of his face are sticking out of the sand. His right hand is moving in the tide as if it is beckoning: 'Follow me. Follow me.' I saw that guy on the second day."

All combat produces unshakable memories. But consider Cliff Langley, who as Corpsman Langley labored side by side with my father on Iwo—3rd Platoon, Easy Company.

He went on to serve in Korea and Vietnam with the Army. But there's one battle that rules: "The dreams have lasted for years. At seventy-three I still get 'em. I've been in three wars and I haven't got past Iwo yet."

After studying in Japan I was convinced I was an expert on Pacific history. At a Thanksgiving dinner at our family home in 1975, I was only too happy to enlighten my father and the assembled family as to the "real" reason we fought Japan in World War II: American insensitivity to Japanese culture and FDR's severing of their oil lines forced Japan—an industrial beached whale—to attack Pearl Harbor in self-defense.

The 350,000 "liberated" victims of the rape of Nanking and the millions who perished in the Asian Holocaust might have taken some exception to this point of view. But I was entranced with it, and confidently explained to the veteran of Iwo Jima seated across the table from me that it was his side that was to blame. Japan was the victim.

Typically, my dad did not take offense that day of thanks. He nodded thoughtfully, his glasses glinting, and reached for his knife to cut the turkey.

It would be years before I read of the atrocities the Japanese military machine had perpetrated on millions of people; years before I discovered that the "self-defense" rationale I was spouting off about had been rejected by the Tokyo War Crimes Tribunal as bogus.

John Bradley was fifty-two in 1975, and he knew a hell of a lot more about why we got into America's War than I did. But rather than challenge me, he just nodded.

He was secure in himself, his marriage, his family. He was a successful man. He owned a large home in Antigo, a summer cottage at Bass Lake several miles to the north, and a thriving funeral business.

He possessed the things that mattered most to him: not fame or adulation, but a large, secure family and the respect of his fellow townspeople, respect that devolved from years of hard work, his attitude of service, and his contributions to his community.

He could afford to nod in silent understanding and hand me another slice of turkey. In return for the slice of baloney I had just handed him.

John's heart was in bad shape by Christmas of 1993. Open-heart surgery, irregular heartbeat.

He was seventy, and had mortality on his mind. He wrote his own Christmas cards that year. He reached down through the years and sent them out to his Easy Company buddies. When I met and interviewed those men after his death, they told me that John had sporadically written little Christmas notes over the years. But his 1993 card was downright chatty and included a photograph of his extended family. Did he know it would be his last?

To Dave Severance, his old company commander, Doc confided: "I am not progressing as I should. My heart is not beating in its proper rhythm."

Betty, making the bed, discovered John's rosary beads under his pillow.

John Bradley's death of a stroke in January 1994 was reported around the world. All the newscasts spoke of John Bradley's passing, and we received clippings from as far away as Johannesburg, Hong Kong, and Tokyo.

Everyone in the world media reported that the last surviving flag-raiser had died. But to us that title seemed distant, disconnected from our dad.

Fred Berner, editor of the Antigo *Daily Journal*, got it right when he wrote:

> John Bradley will be forever memorialized for a few moments' action at the top of a remote Pacific mountain. We prefer to remember him for his life.
>
> If the famous flagraising at Iwo Jima symbolizes American patriotism and valor, Bradley's quiet, modest nature and philanthropic efforts shine as an example of the best of small-town American values.

I will always remember my dad for a little favor at the very end of his life.

When he suffered his stroke, I was the only Bradley unable to drive to the Antigo hospital. I flew in from New York, the pilot holding the connecting plane in Chicago for me.

At about one a.m. on Tuesday, January 11, I pulled into the hospital parking lot. I had been traveling for seven hours.

I rushed into the Emergency entrance. The nurse on duty, who had never met me before, looked up and recognized one of "Johnny's boys." Without a word from me she said, "I'll take you to your father."

I heard him before I saw him: loud, labored breathing. Extreme heavy breathing like that which results in fainting or death. "He can't keep that up!" I blurted out to the nurse.

Approaching his bedside, I was struck by how good he looked in spite of the chest wheezing up and down. His color was up, and he looked like my dad of old, my healthy dad.

I tried to talk to him. But my words could not compete with his loud breathing. And I was crying, besides.

I silently thanked him for being a good man, a good father, someone whom I could admire. I told him all the reasons I loved him.

After about twenty minutes, I left the room to shed my winter coat and rinse my face. When I reentered the room about five minutes later, Dad's breathing had dramatically changed. His chest rose slowly now. Within a couple of minutes, his breathing slowed some more.

I summoned the nurse. She put an oxygen mask on Dad's face. I told her that the family had decided against intervention.

"This will just ease his last moments," she said quietly.

I telephoned my mother. Then Steve, who called Tom; both of them lived nearby. I telephoned Barb, Patrick, and Mark in Wausau, forty miles away.

Within twenty minutes the nearby Bradleys—Steve, his children Paul and Sarah, Tom, Joe, my mother, and me—were all by his side.

My mother cradled his head, brushed his hair, kissed his forehead. We all touched and kissed him. His breathing got weaker.

"Jack, are you leaving us now?" Betty Van Gorp Bradley whispered. "It's all right if you leave us when you're ready," his wife whispered. "It's all right, Jack."

At 2:12 a.m. on Tuesday, January 11, 1994, John Bradley took a small breath, exhaled, and died.

Several hours later, while my brothers were taking care of the arrangements, I sat peacefully in the dark looking at Dad, just sitting and thinking and, perhaps, praying. I noticed the nurse standing slightly behind me. The one who had eased my dad's last minutes.

"He waited for you," she whispered.

We both gazed at John Bradley for a few seconds.

She put her hand on my shoulder. "He waited for you," she repeated.

His wake was held in the funeral home where he had comforted so many. It was the largest anyone could remember. When the well-wishers shook our hands to express their condolences, we could feel that they were bone cold, chilled after waiting in the long line outside in the freezing winter.

We heard many stories about our father that evening, stories of silent kindness that he never brought home with him. But no one mentioned Iwo Jima or The Photograph. One woman said she had read the obituaries but did not know the war hero who was on the monument in Arlington or the sailor on the postage stamp. She said she knew a man who helped her parents with their parents' funerals and had become a friend of the family. She knew a man who had raised his family in Antigo and worked to make Antigo a good place to live. She said that was the man she would miss.

So John Bradley had achieved his goal and died as more than a figure in a photograph.

The morning after the wake, just before the church service, we had the closing-of-casket ceremony at the funeral home. This was the family's last chance to say good-bye to husband, father, father-in-law, grandpa.

Some of our family placed small personal items in his casket: a poem, a ring. I walked down the hall of the Bradley Funeral Home and entered my father's office. I faced the only photo hanging there. I gently removed it from the wall and returned to my father's side.

I turned to my family to get their attention. I held the photo high.

All could see themselves in it, posed in a family reunion shot that John Bradley had never tired of bragging about.

"That is the only photo he cared about," I said, and then slid it into his casket.

We six "Johnny's boys" were his pallbearers. Rolling his casket up the aisle of St. John's, I was surprised that even though the church was packed to the gills, it was utterly silent. Like a void, more silent than when empty. The silence of a community's utter sadness.

At the end of the ceremony we all stood in our pews silently facing Dad's casket. The back doors to St. John's Church were opened. Outside, beyond the back door and down the steps, stood a lone bugler bathed in frigid sunshine. He played "Taps." The crisp and somber notes swept through the mourners and we wept.

Chiseled on John Bradley's simple gray headstone in the Queen of Peace Cemetery are the words he learned from his mother, the words that got him through Iwo Jima, the words he repeated with his wife every night before sleeping: Blessed Mother Help Us.

After he was gone, his actions continued to speak louder than words. I was stunned to learn that my father had been awarded the Navy Cross. Stunned. I read his citation over and over and was so proud of him and his life-saving actions on Iwo Jima.

I'll never truly understand the structure of my dad's wall of silence. Perhaps my daughter Alison's "Letter to Grandpa" comes close to describing the bewilderment and awe left in John Bradley's wake.

Alison was a fifteen-year-old high-school student with an assignment: Write a short letter to the person you admire the most.

She chose her Grandpa Bradley, who had been dead for three years.

> Dear Grandpa,
> You'll see on the envelope there is no address. I sat for a

long time and wondered where to address it. Heaven? Is that where you are? I had no way of knowing, so I hope that this ends up getting to you.

I've been thinking a lot about you lately. I just have a few questions I need answered.

This past holiday Daddy took us to Washington, D.C., for a few days to learn more about you. Daddy told us stories of your youth.

He told us how as a young, unmarried man you boarded a cramped boat with thousands of other young Marines and shipped off to Iwo Jima to either live or die. World War II was such a horrible thing for your generation.

I saw the letter you wrote to your mother from Mount Suribachi. You described how filthy you all were and how you would give your "left arm for a good shower and a clean shave." How did you do it? I'll never know.

Finally, Daddy showed us the original footage of the flagraising in 1945. Over and over we saw you and your friends raise that flag.

This was our background to the trip, no more, no less.

But once in Washington, D.C., the enormity of the event and your contribution sank in. In our four days we climbed up your leg at the Marine Corps Memorial, had a personal tour of Congress, and a private tour of the White House.

I have finally obtained knowledge and understanding of the love and respect that the world has for you. In four days there I learned more about you than I did in the twelve years that I knew you.

Why did you not tell us about the Navy Cross?

And how about the time that Congress stopped and the Senate lined up to shake your hand? Why did you never sit us on your knee and tell us these stories?

The only answer I can give myself is that you were a quiet, modest, and honorable man who did not bask in glory. The only words that you ever spoke in front of a camera were, "I was in a certain place at a certain time. None of us are real heroes; we all just jumped in and lent a hand."

These words illustrate your feelings exactly. You just wanted a normal, ordinary family life with your wife and eight children. And that is exactly what you had. After you died a local newspaper wrote, "Bradley was the sole survivor of the flagraising for more than 14 years. He often was asked to attend banquets and dinners and give interviews. But Bradley was a quiet man who operated the Bradley Funeral Home in Antigo. He declined."

The article ends, "His silence has been honorable. And now it is eternal."

I write this letter exactly fifty-two years to the day since the flagraising on Iwo Jima. I sat for about an hour before I started writing to you and tried to picture exactly how you felt and what it was like being on that little island thousands of miles from home. To you there was no glory in an operation that cost two nations so dearly.

Every year on your birthday, Grandpa, we all go off to your grave and tell stories about how it was when you were alive. We always sing your favorite songs. Can you hear us?

My questions are pointless seeing as I'll never know the answer. I just needed to ask them. I cannot send this to you so it will go into my drawer, but wherever you are, heaven or otherwise, I do hope you receive my letter.

We are all healthy and our lives are going well.

Your loving Granddaughter,
Alison Bradley

In the saga of the figures in The Photograph, my dad came to play a unique role. He was the "last survivor" for fifteen years. For a decade and a half he was the only one.

And being the last survivor, he endured increased demands from

authors, journalists, and documentarians. He politely refused all their
entreaties. Until Betty asked. She wanted him to endure his first and last
taped interview in 1985. "Do it for your grandchildren," she implored.

The transcript of this interview has never been published. I obtained
it after my dad's death. My father answers the interviewer's questions
carefully, weighing every word. Asked to describe his participation in
the raising of a pole, John Bradley says:

> When I came upon the scene, they were just finishing
> attaching the flag to the pole and they were just ready to
> raise it up.
>
> I just did what anybody else would have done. I just gave
> them a hand. That's the way it is in combat. You just help
> anyone who needs a hand.
>
> They didn't ask for my help. I just jumped in and gave
> them a hand.

Then the last survivor smiles, and recalls his buddies:

Harlon: "A tall Texan. Always had a smile . . ."

Franklin: "We loved his stories told in that Kentucky brogue."

Rene: "I was best man at his wedding, you know."

Mike: "A great teacher. We all respected Mike."

Ira: "I always had a lot of respect for Ira Hayes. He was one
great guy."

John then speaks for all the flagraisers, something he had never
done before. He wanted to convey a message that he was sure the other
guys would endorse: "People refer to us as heroes. We certainly weren't
heroes. And I speak for the rest of the guys as well."

". . . certainly weren't heroes."

After spending five years researching their lives, the boys certainly
seem like heroes to me. I admit it.

But I must defer to my father. He was there. He knew the guys, knew what they did. His hands were on that pole. And John was a straight arrow all his life. He said the same things about the flagraising at sixty-two as he had at twenty-two. And he was confident enough in his conclusion to claim the right to speak for the other guys.

So I will take my dad's word for it: Mike, Harlon, Franklin, Ira, Rene, and Doc, the men of Easy Company—they just did what anybody would have done, and they were not heroes.

Not heroes.

They were boys of common virtue.

Called to duty.

Brothers and sons. Friends and neighbors.

And fathers.

It's as simple as that.

from The Long Road of War
by James W. Johnston

Machine gunner Jim Johnston's squad of Marines suffered a mortality rate of more than 83 percent during the campaigns on New Britain, Peleliu and Okinawa. Johnston during the Okinawa campaign took up residence in a pig sty, which offered limited shelter from the frequent artillery attacks.

One night, while I lay in the Okinawan pig sty during a prolonged Jap artillery barrage, I was stricken with a series of convulsions. It was beyond my power to control them. First I tried to tighten every muscle in my body. Then I tried to relax every muscle. I tried to control my reflexes with my mind but to no avail. I prayed that the artillery rounds, as they came in, would either light far away in an open field, where they would hurt no one, or that they would light in the sty with me and make a quick job of it. I did my best to keep little Bako, the replacement who was in the sty with me, from sensing my spasms. Everything I tried was futile. I finally just gave up and let the convulsions run their course. After a while they subsided. Later they ceased entirely and I fell into a deep sleep. I didn't tell the corpsman, or anyone, about the convulsions. I would have died there rather than leave because of the convulsions.

Battle is extremely demanding, menial, arduous endeavor. It is unbelievably depleting both physically and mentally, and the nature of our circumstances was starting to take its toll on me. In addition to the exertion required to fight, I worried a great deal about my responsibility to my men.

In battle, you seldom have a chance to rest until you are near a state of total exhaustion. Even when you sleep under those conditions, your instincts are so finely honed in the interest of survival that the tiniest sound, such as a twig snapping, will sometimes shock you instantly wide awake. Strangely enough, on the other hand, you can sometimes sleep soundly through a mortar barrage. It is often difficult to discern between the conscious and the subconscious—dreams or reality, being asleep or being awake.

Sometime during that night I became aware of something close above me. When I looked up, I saw the countenance of a beautiful Lady. Beneath her smiling face there were wisps of veil-like garments but no recognizable form. She spoke quietly but clearly, saying, "Don't be afraid. You will go home in a strange way." I was instantly wide awake. I searched the darkness of the Okinawan night for some lingering evidence of what I had seen. Silently, I earnestly beseeched the Lady to return and explain her meaning. I lay awake for some time, then eventually went to sleep. In the morning, when I awakened, I could not have been positive whether I had seen the Lady while I was asleep or awake. There was one thing for certain, though. There was a great transformation in me. I was no longer afraid. In the days that followed, when I thought of the Lady and wondered about it all, I sometimes thought of the old verse: "Goodbye cruel world, / I'm going home. / Thou art not my friend / and I'm not thine." Perhaps that was the "home" to which I would go "in a strange way." But I was at peace with myself. I had made up my mind that I wouldn't give up. I would do the very best I could, but whether I lived or died, it was OK by me. I still clung to life, but the words kept coming back to me, "By my troth I care not. / A man can die but once."

I consciously began a different personal behavior pattern after that.

I always kept the lives of my men uppermost in my mind and tried watchfully to care for them. However, I looked especially for tasks that I could do alone, or with just a few of the men, work that would give me the satisfaction of doing something. Something, like Brown had said, even if it was wrong.

In the years since Okinawa, thousands of times I have thought of the Lady who came to me that night in the little pig sty. In my darkest hours, the memory of Her has brought me peace, and I have often wondered if I shall ever see Her again.

When we left Awacha Pocket, we fought night and day from one ridge to the next hill—Wilson Ridge, Wana Ridge, Hill 55, Wana Draw—fighting nearly as hard to get down the forward sides of promentories as we had fought to get up them in the first place.

In the proximity of that time and place, we had two new experiences with Jap weapons. First, the Japs started sending over a huge explosive missile that we called buzz bombs because of the sound they made in flight. I've heard them called other things, such as mallet mortars, because of the way their propelling charge was fired. In flight they sounded *buzz-buzz-buzz.* When that sound quit, you wanted to be out of their line of flight, if possible, because that was when they started down. They carried a very large explosive charge and made a hell of a noise when they went off. Fortunately, none of them ever came down in our midst.

The second new sound came when the Japs turned twin 20mm automatic anti-aircraft guns down on us as antipersonnel weapons. The twenties had explosive projectiles like artillery. When they were directed at us, the firing of the gun, the sound of the shell in flight, and the explosion of the shell when it hit made a very weird, disturbing sound. They were very lethal.

One time in that tangle of days, I was on a little hill where we had captured one of the twin 20mm positions. I was looking at the Jap guns when I noticed some of our riflemen start across a small depression fifty yards to my left. As the marines moved against a hill on the other side of the valley, a Jap threw a grenade into their midst. One of the marines smothered it with his body, killing himself but saving some of his friends.

He was a tall, slim, stoop-shouldered southerner (from one of the Carolinas I think, though I didn't know him well). To my knowledge, several Medals of Honor have been given posthumously for exactly the same well-defined, selfless, and brave act of sacrifice.

Knowing that, I tried to get someone to acknowledge the man's deed that I had witnessed, but to no avail. Everyone was too occupied, or indifferent to the man personally, or unapproving of something he had done that didn't fit the corps's mold. It was but another incident that strengthened my feelings about medals for valor. Courage is in a man's own heart. No one but God can measure the courage in a man's heart or compare it with the courage in other men's hearts.

We eventually made our way to a ridge about five hundred yards from the town of Shuri, approximately half a mile inland from Naha.

From that ridge we could see at our front the remains of the concrete barracks in the town. At the time we thought those were the remnants of Shuri Castle, a renowned structure that had been visited by Admiral Perry in the nineteenth century. There had been another unit of marines on the ridge before we got there. That is the only place I ever saw where marines had dug trenches between their foxholes. Once again we were on the receiving end of intense concentrations of artillery, mortar, and small arms fire. Little Gines of the rifle grenade, and my friend Jack Davis from Lyman, Nebraska, were wounded there. A man named Gosman in one of my gun crews was killed. The bullet that killed him first passed closely in front of my face. When the bullet hit Gosman's head, it sounded as if someone had hit a ripe watermelon with a baseball bat. He fell where I could reach him by extending my arm, but he might as well have fallen alone in the desert, for he was dead when he hit the ground.

We moved a little way to tie in with an outfit on our right. We established our position and toward evening Utter came up and told me to expect a tank attack after dark. Reports had come in of someone hearing tank motors directly to our front. I asked, "What should I do, Leon, throw rocks at them? Can you get a bazooka?"

Utter said he would arrange for a battery of artillery to zero in a few yards in front of us, so if the tanks did attack us we could call for the artillery support in the night. Minutes after Utter left us, a few rounds of our artillery hit sixty or seventy yards in front of us, to designate and verify the area. I felt a lot better. We knew how to place grenades on the tank tracks to disable them but that wasn't a pleasant experience to anticipate.

We stayed on the ridge for a couple of days, attempting two assaults across the valley that was between us and Shuri.

Earlier in the campaign, following one of our unsuccessful assaults on Awacha Pocket, we had been given the word to return to our original positions. I had led my section out by habit, because I always went in front of my men. Brown, on the other hand, had waited 'til last and had followed his men out. That is what I should have done. Brown wasn't any braver than I was, but in some ways he was smarter.

I was happy when I got another chance to handle a withdrawal. My chance came in our first attempt to move across the valley in front of Shuri. In the vernacular of World War I, we went "over the top," out of our trenches into the attack on the Jap stronghold. We met formidable, efficient resistance. Again, as at Awacha, we took too many casualties, and it was obvious that our approach wasn't practical. When the word came to return to our original position, I told Brown to take the section back. I waited 'til everyone else was out and I came back last. It was very gratifying. I think even Brown appreciated it. I know he was glad to get moving quickly, for we were catching a barrage of pretty good-sized mortars. Blood was running out the ears of one of his men as they moved back.

Something happened in front of Shuri that was funny, in a morbid sort of way. Old bitcher Brown came over where Joe and I were holed up and started his chant about how we should change positions with his squad because they had been catching a lot of fire for quite a while. I pointed at the track of an artillery shell that had caught the edge of our foxhole that morning and said, "Are they coming any closer than that, Wiley?"

The place I pointed to was an indentation where a Jap artillery shell had hit the sloping rear edge of our foxhole. If it had hit half an inch lower, its point would have struck the dirt and sent Joe and me to kingdom come. As it happened, the curved surface of the shell made contact with the edge in such a way that it skipped off the ground, much like the flat rocks you throw to skip on water. The shell ricocheted back up into the air, hit a little tree fifteen or twenty yards behind us, and blew away the whole top of the tree.

Brown said, "Shit, Johnston, that didn't happen just now."

I said, "Yeah it did, Wiley. If you'd like to see for yourself, stick around a little while. If things keep up like they have been, it won't be long 'til it happens again." Brown hustled back where he'd come from.

As we began to move down into the valley on our second assault, the rifle squad leader immediately behind me was hit in the leg by automatic small arms fire. The bullets popped the air loudly close by my head. Later, I noticed two bullet holes in the left side of the flap on my back pack, and it was easy for me to hypothesize that the bullets that hit the rifleman's leg had first gone through my pack.

We attacked across the valley, taking casualties as expected. A Mexican-American lad who was one of our gunners was killed. His wife had written that she was sleeping with one of his friends and that, after all, he'd been gone three months and he surely couldn't expect her to wait forever. That had made me feel angry at her and bad for him, even before he died.

As we moved forward we came to a ridge that stretched across our front. We paused there. Some of the marines in the unit on our right flank (I believe it was the Fourth Marines) hollered to us that there was a cave on the back side of the knoll we were on, and that they were exposed to fire from that cave. I took Wiley and Joe to cover me and we went over the crest on the right side, to a point where I could drop a couple grenades in the cave. They must have gone down quite a way, for when the grenades exploded there was just a very muffled "poof" on the surface. We waited a little while by the cave but nothing more came from it. We watched the boys from the Fourth and the Japs throwing grenades back and forth over the little ridge they were on. The marines soon killed the Japs, or drove them off, and we returned to the opposite side of the ridge, where we would have some protection from small arms and artillery fire.

We got a new lieutenant there that the replacement depot sent because we had lost ours. He was a big, brave, pleasant Irishman, a ninety-day wonder, and this was his first dose of combat. That night when the mortars started falling on us, he wanted to charge the Jap mortar positions. Some of us finally got him convinced that that wasn't a prudent thing to do at night. Their batteries were probably fifteen hundred or two thousand yards away, and there would be a lot of Jap machine guns and riflemen dug in between us and the mortars. If we had been lucky enough to get through those troops to the mortars, we would unquestionably have been so disorganized that we would have been as likely to shoot each other as the Japs.

In the daylight the lieutenant wanted us to charge over the crest and set up on the front face of the ridge. I told him I didn't think that would be a good idea, either. He said he thought there might be Japs over the ridge and we should go rout them out.

I was certain there would be hell to pay if we did that. Shuri was only a few hundred yards in front of us. I asked the lieutenant if it would be OK if I went over there and checked it out. That suited him.

Some of our men had been listening to the lieutenant and me talking. I asked if anyone wanted to go along, and one young rifleman said, "I'll go with you, Johnsey." How I wish I could remember his name. What he did might not sound like much in the warm glow of your parlor, but on Okinawa that day it was a very significant act. He had stuck his neck out a long fucking way and he knew it, but still he volunteered.

So over the ridge we went. Jap trenches had been dug back and forth all over the area. I don't think the Japs had been gone long because I could still smell them, literally, and the odor was very strong. The rifleman and I went quickly through all the trenches, trying always to be mindful of trip wires and areas likely to be trapped. He was a big help. Two of us could cover the ground faster and we could be on the watch to help each other, if need be. When we were sure there was nothing there, we hustled back over the ridge.

We had worked very hard in making a thorough search very quickly. I lay down on my back against the slope of the hill. Wiley came over and stood at my feet as he looked forward over the crest. He wanted to learn what we had found on the other side.

I was looking at Brown as I talked to him. Suddenly, there was a loud swishing noise as something passed by us very close, and his eyes widened. Almost simultaneously, a large round of artillery hit close in the valley behind us. Brown said, "Jesus Christ, Jim, that almost hit me in the face."

The round had been coming so nearly straight at his eyes that, even as fast as it was going, Brown could see it in flight.

It is odd how things that are nearest to tragedy when they happen sometimes become laughable when you recall them. I still giggle inanely when I think of Brown getting bug-eyed as a five-inch round of Jap artillery nearly hit him full in the face. Of course it would have killed us both, so I'm not laughing at Brown, I am laughing at us.

The little rifleman and I had barely gotten back from our two-man patrol of the south side of the ridge when the Jap artillery blew hell out of the place we had just left. If we had all gone over there and stayed, only a lucky few would have had any chance to survive. As it was, the poor lieutenant was killed, later. It looked as though he was shot in the arm. If so he either died of shock or the bullet that hit him in the arm continued into vital organs. It was a shame. He was a great fellow. If we could have kept him alive long enough for him to get some idea about the war to go along with his book learning, I know he would have made a good officer.

We found out that the big part of the Jap defenders of Shuri had either taken off or died. The trenches on the ridge in front of the town were empty. What was left was not the original strong line of defense. In the night another battalion of the Fifth Marines, the First, took over our positions and moved into Shuri with less trouble than they expected. I read about a marine officer raising the Confederate flag on Shuri, and I wonder how many of the marines who died making that possible for him were Confederates and how many were Union. I wonder how many were like me, born on one side and raised on the other, with a father from one side and a mother from the other. I wonder how many are like me, deathly ashamed of all the bastards in charge on both sides that ever allowed the tragedy of the Civil War to happen.

We went back over a few hills to the area near where our company mortars were set up and awaited our next assignment. It was such a relief to be able to stand up and walk around without the Jap machine guns and snipers working us over.

We drew new rations, including canned heat, tooth powder, and such, most precious of which was plenty of water. After a little while (the exact time period gets away from me again) we began another offensive.

The army on our left flank had advanced several hundred yards along the east coast. A plan was devised whereby we would move down the coast as far as possible and then turn, at right angles, to the west and send a pincer into the Jap area behind their lines in the central part of the island. The burden of being the point on this assignment fell on the First Platoon of E-2-5.

When we had made the flanking movement into the Jap area and had advanced several hundred yards, we came to a rather prominent knob of land directly to our front. When "the man" said we should have a couple of strong points—that being machine guns on high ground—it seemed natural for me to say, "I think we can make it." I took my gunners and the guys that would go with us up to the top of the ridge on Hill 57. At least I was told it was Hill 57. I couldn't swear to that but I'll refer to it as such. To me it was just another hill.

We passed some caves on the reverse sides of some of the higher ground as we made our way to the crest. When we got to the top, some of us started to work the caves we had bypassed. One of them looked especially foreboding. The opening was a fairly large hole in the bank. You could see to the back of the cave, but there were tunnels going both ways, right and left, from the main opening. As we began dumping grenades into the cave we could hear the Japs inside working themselves into a frenzy. With each assault we made on the cave their frenzy increased.

Quite suddenly a black, acrid smoke started to roll thickly from the cave opening. I told the guys we had better back off some because it looked like something was going to blow. Before we could move more than a few yards, there was the biggest explosion I was ever near. One whole side of that pretty-big hill was blown completely away. It erupted like a small volcano and my men were right in the face of it.

I had been standing when the hill exploded. I was blown forward, flat on my belly. When all the ground that had been blown up settled back to earth, I tried quickly to assess the situation. In my back there was a tingling numbness but I seemed able to move all right in spite of it, so I started checking the men. Three of them were dead, two of them close to me on both sides.

I helped patch up all of them I could. One of them couldn't see, one's arm was mostly gone, one's leg was about gone from just below his knee, and one couldn't move from his waist down. Several more were wounded in a variety of ways and places.

The corpsman and I put them back together as best we could, and I went with them back to company headquarters to report. When I had accounted for my men the First Sergeant asked if I was turning in, too, and I said that I was. He asked what was wrong and added, "Need a rest?"

I said, "Hell, yes, I need a rest, but that's not why I'm turnin' in. I got hit in the side." As I was fully dressed and equipped, I imagine he wondered if I was just weary.

I started the trip back with my beat-up outfit. At each med station we would drop off a few and continue.

• • •

It had all happened in the late afternoon. As we went back to the aid stations and mobile hospitals it got later and later. About 2 or 3 a.m. we finally had taken care of all the boys. It was in a rear area field medical unit that I found myself the only one left. The doctor turned to me and asked, "What's your problem?"

I said, "I don't know, sir, but something is starting to hurt pretty bad in my back and side."

He told me to peel off my gear and he'd have a look. I was still wearing all my clothes, my pack (minus the shovel, since its handle had been broken in two by the big blow), and my cartridge belt, and I was carrying my carbine.

I laid down my weapon, took off the pack, cartridge belt, and my dungarees. My cartridge belt had one hole in it. The doc looked at me a moment and said, "Son, lie down on the stretcher on your belly and don't move until I tell you to."

For seven months I had done my best to take care of that bunch of kids and old man Brown. Sometimes pissed off at them for getting lazy or indifferent about what they needed to do, and most of the time so very proud of them. But however I felt, always trying to act with their best interests uppermost in my conscious efforts. I tried to teach them what they needed to know and to take care of them as best I could. I had done a pretty good job, too. I'd mothered them through some terribly tough spots without losing too many. Up to this time, that is, up to the hill I know as Hill 57. There I lost damn near all of them. I felt so helpless, so futile. As I lay down on the stretcher I took a very deep breath and fell sound asleep. I awakened slightly to the jiggling of someone carrying the stretcher and then I slept in fitful short snatches as the ambulance bounced its way back to an army field hospital. They unloaded me into one of the tents.

I awoke to the sound of someone laughing. It was a unique, very individual laughter and I was certain that I recognized it. Into the darkness I asked, "Anyone here from Nebraska?"

Back from the darkness came, "Who said Nebraska?"

"Kenny? Kenny Yant?" I asked.

"Yeah. Who is it?"

"Jim Johnston."

"My God, Jim. I look at all the incoming cards. I saw your name but your card said you were from Kentucky, so I didn't think it was you."

"The folks moved back to Kentucky after the war started, Ken. What are you doing here. Are you wounded?"

"No, Jim, I'm a medic. Where are you hit?"

I told him, in my side and my back. He said he'd take a look at me. It had been a long time before that, and was a long time after, that I was as glad to see anyone. He was a good friend from home. When I went to the operating room to have the steel cut out of me, Kenny went along. He stood by the operating table and held my hand. They had given me a local anaesthetic to deaden the pain while the doctor cut the shrapnel out of my side. As the surgeon was operating on the side of my body with his scalpel, the pain shot through me like a bolt of lightning. ("Uh oh! Hit a nerve.") My muscles jerked involuntarily. I still remember the feeling right after that, when Kenny's grip tightened on my hand.

I suppose it was in apprehension that the doctor would hit something like that again that I began to sweat quite profusely. A little nurse came over and wiped my face with a damp cloth. She said, "Don't sweat it, marine. The doc's about got it."

Her touch felt like an angel's. She was close enough that I could smell her. She smelled like Camay soap, the kind my mother always bought. All of a sudden I felt better.

As far as the war was concerned, my association with the Marine Corps was about over.

Kenny Yant went back with me to my sack in the ward tent. There I spent most of the next few days lying on my belly. Afterward Kenny would help me walk, a little farther each day.

I wrote V-mail to the folks from the hospital:

Dearest Mom and Dad,

Here it is June 5th and the story goes on. Haven't heard

from you or anyone or been able to write for a little while but everything is still going fine. I am in the hospital now but will be out soon. I got a very little wound—nothing to worry about. It is just a scratch on my side and back. I'll only be in the hospital a couple days and then back to duty.

I saw Kenny Yant yesterday and it is wonderful to see someone from the old home town. He talks to me quite often and is a lot of fun.

I will close for this time and write again when I can.

God be with you til we meet again,

Jim

I never did tell Mom about the doc cutting the steel out of me. I just kept writing that all was well and the wounds were nothing but a scratch. I know the folks knew that something didn't exactly add up when I was still writing them from the hospital on June 21.

Dearest Mom and Dad,

June 21st and my heart is a little low. In spite of myself I write that. You know how it is—sometimes a person thinks too much.

I am still in the hospital but will probably go back either tomorrow or the next day. I am fine and all is well. I am hoping and praying that I can come home soon.

I have four little bronze battle stars in my South Pacific campaign bar now and a purple heart with a star.

If I'd been with my outfit (instead of in the hospital) last week I'd have made sergeant. Might have made it anyway but I doubt it. They don't give rates, to guys in the hospital. It doesn't worry me, but I've been doing a sergeant's job for seven months and would surely like to have gotten the rank to go with it. If I don't make it here I'll never make it. They'll never advance my rate in a new outfit where I'm unknown and unproven.

Be that as it may—it is of little consequence. [I write] mainly to let you know that up to now I am OK.

Jim

When I wrote, "My heart is a little low," there were several reasons. When I had left E Company with my wound, there were eleven men left on the line in the first platoon (which originally consisted of three rifle squads and two machine-gun squads). Those eleven were all that was left of the original outfit and an unknown number of replacements. Nine riflemen remained. As I recall, of my gunners (thirteen to begin with and an estimated six replacements), there were two remaining. Two. One of them had been shot through the leg and had returned to duty to be wounded again, and the other (it was reported to me) was later killed in action.

I have read accounts that describe machine gunners as support troops. When I do so, I begin to question the writers' credibility, or at least their judgment. I know they were either never where I was or they are careless about honoring the facts. I served enough duty as a scout to know firsthand the perils of that job. I watched enough riflemen die in front of me to ingrain the deep respect I have for them. But there were a great many days when I set our machine guns out on top of the ground in salients and on hilltops with no one but the enemy in front of us. And it was *every* long, fucking lonesome night that we manned those positions. Is experience like that grounds for lumping us off with the support troops? When there was *nobody* between you and the Japs all night, every night, it was a different ball game entirely—different from anywhere else.

While I had been caring for the wounded on Hill 57, I noticed that the serial numbers on the dog tags of some of the dead, who were recent replacements, were 250,000 less than mine. Serial numbers were a big deal in the corps. Supposedly, they indicated how long you had been there. The size of a serial number didn't have any significance to me. Much more important to me was what you were, where you

were, and what you had been doing. I think the corps assigned numbers by the batch to certain areas, which might account for men with
lower numbers getting to the war so much later. There were also fairly
large groups of men in ROTC programs, and the like, who were given
serial numbers even though they were a long way from being marines.

I had been in the hospital a week or so after the surgeons had
removed the shrapnel inside me. I was quietly lying on my sack
absorbing the peace and quiet. There were a lot of wounded soldiers
in the ward tent. One afternoon a mouthy first sergeant from some
outfit in the First Marine Regiment was admitted to the ward. He had
come to the hospital for tests to see if he had worms. He didn't know
I was a marine, and I never told him. He talked too much and too
loud, so he wasn't making points with the wounded army boys. I
didn't feel like getting into that discord, however, so I just kept my
mouth shut.

In a couple of days another marine from the first sergeant's unit
came into the ward, and the sergeant asked the boy what was happening. The young marine told him he thought their outfit was going
to relieve some unit of the Fifth on the ridge. The sergeant said,
"Yeah, whenever the Fifth runs into something, the First always has
to relieve them."

Before I had time to think, I said, "Bullshit, sergeant. Where the fuck
were you people after the first few days on Peleliu? Weeks after you had
all left, I got hit working the hills you were supposed to take."

I immediately regretted what I'd said. The sergeant had been badly
out of line, but I served no useful purpose in taking exception to his
absurd remark. I didn't need any more conflict right then, and I'm sure
the sergeant didn't either.

He muttered something about the casualties they'd had, but he was
pretty quiet after that. I was ashamed I'd spouted off. I have never been
able to make myself feel better by making someone else feel bad. I
wish I had just said something to the effect that we always felt the
same about them. There were so many good men in the First

Marines. A lot of them died, a lot were old friends of mine. One of them who lived through Peleliu told me one time, after a few drinks, how he hated it that we had had to spend so many tough weeks in combat on Peleliu after the First Marines had left. Maybe the sergeant felt the same way. I was ashamed then of the way I had hopped on him. I still am.

He left the hospital soon after that. I imagine he went back for the few days—the few nasty days—that were left of the war. I hope he made it through.

While I was in the hospital, one of our anti-aircraft batteries of 90mm guns somehow got out of synchronism and fired a few rounds into the hospital area. The shrapnel cut holes in the tent where I was recovering. I thought what a wicked joke it would be to fight the Japs for two years and then die in the hospital from rounds of our own anti-aircraft.

When I checked out of the hospital, I reported back to battalion headquarters. Instead of being sent on to E Company, I was taken to a casual company to await transportation home. While I was there, some of the people from my old outfit came to see me. They told me that if I would volunteer to return to E Company and stay for the next campaign, I would probably be gunny—top NCO—of our platoon, and my cobber Utter would have the company. It sounded good.

I damn near stayed. Even knowing that I would almost certainly be there forever, my allegiance to my men and the corps had become so strong that I damn near stayed.

Only thoughts of my folks tipped my decision in favor of going home. I could hold Mother and Dad in my arms and tell them how much I loved them. I could then tell them what it was that I would be going back to, tell them the cold truth. Then I could return to hit Japan and die, and all would be OK.

I was sure I had too much experience for the corps to allow me to leave for good. I was sure they would bring me back to the Pacific, certainly for something as critical as hitting the Japanese homeland. And that was fine by me, if I could first see home and the folks once more, if I could say goodbye and tell the girls, "Hey, baby, long time no come see."

The division went to China. When I had arrived overseas, I had two friends who had seen old-time China duty and they were great. I would have given the proverbial "left one" to get a chance at China duty. If I had been lucky enough to live through it, there would have been some tall tales to tell.

I stayed on Okinawa until the campaign was over, but I never went back into the lines. I was there on the Fourth of July, when all our batteries of big artillery turned loose to celebrate our Independence Day. I left for home shortly thereafter, around the middle of July.

I didn't write the folks that I was coming home. I figured if I got home it would be great, but if I wrote I was coming and didn't make it, everyone would be morbid. I waited until I was in the States and called home to say I'd be there in three days, God willing.

If I'd had any idea how things were going to turn out I'd have stayed on Okinawa instead of coming home. The way it was, the United States dropped the atomic bombs on Japan, and the war was over before I was due to return to the Pacific Theater.

From Okinawa I boarded a slow transport and sailed to Pearl Harbor, where we lay at anchor for a few days. I volunteered to take some working parties ashore to load supplies, mainly so that I could say I had done duty in Hawaii, but also as a way to break up the monotony of staying aboard ship, doing nothing.

When our ship was nearing sight of the American mainland, the ship's command notified the troops, and we all climbed to some vantage point where we could see the Golden Gate Bridge as soon as possible. Very impressive, very moving. I had been gone from my homeland for twenty-five months.

There was a band playing on the dock, and I wondered what celebration we had stumbled onto. It was difficult for me to swallow when I learned they were playing for us. We weren't used to much fanfare.

When we went ashore, we were almost immediately granted freedom of the base, to hit the stateside PX and cafe. We could hardly believe that whatever was on the menu was ours to eat and drink. Three of us ordered twelve bottles of chocolate milk and quaffed them in no time flat. Then we started to eat.

It was later at that same station, Treasure Island, that we went before a briefing officer. He was a captain and he made quite a lengthy precautionary reorientation lecture about dealing with the civilian world. One thing that he said tickled me. First, he said that while we were away, we had built a dream world out of home, but in reality it was just part of the same old world. We needed to be ready for many disappointments. Then he added that the blonde who lived down the street had probably gotten married—and worse than that, she'd moved.

I went back to Nebraska for three weeks or so of convalescent leave and then reported for duty at Moffet Field, Mountain View, California. Because of the length of time I had been part of E Company, and the combat experience I had, the company had confidence in me. I carried some weight there. At least half of the old guys who had made it through in E Company owed their continued existence to me and a couple of other guys like me. But when I left my old outfit, I hadn't yet gotten the rating that I had earned as a section leader. So I was just another corporal among a bunch of new acquaintances, among a bunch of strangers who didn't know me from Adam. When I was transferred to the detachment at the Naval Air Station at Moffet Field, I was assigned to a guard unit where I'd be standing post four hours on and four hours off, like a private.

Jesus wept! The Marine Corps was at it again.

I had gotten my ass shot up and seen men killed all around me, leading them into places the devil himself wouldn't go. I had done the job the Marine Corps told me to do, and done it well. They even attested to that fact by a letter of commendation I received, signed by General Roy Geiger. I had given them more than two years of faithful service in the Asiatic-Pacific Theater, but that had ended.

Now who would give me the grade, or the pay, or the consideration I had earned? Nobody in the corps would do so. Once more they had given me the short end of the stick. But there wasn't any changing it and I was resigned to that fact.

My post was in a little wooden shack about the size of a two-holer outhouse. It was located on a perimeter road on the extreme outskirts of an underground ammo dump. Talk about being in the boonies! I was issued a carbine with no live ammo. It was about as useless and absurd a position as you could find in this world. It certainly was not a fitting place to assign a shot-up old section leader. You could tell how critical the guard post was to the corps from the fact that they didn't even issue me live ammo. If someone attacked me, I could hit him over the head with my empty carbine.

Out there on post the first day, I had taken off my cover and leaned the empty carbine up in the corner of the little shack. I was sitting on one of the brace boards inside the shack when I heard something on the road.

Through a crack in the boards of the wall, I saw a jeep slowly, quietly approaching the rear of the shack. The gunnery sergeant driving the jeep was sneaking up on me. I didn't want to risk being seen jumping around after my gear like he'd caught me at something. So I stepped out the door of the shack without my cover or weapon—and casually hailed him. "Hi ya, Gunny. What's going on?"

I knew what was going on. He was wearing an arm band lettered OD. This noncombatant gunnery sergeant was playing officer of the day, and he was looking for someone who would snap to for him. Well, he'd come to the wrong place. Neither he nor the situation rated shit as far as I was concerned.

The gunny was flabbergasted, completely taken aback by my attitude and conduct. "I'm inspecting the guard," he said.

"If you're looking for something exciting, you'll have to go somewhere besides this graveyard, Gunny."

You could see he had decided I wasn't going to play his game, and I guess he was reconciled to it. Still, he said, "If the real OD comes around you'd better report your post in a military manner. He expects the guard to go by the book."

"Then you might tell him in my outfit I was a section leader. I stood sergeant of the guard. If the motherfucker wants to operate by the book, that's what I should be doing now, and some private with a billy club should be watching these piles of concrete."

When he left I wondered if he would put me on report. I didn't really care. I'd joined the marines to help fight a war, and we'd done a pretty good job. The war was over and I didn't want to play their peacetime games. I hoped that I could find something more worthwhile to do than spit-shining boondockers and scrubbing 782 gear. It was time now to start telling myself not to kill whoever got in my way, then praying that I'd listen.

I guess some of my thoughts must have shown in my face, because that was the last I ever heard from the gunnery sergeant. I'm sure he realized that I knew a dozen ways I could get rid of him, and no one would ever be the wiser. Of course I would never have considered doing anything like that, but the sergeant didn't know as much. All he knew was that, like Lawrence of Arabia, I had "sailed many ships and killed many men," and that I wasn't happy with his whole operation. I'm sure the gunny thought it would be more productive, and probably far safer, to try his chickenshit routine on some greener marine.

The war was over. The point system had been devised to start discharging marines who were in the corps only for the duration of the national emergency. When I reported to the station that handled the point system, I found that the corps had lost all my medical records. Down in the sea or up in flames, either way they were gone. My only medical records were the notices of my wounds that the War Department had sent my parents. The folks had kept those notices in their safe.

When I knew the date I would be discharged, I called home. Dad once more scrounged enough gas coupons to drive the old Oldsmobile out to pick me up. Except in my dreams—and in memories of the marines I had known—my association with the corps was over.

One thing I wanted to do before leaving California was to pay my respects to the family of Jack Howell. He had been a replacement on Okinawa, one of the few that I had gotten to know well. He had been a good kid and a solid marine.

He was from a good family, who were very close. He had showed me a picture of his classy Mercury convertible, which his dad was taking care of until Jack got home.

Jack had been killed in the hills toward the south end of Okinawa. The night I went to see his family at their home in Pasadena, his mother answered the door, and I told her Jack Howell had been a close friend of mine. Mrs. Howell introduced me to Jack's sister and brother. His mother told me, "Jack's father died of a heart attack when they brought him word that Jack had been killed on Okinawa."

It was a melancholy place. I told Mrs. Howell her son had been brave and honorable. I hoped that might be some consolation.

When I was leaving she offered me the souvenirs her son had sent home including a fancy Jap sword. I sometimes wish I had taken the items and kept them as mementos of my association with Jack, but at that time they were just Japanese tokens to me, and I had all the memories of the Japs I wanted.

When I left the Howells, I joined my father in the car outside, where he had waited. I put my arms around him and wept in the futility of deep sorrow.

I went back to Nebraska, but not back to life as it had been. I had given the corps the best I had, and it had given me a new set of values. I didn't give a damn about going back to college, or trying to become what our society seems to think of as a success. Wealth and influence had lost all significance. In the dark corners of my mind, the only power under God that meant anything to me came out of the bore of a .30-06—or if you were close enough, a .45. Those dark corners are still there.

At the time I got out of the corps, what I hoped for most was a place where I could be alone and at peace. However, it wasn't long before I found that the Marine Corps had left me with something besides a desire to escape the world, something I don't really understand. It's a feeling, like one of obligation, toward the fucking corps. Can you imagine that? The sons of bitches had short-sheeted me at every association. And yet . . . we had been through too much together. I'm a part of their history, good or bad, whether they like it or not. They can't disavow me. But it works both ways. I can't abandon them either.

It seems entirely inappropriate and undesirable that I should just live out the days. I keep looking for a hill to assault, hoping for a hill to assault, and then another and another until there are no more hills. Or no more me.

from Goodbye, Darkness
by William Manchester

Marine Corps veteran William Manchester is best known for works of history and biography. His 1979 memoir includes some of his most memorable writing, such as this passage on the battle for Okinawa.

Now I enter a period of time in which a structured account of events is impossible. Continuity disappears; the timepiece in the attic of memory ticks erratically. These pages in my war diary are glued together with blood which hardened long ago. Certain incidents and impressions can be recalled, but only as a kaleidoscopic montage. Somewhere in here occurred the Truce of the Fucking Dogs; one of our war dogs got loose, ran out on the killing ground north of Sugar Loaf, somehow met an Okinawan pye-dog, and mounted her while both sides, astounded by this act of creativity in the midst of annihilation, held their fire. Then there was the Matter of the Everlasting D Ration, a chunk of bitter chocolate, supposedly packed with nutrition, which looked like and tasted like modeling clay and was all I ate for five days, combat having destroyed my appetite. More darkly I remember the Execution of the Two Pricks, a supercilious pair of junior army officers who were reconnoitering the front, addressing us as "bellhops," and ordering us to direct them to the best view of the battle. A gunny pointed toward the Horseshoe, and off they went, covering about thirty feet before they were slain. There was also the Great Helmet Debate between me and Bubba. Both of us were wearing our steel chamber pots at the time, facing each other, sitting on the reverse slope of a little rise overlooking no-man's-land. Bubba said helmets were an unnecessary encumbrance and dampened the offensive spirit. The Army of Northern Virginia hadn't needed them, he said. I was trying to introduce the subject of Appomattox when a large chunk of shrapnel whirred through the air and hit Bubba's helmet. He took it off and fingered the dent. No doubt about it; if he hadn't been wearing it, he would have been dead. He carefully put it back on, fastened the strap—and then took up where he had left off, his finger wagging and his voice rumbling, insisting that helmets were completely useless.

One of my clearest memories is of the Arrival of the Six Replacements. Rain was still pelting us mercilessly when we were taken off the line briefly, and I found us a dry cave near Machinato Airfield. The cave faced the shore. I was exhausted, and once inside my dry sanctuary I lay on my side for a few minutes, watching the kamikazes diving and exploding on our warships. It was one of the war's most extraordinary spectacles, but I was too weary to keep my eyes open. I took off my boondockers and lapsed into a coma of sleep without even removing my pack or helmet. Then I felt someone plucking at one of my leggings. A reedy, adolescent voice was saying urgently, "Hey, Sarge! Sarge!" I looked up and saw a half-dozen seventeen-year-old boys who had been brought here directly from boot camp. I vaguely remembered the Top having told me that they were on their way to me. We had heard that back home men were being drafted into the Marine Corps, which was outrageous, if true—*every* Marine had *always* been a volunteer—but sending these children was worse. Between Iwo Jima and Okinawa the Marine Corps was running out of fighting men, so these kids were here, disturbing (I was selfish enough to think of it that way) my siesta. They weren't much of an advertisement for the Corps. All of them looked pallid, mottled, and puffy. "What'll we do?" their spokesman asked anxiously in a voice which was still changing. He wanted orders, and I had none. I knew I should give them a full briefing; if they went into the line without one, they could die fast. It was my duty to protect replacements from that. That was what I was being paid for. I didn't do it; I turned over and again drifted off into deep sleep.

Then black comedy, whose role in war is rarely appreciated, solved the problem. Water was dripping on my face. Incredulous, I opened my eyes and realized that the cave was leaking. Over the past week the porous limestone overhead had become saturated. Now it was raining *indoors*. I ripped out all the filthy words I knew, repeated them, and then noticed that my new wards were still there, earnestly hoping that I could spare a few minutes of my valuable time for them. So I did. I told them how to learn about shell-fire on the job, and the tricks of Jap snipers, and booby traps, and how doubt is more fatal than slowed reflexes, and where they might avoid being enfiladed on the line, adding, however, as gently as I could, that they would seldom be in a position to benefit from that information because they would spend most of their time as runners, and a runner is exposed far more often than a rifleman. Their boondockers, I said, were their best friends; they should dry them whenever possible. If they were overrun by a Jap charge they should play dead, affecting a grotesque pose of death; they would probably be bayoneted anyway, but there was always that chance they might be overlooked. They should be alert for the sharp click of steel on steel, which probably meant trouble, because that was how Japs armed grenades. If they heard it, they should move fast. (I should have told them to leap toward the sound, getting the Jap, but this was a lesson in survival, not heroism.) I saw they were beginning to tremble, but it was better to have it out here than there. Feelings of elation in the moments before combat were normal and OK as long as men didn't become suicidal; the moth-in-the-flame threat was always there. Also OK was the instinct to fantasize, to dramatize your actions to yourself. This was actually helpful and should, in fact, be encouraged. To be avoided, and if necessary ignored, were gung-ho platoon leaders who drew enemy fire by ordering spectacular charges. Ground wasn't gained that way; it was won by small groups of men, five or six in a cluster, who moved warily forward in a kind of auto-hypnosis, advancing in mysterious concert with similar groups on their flanks. These young Marines were going to lose a lot of illusions, but if they lost faith in everything else, including the possibility of winning this fight, including the rear echelon and even the flag, they should keep faith with the regiment. It had an outstanding record, and all its men were proud of it. If it was any comfort to them, I ended, they should know that unfounded fears were worse than founded fears and that this battle was the toughest struggle in the history of the Corps. They nodded dumbly, kneeling there like novitiates, steadied by hands grasping upright MIs propped on the wet cave floor. I wondered whether they had understood any of what I had said or whether I had become as sounding brass or a tinkling cymbal.

Had anybody told *me* all this on my first day, I would have thought he was Asiatic, snapping in for a survey, or, as it was sometimes put, one who had "missed too many boats." Since then I had become a disciplined fighter, however, though until now my own survival had been more a coefficient of luck than of skill. There was just one moment in the war when I saved my own life, and it came right after my soggy nap in that defective cave. Back on our own little amphitheater of war, still soaked to the skin, I started a routine tour of the line companies that afternoon, covering it much as a mailman covers his route, except that I had company, because, if possible, we always moved in pairs. My buddy that day was Chet Przyastawaki, the Colgate athlete with the shrill voice. We followed the embankment as far as it went and then moved from one local feature to another: the Long Square, the Blue Icicle, Grable's Tit, the X, the Iron Claw, Thurston's Trick, and the V, also known as the Hairless Pussy. This was a time when the Japanese were constantly challenging us, trying to infiltrate every night and sometimes, brazenly, by day. If their purpose was to keep us off balance, they were succeeding. This surging back and forth quickened the pulses of the Raggedy Asses. People like us, moving from one CP to another, could get caught by occasional Nips who were testing us, penetrating as deeply as they could and then, when found, trying to slip back.

Chet and I had covered the companies, Fox to Easy to Dog, as smoothly as Tinker to Evers to Chance. Positions around Sugar Loaf were in constant flux—at one time or another nine Marine battalions fought on the hill—and we had been told to skirt enemy lines on our way back, scouting every dip, crease, cranny, and rut in the ground that might be useful in combined attacks. The last leg of our journey, before we reached the lee side of the railroad embankment, took us past the crevice called McGee's Closet and down Windy Alley, a rock gulch which, like Sugar Loaf itself, had changed hands repeatedly. We arrived there at the worst possible time. The Japs had launched a reconnaissance in force; no sooner had we entered the lower throat of the alley than we heard the unmistakable sounds of an enemy patrol sealing it off behind us, closing our option of retracing our steps. Then we heard a familiar, husky sob in the air, directly overhead. We hit the deck, and a mortar shell burst a hundred feet away, followed by another, and then another. Silence followed. Chet crossed himself. Another shell burst. The stupid Japs were falling short of their targets, our lines, mortaring us in. When mortared, you are supposed to flee in almost any direction, but, as we were about to discover, it is not always that easy. As we rose cautiously, we heard jabbering on the opposite slopes of both sides of Windy Alley. So much for our flanks. We darted ahead, toward the embankment, and that was when the pneumatic whuff of the first bullet from that direction sang between us. It wasn't from an MI; it had that unmistakable Arisaka whine. We hit the deck again and rolled rightward together, toward the protection of a huge boulder, a rough slab of rock. Two more bullets whuffed past before we made it. Our problem now, and I cannot begin to tell you how much it discouraged me, was that a Nip sniper was in position at the alley's upper throat, behind another boulder, blocking the maze of intersecting paths there, cutting us off at the pass. We were trapped, the nightmare of every foot soldier. All I had going for me was sheer desperation. *Warning: this animal is vicious; when attacked, it defends itself.*

Lying in tandem, Chet and I exchanged wide-eyed glances. The coral had cut both his hands, but I was in no mood to comfort him. I felt a wave of self-pity. For several seconds I was completely mindless. Fear is the relinquishment of reason; we yield to it or fight it, but there are no halfway points. Then I struggled and shook off the panic. It was one of Napoleon's maxims that in war you must never do what the enemy wants you to do. This Jap expected us to stay put. So we wouldn't. Each of us had two grenades hooked on his harness. I hunched up and reached for one. Chet shook his head. "Too far," he whispered. If the range was too great for a Colgate halfback, a scrawny sergeant didn't have a chance, but I already knew the distance was too great; reaching the Nip with a pitch wasn't what I had in mind. I didn't tell Chet now what was there, because as I unlooped the grenade I had to think about a weapon which would reach our man. I was carrying a carbine and a .45, both useless in a sniper's duel. Chet had an MI. I asked, "Did you qualify?" He said, "Sharpshooter. Under three hundred." I shook my head. It wasn't good enough. For once I was going to do what the Marine Corps had taught me to do best. I said to Chet, "Give me your weapon and an extra clip."

My problems were complicated. I knew nothing, for example, of the Japs' timetable. If this was a quick in-and-out operation, the sniper might disappear, running back to his hole in Sugar Loaf. But that wasn't the way their snipers worked; if they had quarry, they usually hung around until they flushed it. And this one now confirmed his personal interest in us in a thin, falsetto, singsong chant, a kind of liquid gloating: "One, two, three—you can't catch me!" Chet muttered in an even higher register, "No, but he can catch us." I was looking up at the sky. The light was clouded. Soon waves of darkness would envelop us, and conceivably it could come to the knife. I couldn't even think about that. Instead, I asked Chet, "Is your piece at true zero?" He said, "It throws low and a little to the right." I took it, leaving him the carbine, and said, "His piece must throw high, and he probably doesn't know it. He had three clear shots at us and drew Maggie's drawers every time." Chet said, "But from where he is . . ." I nodded grimly. That was the worst of it. An invisible line lay between his position and ours. It was diagonal. The azimuth of his lair was about 45 degrees west; mine was 135 degrees east. On a clock this would put him at eight minutes before the hour and me at twenty-three minutes past—northwest for him, southeast to me. Since both our slabs of rock were set dead against the alley's walls, I couldn't use my weapon and my right arm without stepping clear of my boulder, exposing myself completely. All he needed to show was an arm and an eye, unless, by some great stroke of luck, he was left-handed. I had to find that out right now.

Peering out with my left eye I caught a glimpse of him—mustard colored, with a turkeylike movement of his head. He was right-handed, all right; he snapped off a shot. But he wore no harness, and I had been right about his rifle. It wasn't true; the bullet hummed overhead and hit the gorge wall, chipping it. So much for the marksmanship of the Thirty-second Manchurian Army. My job was to beat it. Luckily Windy Alley was calm just now. I checked the cartridge in the chamber and the five in the magazine. Now came the harnessing. The full sling I had perfected during my Parris Island apprenticeship involved loops, keepers, hooks, feed ends, and buckles. It took forever, which I didn't have just then, so I made a hasty sling instead, loosening the strap to fit around and steady my upper arm. My options were narrowing with each fading moment of daylight, so I didn't have time to give Chet an explanation. I handed him the grenade now and said, "Pitch it at him, as far as you can throw. I'm going to draw him out." He just stared at me. What I loved about the Raggedy Ass Marines was the way my crispest commands were unquestioningly obeyed. He started to protest: "But I don't understa—" "You don't have to," I said. "Just do it." I started shaking. I punched myself in the throat. I said, "*Now.*"

I turned away; he pulled the pin and threw the grenade—an amazing distance—some forty yards. I darted out as it exploded and rolled over on the deck, into the prone position, the MI butt tight against my shoulder, the strap taut above my left elbow, and my left hand gripped on the front hand guard, just behind the stacking swivel.

Load and lock
Ready on the left   Ready on the right   Ready on the firing line
Stand by to commence firing

My right finger was on the trigger, ready to squeeze. But when I first looked through my sights I saw dim prospects. Then, just as I was training the front sight above and to the left of his rocky refuge, trying unsuccessfully to feel at one with the weapon, the way a professional assassin feels, the air parted overhead with a shredding rustle and a mortar shell exploded in my field of fire. Momentarily I was stunned, but I wasn't hit, and when my wits returned I felt, surprisingly, sharper. Except for Chet's heavy breathing, a cathedral hush seemed to have enveloped the gorge. I could almost hear the friction of the earth turning on its axis. I had literally taken leave of my senses. There remained only a trace of normal anxiety, the roughage of mental diet that sharpens awareness. Everything I saw over my sights had a cameolike clarity, as keen and well-defined as a line by Van Eyck. Dr. Johnson said that "when a man knows he is to be hanged in a fortnight, it concentrates his mind wonderfully." So does the immediate prospect of a sniper bullet. The Jap's slab of rock had my undivided attention. I breathed as little as possible—unlike Chet, who was panting—because I hoped to be holding my breath, for stability, when my target appeared. I felt nothing, not even the soppiness of my uniform. I looked at the boulder and looked at it and looked at it, thinking about nothing else, seeing only the jagged edge of rock from which he had to make his move.

I had taken a deep breath, let a little of it out, and was absolutely steady when the tip of his helmet appeared, his rifle muzzle just below it. If he thought he could draw fire with that little, he must be new on the Marine front. Pressure was building up in my lungs, but I thought I would see more of him soon, and I did; an eye, peering in the direction of my boulder, my last whereabouts. I was in plain view, but lying flat, head-on, provides the lowest possible profile, and his vision was tunneled to my right. Now I saw a throat, half a face, a second eye— and that was enough. I squeezed off a shot. The MI still threw a few inches low, but since I had been aiming at his forehead I hit him anyway, in the cheek. I heard his sharp whine of pain. Simultaneously he saw me and shot back, about an inch over my head, as I had expected. He got off one more, lower, denting my helmet. By then, however, I was emptying my magazine into his upper chest. He took one halting step to the right, where I could see all of him. His arms fell and his Arisaka toppled to the deck. Then his right knee turned in on him like a flamingo's and he collapsed.

Other Nips might be near. I knifed another clip into the MI, keeping my eyes on the Jap corpse, and crept back to the boulder, where Chet, still breathing hard, leaned against me. I turned toward him and stifled a scream. He had no face, just juicy shapeless red pulp. In all likelihood he had been peering out curiously when that last mortar shell burst. Death must have been instantaneous. I had been alone. Nobody had been breathing here but me. My shoulder was all over blood. Now I could feel it soaking through to my upper arm. I shrank away, sickened, and the thing he had become fell over on its side. Suddenly I could take no more. I jumped out and dodged, stumbling, up the pitted, pocked alley. I braked to a halt when I came to the body of the dead sniper. To my astonishment, and then to my rage, I saw that his uniform was dry. All these weeks I had been suffering in the rain, night and day, this bastard had been holed up in some waterproof cave. It was the only instant in the war when I felt hatred for a Jap. I swung back my right leg and kicked the bloody head. Then, recovering my balance, I ran toward the safety of the embankment. Just before I reached it I glanced to my right and saw, on the inner slope of a shell hole, a breastless creature leaning backward and leering at me with a lipless grin. I couldn't identify its race or sex. It couldn't have been alive.

Back at battalion, the news of Chet's death deepened the section's numbness, but the days of cathartic grief, of incredulity and fury, were gone. One by one the Raggedy Ass Marines were disappearing. The Twenty-ninth was taking unprecedented casualties.

On April 1 the regiment had landed 3,512 men, including rear-echelon troops. Of these, 2,812 had fallen or would fall soon. The faces in the line companies became stranger and stranger as replacements were fed in. In our section we had already lost Lefty, of course, and Swifty; now Chet was gone, too. Death had become a kind of epidemic. It seemed unlikely that any of us would leave the island in one piece. The Jap artillery was unbelievable. One night Wally Moon was buried alive, suffocated in his one-man foxhole—he always insisted on sleeping alone—by sheets of mud from exploding shells. We didn't miss him until after the bombardment, when I whispered the usual roll call. Everyone answered "Here" or "Yo" until I came to Wally. There was no answer; we hurriedly excavated his hole, but it was too late. Wally, who had told us so much about time, was eternally gone.

Inside, though I was still scared, I felt the growing reserve which is the veteran's shield against grief. I was also puzzled. I wondered, as I had wondered before, what had become of our dead, where they were now. And in a way which I cannot explain I felt responsible for the lost Raggedy Asses, guilty because I was here and they weren't, frustrated because I was unable to purge my shock by loathing the enemy. I was ever a lover; that was what Christianity meant to me. I was in the midst of satanic madness: I knew it. I wanted to return to sanity: I couldn't. All one could do, it seemed to me, was to stop combat from breaking you in half, to keep going until you reached the other side of your immediate objective, hoping it would be different from this side while knowing all the time, with the weary cynicism of the veteran, that it would be exactly the same. It was in this mood that we scapegoated all cases of combat fatigue—my father's generation of infantrymen had called it "shell shock"—because we felt that those so diagnosed were taking the dishonorable way out. We were all psychotic, inmates of the greatest madhouse in history, but staying on the line was a matter of pride. Pride was important to young men then. Today it is derided as machismo. But without that macho spirit California and Australia would have been invaded long before this final battle.

Looking back across thirty-five years, I see the Raggedy Ass Marines, moving in single file toward the front, glancing, not at their peerless leader, in whom they justifiably had so little confidence, but back over their shoulders toward all they had left on the other side of the Pacific. They are bunching up, enraging the colonel, and their packs are lumpy and their lack of discipline is disgraceful. Griping, stumbling, their leggings ineptly laced, they are still the men to whom I remain faithful in memory. And as I had pledged myself to them, so had they to me. In retrospect their Indian file tends to blur, like movie dissolves, each superimposed on the others, but they keep moving up and keep peering over their shoulders, their expressions bewildered, as though they are unable to fathom why they are where they are and what is expected of them; anxious, under their collegiate banter and self-deprecation, to remain true to the principles they have been taught; determined not to shame themselves in the eyes of the others; wondering whether they will ever see the present become the past. And then, as their single file disappears in the mists around the bottom of Sugar Loaf, I remember how they were hit and how they died.

Lefty had been Harvard '45 and premed; Swifty had been Ohio State '44 and an engineering major; Chet, Colgate '45, hadn't picked a major; Wally, MIT '43, would have become a physicist. The class dates are significant. That was our generation: old enough to fight, but too young for chairborne jobs. Most of us—I was an exception—had been isolationists before Pearl Harbor, or at any rate before the fall of France. Unlike the doughboys of 1917, we had expected very little of war. We got less. It is a marvel that we not only failed to show the enemy a clean pair of heels, but, on the whole, fought very well. Some were actually heroic. Knocko Craddock had quivered all over as we approached the line. But on Horseshoe Ridge he found a Japanese knee mortar and carried it to his foxhole. When the Nips rushed him, he fired eight rounds at them with their own ammunition and then stood erect in his hole, blazing away with a tommy gun until they cut him down. Knocko was Holy Cross '45. He would have become a lawyer.

Bubba Yates, Ole 'Bama '45 and a divinity student, spent his last night of combat on the forward slope of Half Moon. He fired BAR bursts at the enemy till dawn. Six Nip bodies were found around him. He was bleeding from four gunshot wounds; corpsmen carried him back to a field hospital. All the way he muttered, "Vicksburg, Vicksburg . . ." I heard he was going to be written up for a Silver Star, but I doubt that he got it; witnesses of valor were being gunned down themselves before they could report.

Barr—I never learned his first name—came up as a replacement rifleman and disappeared in two hours. He and Mickey McGuire went out on a two-man patrol and became separated. No one found any trace of him, not even a shred of uniform. He simply vanished. I don't even recall what he looked like. Our eyes never met. One moment he was at my elbow, reporting; an instant later he was gone to wherever he went—probably to total obliteration.

Killer Kane, autodidact, was dug in for the night near the crest of Sugar Loaf when a Jap loomed overhead and bayoneted him in the neck, left shoulder, and upper left arm. The Nip was taking off his wristwatch when Kane leapt up, wrapped him in the strangler's hold, choked him to death, and walked to the battalion aid station without even calling for help.

Pip Spencer, aged seventeen, who wanted to spend his life caring for handicapped children, had his throat cut one night in his foxhole. Nobody had heard the Jap infiltrators.

• • •

Mo Crocker, with an IQ of 154 but no college—scholarships were hard to come by in the Depression—had worked in a Vermont post office. He was deeply in love; his girl wrote him every day. He disintegrated after one of our own 81-millimeter mortar shells fell short and exploded behind him.

Horst von der Goltz, Maine '43, who would have become a professor of political science, was leading a flamethrower team toward Hand Grenade Ridge, an approach to Sugar Loaf, when a Nip sniper picked off the operator of the flamethrower. Horse had pinpointed the sniper's cave. He had never been checked out on flamethrowers, but he insisted on strapping this one to his back and creeping toward the cave. Twenty yards from its maw he stood and did what he had seen others do: gripped the valve in his right hand and the trigger in his left. Then he pulled the trigger vigorously, igniting the charge. He didn't know that he was supposed to lean forward, countering the flame's kick. He fell backward, saturated with fuel, and was cremated within seconds.

Blinker Reid, Oberlin '45, a prelaw student as angular as a praying mantis, was hit in the thigh by a mortar burst. Two Fox Company men carried him to the aid station between them, his arms looped over their shoulders. I saw the three of them limp in, all gaunt, looking like Picasso's *Absinthe Drinker.* Blinker's face was a jerking convulsion, his tics throbbing like a Swiss watch. He wanted to talk. I tried to listen, but his jabbering was so fast I couldn't understand him. He was still babbling, still twitching, when a tank—no ambulances were available— carried him back to the base hospital.

Shiloh Davidson III, Williams '44, a strong candidate for his family's stock-exchange seat, crawled out on a one-man twilight patrol up Sugar Loaf. He had just cleared our wire when a Nambu burst eviscerated him. Thrown back, he was caught on improvised wire. The only natural light came from the palest wash of moon, but the Japs illuminated that side of the hill all night with their green flares. There was no way that any of us could reach Shiloh, so he hung there, screaming for his mother, until about 4:30 in the morning, when he died. After the war I visited his mother. She had heard, on a Gabriel Heatter broadcast, that the Twenty-ninth was assaulting Sugar Loaf. She had spent the night on her knees, praying for her son. She said to me, "God didn't answer my prayers." I said, "He didn't answer any of mine."

Barney, with his hyperthyroidism, hypertension, and the complexion of an eggplant—I had thought he would be our first casualty—became one of the section's survivors, which was all the more remarkable because after I had been evacuated on a litter, I later learned, he perched on a tank barreling into a nest of Japs, firing bursts on a tommy gun and singing:

> I'm a Brown man born, I'm a Brown man bred,
> And when I die I'll be a Brown man dead . . .

Once the battle was over, once the island was declared secure, Barney hitchhiked to the cemetery near Naha where our dead lay. He was wearing dungarees, the only clothing he had. An MP turned him away for being out of uniform.

At various times Sugar Loaf and its two supporting crests, Half Moon and Horseshoe, were attacked by both our sister regiments, the Twenty-second Marines and the Fourth Marines, but the Twenty-ninth made the main, week-long effort. In one charge up Half Moon we lost four hundred men. *Time* reported after a typical night: "There were 50 Marines on top of Sugar Loaf Hill. They had been ordered to hold the position all night, at any cost. By dawn, 46 of them had been killed or wounded. Then, into the foxhole where the remaining four huddled, the Japs dropped a white phosphorus shell, burning three men to death. The last survivor crawled to an aid staion." In another battalion attack, all three company commanders were killed. Now that Germany had surrendered, Okinawa had become, in *Time*'s Phrase, "the vortex of the war."

Infantry couldn't advance. Every weapon was tried: tanks, Long Toms, rockets, napalm, smoke, naval gunfire, aircraft. None of them worked. If anything, the enemy's hold on the heights grew stronger. The Japanese artillery never seemed to let up, and every night Ushijima sent fresh troops up the side of the hill. We kept rushing them, moving the somnambulists, the weight of Sugar Loaf pressing down on us, harder and harder. And as we crawled forward, shamming death whenever a flare burst over us, we could almost feel the waves of darkness moving up behind us. In such situations a man has very little control over his destiny. He does what he must do, responding to the pressures within. Physical courage, which I lacked, fascinated me; I wanted to know how it worked. One of Sugar Loaf's heroes was a man I knew, a major, named Henry A. Courtney, Jr., a fair, handsome man who looked like what we then called a matinee idol. No man bore less resemblance to John Wayne. There was something faintly feminine about Courtney, a dainty manner, almost a prissiness. Yet he rallied what was left of his battalion at the base of Sugar Loaf, asked for volunteers to make "a banzai of our own," and led them up in the night through shrapnel, small-arms fire from Horseshoe and Half Moon, and grenades from Sugar Loaf's forward slope. Reaching the top, he heard Japs lining up on the other side for a counterattack. He decided to charge them first, leading the attack himself, throwing hand grenades. His last cry was, "Keep coming— there's a mess of them down there!" He was awarded the Congressional Medal of Honor posthumously. After the war I called on his widow in Oklahoma. Apart from our shared grief, I was still trying to understand why he had done what he had done. I thought she might know. She didn't. She was as mystified as I was.

The odd thing, or odd to those who have never lived in the strange land of combat, is that I never had a clear view of Sugar Loaf. I was on its reverse slope, on the crest, and eventually on the forward slope, but there were always coral dust, high-explosive fumes, and heavy clouds of bursting ammunition on all sides. It would be interesting to see a study of the air pollution there. I'll bet it was very unhealthy. In that smog, grappling with whatever came to hand, we were like the blind man trying to identify an elephant by feeling his legs. After the war I saw a photograph of the hill, but it had been taken from a peculiar angle and was out of focus. That was also true of my memory, which was blurred because, I think, there was so much that I did not want to remember. There, as in the months following my father's death, I suffered from traumatic amnesia. Some flickers of unreal recollection remain: standing at the foot of the hill, arms akimbo, quavering with senseless excitement and grinning maniacally, and—this makes even less sense—running up the slope, not straight up, but on a diagonal, cradling the gun of a heavy machine gun in my left elbow, with a cartridge belt, streaming up from the breechlock, draped over my right shoulder. The gun alone weighed forty-one pounds. Nobody runs uphill with such an awkward piece of machinery. And where was the tripod? I don't know where I had acquired the gun, or where I was taking it, or why I was there at all.

Mostly I remember a lot of scampering about, being constantly on the move under heavy enemy fire, racing from one company CP to another, always keeping an eye open for the nearest hole. Usually I was with either Alan Meissner, skipper of Easy Company, or Howard Mabie, Dog Company's CO until he was hit. There were dead Japs and dead Marines everywhere. Meissner's company went up the hill with 240 men and came back with 2. On the slopes the fighting was sometimes hand-to-hand, and some Marines, though not I, used Kabar knives, the knives being a more practical implement for ripping out a man's guts than a rifle or bayonet. At close range the mustard-colored japs looked like badly wrapped brown-paper parcels. Jumping around on their bandy legs, they jabbered or grunted; their eyes were glazed over and fixed, as though they were in a trance. I suppose we were the same. Had I not been fasting I'm sure I would have shit my pants. Many did. One of the last orders before going of action was "Keep your assholes tight," but often that wasn't possible. We were animals, really, torn between fear—I was mostly frightened—and a murderous rage at events. One strange feeling, which I remember clearly, was a powerful link with the slain, particularly those who had fallen within the past hour or two. There was so much death around that life seemed almost indecent. Some men's uniforms were soaked with gobs of blood. The ground was sodden with it. I killed, too.

By sundown on May 17 we had just about lost heart, ready to withdraw from the hill because we were running out of ammunition. There wasn't a hand grenade left in the battalion; E company had used the last of them in two futile charges. As it happened, we not only stayed; we won the battle. That night Ushijima tried to reinforce his troops on the opposite slope, but our flares lit up his counterattack force just as it was forming, and twelve battalions of Marine artillery laid down so strong a concentration that he withdrew. Our battalion commander called Whaling on the field telephone and said, "We can take it. We'll give it another go in the morning." His faith was largely based on news that other Marines had captured Horseshoe Ridge, while our Third Battalion—Baker's, beefed up with replacements and back on the line—was digging in on the slope of Half Moon. At 8:30 a.m. on Friday, May 18, six U.S. tanks tried to reach the hill but couldn't; all were destroyed by enemy mines. New tanks arrived, however, and maneuvered their way through the minefield. At 10:00 a.m. a combined tank-infantry assault, half of Mabie's D Company swarming up one side of the hill while the other half lunged at the other side, sprang at the top. It worked. There was a terrific grenade battle at close quarters on the summit, and the Japanese sent a heavy mortar barrage down on our people, but the remnants of D Company, with the fire support from F Company, which was now on the forward slope of Horseshoe, didn't yield an inch. As night fell on the embattled army, the Twenty-ninth Marines held the hill. The Twenty-ninth holds it still.

Newsweek called Sugar Loaf "the most critical local battle of the war," but I felt no thrill of exultation. My father had warned me that war is grisly beyond imagining. Now I believed him. Bob Fowler, F Company's popular, towheaded commander, had bled to death after being hit in the spleen. His orderly, who adored him, snatched up a submachine gun and unforgivably massacred a line of unarmed Japanese soldiers who had just surrendered. Even worse was the tragic lot of eighty-five student nurses. Terrified, they had retreated into a cave. Marines reaching the mouth of the cave heard Japanese voices within. They didn't recognize the tones as feminine, and neither did their interpreter, who demanded that those inside emerge at once. When they didn't, flamethrowers, moving in, killed them all. To this day, Japanese come to mourn at what is now known as the "Cave of the Virgins."

So my feelings about Sugar Loaf were mixed. As I look back, it was somewhere on the slopes of that hill, where I confronted the dark underside of battle, that passion died between me and the Marine Corps. The silver cord had been loosed, the golden bowl broken, the pitcher broken at the fountain, the wheel broken at the cistern. Half the evil in the world, I thought, is done in the name of honor. *Nicht die Kinder bloss speist man mil Märchen ab.* I now caught the jarring notes in the "Marines' Hymn"—which, after all, was a melody lifted from an obscure Offenbach operetta—and the tacky appeals to patriotism which lay behind the mass butchery on the islands. I saw through the Corps' swagger, the ruthless exploitation of the loyalty I had guilelessly plighted in that Springfield recruiting station after Pearl Harbor. On Sugar Loaf, in short, I realized that something within me, long ailing, had expired. Although I would continue to do the job, performing as the hired gun, I now knew that banners and swords, ruffles and flourishes, bugles and drums, the whole rigmarole, eventually ended in squalor. Goethe said, "There is no man so dangerous as the disillusioned idealist," but before one can lose his illusions he must first possess them. I, to my shame, had been among the enchanted fighters. My dream of war had been colorful but puerile. It had been so evanescent, so ethereal, so wholly unrealistic that it deserved to be demolished. Later, after time had washed away the bitterness, I came to understand that.

a humor magazine. He was friendly on campus with Frank Gifford, the All-American football hero; David Wolper, later one of Hollywood's most successful producers; and Pierre Cossette, who became the man behind the televised Grammy Awards. It was a fantasy come true for this funny little man from a succession of foster homes in New York.

His Walter Mitty life took an even more romantic turn when he learned the GI Bill was good in Paris as well as in the United States. Determined to become another Hemingway or Fitzgerald, Buchwald hitchhiked to New York and caught an old troop ship for France. He lived the life of an expatriate on the modest stipend the GI Bill provided him for classes at the Alliance Française, drinking Pernod late into the night in Montparnasse, stringing for *Daily Variety* back in the States, and hanging out with new friends who would later become famous writers: William Styron, Peter Matthiessen, James Baldwin, Mary McCarthy, Irwin Shaw, and Peter Stone. As he recounted in *I'll Always Have Paris*, Buchwald loved the life. "We had come out of the war with great optimism," he said. "It was a glorious period."

It became even more glorious when Buchwald talked himself into a job at the glamorous *International Herald Tribune*, the English-language newspaper that was distributed throughout Europe and served as a piece of home for American tourists. In 1949, just seven years after he'd been rejected by his summertime sweetheart and joined the Marines in a desperate attempt to find a new life, Art Buchwald had talked his way into one of the most sought-after jobs in journalism. "Paris After Dark," Buchwald's column, quickly became one of the most popular items in the paper, and it led to the byline humor column that made him the best-known American in Paris. He was the city's most popular tourist guide for visiting stars such as Frank Sinatra, Humphrey Bogart, Lauren Bacall, and Audrey Hepburn.

His books became bestsellers, and when he came home, sixteen years later, he was an even bigger star in Washington, with his own table at the most popular restaurant in the capital and lecture fees now at five figures, often with a private plane for transportation. He was practically an uncle to the various Kennedy offspring. When he went to Redskins games, he sat in the owner's box. He summered on Martha's Vineyard with pals Katharine Graham, Mike Wallace, Bill Styron, and Walter Cronkite.

However glamorous his life had become, he never forgot he was a Marine. When Colin Powell was preparing to leave the military and enter civilian life, Buchwald offered to advise him on what lecture agencies would serve him best. Powell's assistant called Buchwald, inviting him to lunch with the general at the Pentagon. Buchwald said, "Lunch? Don't I get a parade? I was in the Marine Corps three and a half years and I never had a parade." When Buchwald arrived at Powell's office, the general said, "Follow me." He took Buchwald into a large room where Powell had assembled fifty of his staff. As Buchwald entered, they all came to attention and gave him a salute. After all those years of people not believing he had been a Marine, Buchwald had a parade, with the Chairman of the Joint Chiefs at his side, in the Pentagon.

He laughs now when he thinks of how much attention he received from Marine brass once he moved to Washington. "They said I was a great Marine. I was a *lousy* Marine. But at the last Marine Ball I attended, colonels were coming up to have their pictures taken with me. I loved that."

Buchwald's feelings go well beyond the attention he gets at Marine ceremonies. "I had no father to speak of, no mother. I didn't know what I was doing. Suddenly I'm in the Marines and it's my family—someone cared about me, someone loved me. That's what I still feel today."

Despite his lovably rumpled appearance, Buchwald also maintains certain habits he learned at Parris Island. He keeps his personal effects neatly arranged, just as he did in his footlocker during basic training. His shoes are always shined to a high gloss. He always has an extra pair of socks, just as the Marines taught him.

During the Vietnam War, he was caught between conflicting emotions. He was against the war, yet when the Marine Corps asked him to record some radio commercials for their recruiting efforts he happily complied. He was flattered, in fact; after all, he was a Marine. He realized that his old loyalties and his current thinking were in conflict only when friends began to point out the inconsistencies of his behavior. He stopped recording the commercials.

Buchwald has written about his Marine Corps experience so often that fellow leathernecks often approach him to compare notes, inevitably saying, "You think *your* drill instructor was tough. *Mine* was the toughest in the Corps." Buchwald never concedes. He *knows* Pete Bonardi was the toughest.

In 1965, *Life* magazine asked Buchwald to return to Parris Island for a week of basic training, to recall the old days. He agreed, if he could take along his old drill instructor, Pete Bonardi.

He found Bonardi working as a security guard at the World's Fair in New York and arranged for him to get the time off work. Bonardi remembered Buchwald from basic training, saying, "I was sure you'd get killed," adding warmly, "You were a real shitbird."

In his book, Buchwald recalls that they had a nostalgic week at Parris Island and that nothing much had changed. He may have been famous, but he was still a klutz. On the obstacle course, Bonardi was still yelling things like "Twenty-five years ago I would have hung your testicles from that tree." At the end of the week, they shook hands and parted friends.

A quarter century later, Buchwald received a call from a mutual friend telling him Bonardi was gravely ill with cancer. Buchwald telephoned his old drill instructor, whose voice was weak as he told Buchwald he didn't think he could make this obstacle course.

In *Leaving Home*, Buchwald describes taking a photo from their *Life* layout and sending it to Bonardi with the inscription "To Pete Bonardi, who made a man out of me. I'll never forget you." Bonardi's wife later told Buchwald that the old D.I. had put the picture up in his hospital room so everyone could read it.

Bonardi also had one final request. That autographed picture from the shitbird, the screw-up Marine he was sure would be killed, little Artie, the guy he called "Brooklyn" as he tried to make a leatherneck out of him? Corporal Bonardi, the toughest guy Buchwald ever met, asked that the picture be placed in his casket when he was buried.

I confess that I weep almost every time I read that account, for it so encapsulates the bonds within that generation that last a lifetime. For all of their differences, Art Buchwald and Pete Bonardi were joined in a noble cause and an elite corps, each in his own way enriching the life of the other. Their common ground went well beyond the obstacle course at Parris Island.

from # The Coldest War
by James Brady

*James Brady arrived in Korea Thanksgiving weekend, 1951,
17 months into the war. He joined American and Allied
troops hunkered down opposite Chinese and North Korean
troops. By spring, Brady was a seasoned veteran.*

On Sunday at four o'clock precisely, Chinese guns began firing all the length of the marine lines. The targets were behind us, the marine Divisional artillery batteries. The Chinese intelligence was very good, and they hit in or around every battery but two. I was asleep, and Mack was wrestling outside the tent with Buscemi, the football player who was now communications officer. It was just a routine, peaceful Sunday afternoon, and then the shells came over. It only lasted a few minutes, but I was lying facedown in a slit trench, and Mack and Buscemi were tangled up in another trench. No one was hit in the Battalion; they weren't aiming at us. Casualties were light all along, only a couple of artillerymen killed. Still, it was disturbing when things like this happened. You hoped the chinks weren't that good, that coordinated. But they were.

The next morning, at the staff meeting, the colonel talked about the shelling. He said Regiment suggested the Chinese must have pretty good observation posts to be able to pull off a stunt like that. They were probably getting good information from infiltrators and the natives. When I heard that I felt pretty good about having burned out the village.

"Lieutenant Brady, are there Chinese on Yoke?"

Yoke was a modest hill halfway between the lines, directly in front of 212, where Dog Company sat, about a mile out in front of the line. I started to make a little speech about Yoke, not knowing really. This was something I had a tendency to do when I lacked knowledge, make a little speech, but Gregory wasn't having any of it.

"Are there or aren't there?"

I fell back on honesty. "I don't know, Colonel. We haven't seen any, but that doesn't mean to say they aren't there."

"Thank you, Mr. Brady. It's always helpful to have expert opinion." The colonel could be cutting when he chose.

"I suggest, or rather Regiment has suggested to me, that we send a patrol out there to see if there really are any Chinese on Yoke operating an observation post. When Regiment suggests something, I generally go along." He permitted himself a brief cackle.

Nicholson had obviously worked this out. He outlined the battle plan. A full rifle platoon would go out, supported by a section of light machine guns. The guns would set up on the last little hump before Yoke and cover the platoon as it climbed the hill. Simple enough. After that, well, that would depend on whether there were Chinamen there. The patrol was scheduled for that night.

"What do you think, Brady?" the colonel said.

"Sounds fine, Colonel. Fine."

"Now, Brady, since you're the intelligence officer of this Battalion and since you don't know if there are Chinese out there and such information might interest you, don't you think it would be a nice idea if you went along?"

The colonel was a lot of laughs at staff meetings. "Well, yes, sir, I guess it would."

"That's dandy. You might take an interpreter along, just in case those Chinese you don't think are there play us a dirty trick and be there when you arrive."

I was cleaning and oiling my .45 when Mack came in.

"The old man got something against you?"

"Oh, he just likes to needle, and on this one he's right. I don't know what's out there and I guess I should."

We were jumping off at 2 a.m. so we'd be on Yoke before light. I climbed the hill to Dog Company alone, just before dark. Two of my scouts and two interpreters had gone ahead.

It was dark on the hill, with stars. There would be no moon, which was good. Stars were enough to find your way; a moon showed you up. It was nice being back with the Company. There weren't too many people I knew anymore, but there was the familiar feel of an old neighborhood. McCarty, the exec who succeeded me, was still there and so was Maki, but this wasn't his patrol. I was glad about that. I didn't see him and that, too, made me glad. Charley Logan still had the Company. One night in reserve Logan got drunk and blubbered about how Mack and I and the old-timers were always comparing him to Chafee and how it hurt. He was right. We did. But it was nothing personal. We would have felt that way no matter who replaced John Chafee. It was even good seeing Charley again, especially since he wasn't brushing his teeth.

Logan and McCarty had me to dinner, the usual cans heated over a burner, arid coffee. Their bunker had a port, and you could see Yoke out there in front, a black bulk looming, no details. I'd seen it plenty; I was just refreshing myself. There was still a high-tension steel tower on Yoke, a leftover from the Japanese power grid that was all shot to hell now, and that was how you could easily pick out Yoke by day. After dinner we lay around the bunker, a bit crowded, smoking cigarettes and talking. The first sergeant said he was taking his bag down to the supply tent for the night so I could sleep for a couple hours before going out. I thought I wouldn't, that it wasn't worth it, but by nine I was yawning. I lay down on the bare ground, my field jacket buttoned up, my face toward the sandbagged wall and away from the candlelight and the low murmur of Logan and McCarty's talk. McCarty had decided to go along with us. He was being transferred soon, and being a regular he wanted to see as much as he could this last tour on the line. He'd always wanted to make a big patrol and this might be his last chance. He had a new movie camera, a Jap jobbie, and he hoped to get some shots of the chink MLR from the crest of Yoke. I didn't care if I never went on patrol again; McCarty was eager to go.

I didn't fall asleep immediately. I kept yawning but sleep didn't come. That was nerves. You never knew when you went out through the lines, you really never knew, and for the first time, I'd begun thinking about being rotated home. It was obvious that I was never going to become a rear-echelon pogue, that so long as I was in Korea I would be with a Marine rifle battalion on the line. Now I had nearly seven months in and not many more to go, two months, maybe three or four tops. I could count. Quantico was turning out platoon leaders by the hundreds, and for the first time in two years the Division had enough lieutenants. They were still short of certain NCOs and a few specialists and captains. But they had plenty of lieutenants. It might mean going home this summer. Now I was going on patrol, as I'd done that first tour when I was scared because I didn't know anything. Now I knew a lot. And I was still scared. I turned again on the hard ground of the bunker, and that was the last thing I remembered until Logan was shaking me awake and shoving a can of hot coffee into my hand.

McCarty and I went outside. Logan came after us, clapping us both on the shoulder. I think Charley was glad he wasn't going. Never mind the heat of the day, now it was cold outside. The day's heat had drained off into space, and from a clear, cloudless sky, heavy dew fell on the hill. I shivered, part of that the sudden waking, and I was glad I had worn my field jacket and wasn't going out there in a T-shirt, like Mack's people had. I tightened my gun belt, having lost a few pounds since the weather turned hot. McCarty held out a couple of grenades.

"Want them?"

"Sure." I shoved them into the breast pockets of my shirt. They hung there heavy, like breasts swollen with milk, but cold and dead. Then, on impulse, I stripped off the field jacket and gave it to Logan to keep for me. Even with the night chill, we might be out there all day and it was going to be hot. By morning I'd be swearing and tired in a field jacket; this way I was cold at the start but would warm up. The armored vest was enough to wear, and I let it hang open. I had the .45. They'd taken personal weapons like my .38 Smith & Wesson and locked them up months ago. Too many accidental discharges, too many people shot. The .45 was a joke but you wore it. Close enough, you could knock someone down, maybe even kill him. Fifty yards away, you couldn't hit shit. The carbine wasn't much better and it was silly carrying a rifle. If we got into a firefight, there would be rifles around. Plenty. I'd learned that much.

The platoon was moving through the wire, quiet at the start, placing their feet cautiously, not to slip on the shale of the forward slope. Jack Rowe had the platoon, a replacement from Philadelphia, a slim, nice-looking boy who'd graduated from Villanova. Rowe was only a second lieutenant and green, but on a patrol both McCarty and I, who out-ranked him, would be under his orders. I fell back with my scouts to the rear of the single line the patrol had assumed. Only the machine gunners were behind us. We moved out briskly, the stars giving plenty of light. Once your eyes adjusted stars were enough. We went down the hill with very little noise, and onto the flat, sixty men and their weapons moving quietly and fast. Yoke loomed black ahead of us.

The line snaked out across the valley and I could see neither head nor tail. But you began to sense the accordion effect as we spread out, the rear end of the file closing suddenly on the people ahead, then the head of the file opening up so that men had to trot to keep up. Any-time this many men moved in file on rough ground you had the same problem. Still, it wasn't so bad, the stars giving light, and no one fell. But we were beginning to make noise. We were no longer moving quietly. I knew we were making a hell of a lot of noise, no talk, nothing really loud, but the sum total of sixty men on the march, carrying machine guns and BARs and wearing web gear, created a steady rasp and rattle that had to carry. I hoped it didn't carry too far. I didn't think there were chinks on Yoke but I wasn't all that sure. Before me the file began to climb the lower slopes of Yoke, the first people on Yoke itself, the point that led every patrol. I was still on the flat but it was only three o'clock, not bad time. We would be at the top before dawn caught us. Now I began to climb, Sasso with me and Wrabel, a scout corporal and a good one, a big, rangy kid. The two of them moved quietly, if no one else did. The machine gunners had dropped back to set up, and I could hear metal on metal as they ran belts through the guns and set up for overhead fire. Somewhere a bird chirped, the first to wake. No distant artillery rumbled, masking sound. All along the line the night gunners had gone to bed and the day gunners had not yet risen. We'd crossed the open flat without difficulty and now were on Yoke, and it looked as if the chinks weren't there, maybe never had been there. For once, we were lucky.

The first explosion was so shocking, I thought we'd set it off ourselves and wondered why we were so stupid and noisy. Then I wondered if it had really happened. One moment the night was black, the next brilliantly lighted, then dark again, the sound fading into echoes. It lighted the hill and then died, just bright enough to blind us for the confused seconds that followed. I knew by now it wasn't imagination. Someone must have hit a mine, some point man got it. Then there came a *rrripp* of burp guns from above, and I realized it wasn't a mine but a grenade; there were chinks up there. There were more crashes, grenades, and shouts in English, and the start of firing back. I'd dropped prone and lay there, head up, trying to see, but not giving a target. Up ahead someone called for the third squad to move up. Behind me and around me men got to their feet and started heavily up the incline. I looked around. Wrabel was nearest me. It was his first firefight.

"Wrabel, okay?"

"Great, Lieutenant. I didn't think we'd be this lucky first time out."

Well, that was a healthy, positive attitude. There was more firing, and when I turned right I could see the sky had cracked and the light was coming, the stars fading and the black turning dull gray. Oh, shit. It was going to be Tu-mari and 104 all over, caught by daylight assaulting a Chinese position. There was plenty of firing, grenades and the burp guns and our stuff, too, plenty active up ahead. I got to my knees.

"Wrabel, Sasso, get the interpreters. Let's go. We'll act as an independent fire team. Watch me."

We got up and began to climb the hill, no one behind us now but the machine gunners a few hundred yards back, out of sight. Up the slope I found McCarty. There were marines lying all over the hill, rifles and BARs pointed uphill. The firing had died down "What happened?"

"They got the point man," McCarty said. "Dead. I don't know if it was a grenade or a trap. They're up top, on the crest. You'll be able to see from a little higher up. Rowe has two squads up there tying to take them. We're reserve."

"Did he call in the machine guns?"

"Not yet. Not till Rowe gives it a try or stalls. If he gets stalled I'll call in the machine guns. Can't shoot now, with Rowe trying to crawl up there."

Now the firing erupted again, with grenades going off in strings like firecrackers on the Fourth. It was real dawn now, gray, and the grenades no longer lighted up the place. There were some shouts and then the cry.

"Corpsman, corpsman!"

"Well," McCarty said, "I don't think they made the top."

He got up very slowly, his movie camera looking silly slung around his neck. I didn't think he was going to get much use out of it.

"This fire team come with me," McCarty ordered. Then, to me, "Want to come?"

"Sure." We started up the path again, easy to see now without straining for footholds. There was very little firing. Before we'd gone very far we met marines coming down. The first three were bloody, but you couldn't tell how badly they were hit. None of them were crying or looked to be in shock. They were just bloody and they were walking back, doing all right. I nodded to them as they went past, but they didn't look at me.

"Where's Mr. Rowe?" McCarty asked.

"Up there," one of the wounded said over his shoulder. "He got hit."

McCarty and I went up until we reached a bunch of wounded marines lying on the hillside while off to the right and left of them a skirmish line of marines was lying prone. Every so often someone squeezed off a shot. I don't think they had targets; they were just firing.

"Here's Rowe," McCarty said. He was lying flat. His face was hit and there was something wrong with his hands. A corpsman was kneeling over him doing something. I called Rowe's first name, "Jack?" but he didn't move or answer. I turned to look at McCarty.

"He's bad. You want to take it or shall I?"

"What the hell," McCarty said, "I just came along for the ride, to take pictures. Whatever you want."

"Okay," I said, "you're the exec and you're senior. You take over. Just tell me what you want done."

"Swell," McCarty said. "Sergeant, how many Chinese up there?'

A marine crawled over to us. He was bloody, too, but I couldn't see where he was hit. He talked fast, excited, but he didn't seem badly hurt.

"Could be a platoon, probably less. We got up to the wire and then when we started through they hit us with grenades. They got grenades up the ass. They was throwing them down and we was throwing them back. That's how Mr. Rowe got it. He caught a grenade and it went off. He's shy an eye and it looks like some fingers."

"How many dead have we got?"

"Just the point man so far, unless some of these hit guys croaked. But we got a lot of woundeds. Just about everyone picked up something in the wire."

I looked up and could see the wire, a triple-apron fence. I wondered why we hadn't seen it before, from the OPs, through glasses. It would have told us the chinks were here, maybe. McCarty was taking a head count, and then he sent down for the last squad to come up.

"Give me the radio." He called the machine gunners. "Look, we got chinks on the crest of the hill, the very crest. You think you can hit them and not hit us? We're just below the wire. Can you see the wire now? Got enough light?"

He turned to me, "The machine guns can see us. They say they've got light." He punched the radio button again. "Okay," he said, "hit them."

Both machine guns began to fire, and I crouched lower, head down, neck bowed. It was instinctive. At this range the guns fired with extreme accuracy, and anyway their target was fifty yards or more above where McCarty and I had set up. You could hear the bullets hitting earth, or sandbags or logs or whatever they had up there. Occasionally one hit the steel tower and whined away. Now it was four o'clock and full light, and I wished I could back up and see what the crest of Yoke really looked like. Here we were under it and too close to see. There was no firing from the Chinese. The radio squawked at McCarty and he put it to his ear. "Sure," he was saying, "sure. If they think they can lay it in and not hit us." He put down the handset and looked at me.

"They can give us 105s, too."

"We're pretty close for 105s," I said. Boy, that was an understatement.

"Well, they say they've got a good fix on the crest and they say they can do it. What the hell, they know their stuff. I say let them try."

"Okay," I said, "you've got the wheel."

I didn't like this at all, but McCarty seemed relieved to have a second opinion and that I was going along with him. "Tell them give us one round of 105. We'll adjust."

There was a weird silence, the machine guns stopped, probably changing belts, cooling the barrels so they wouldn't get stoppages. Then the first shots from the 105s came in over our heads, sounding like freight trains, to burst forty, fifty yards up the hill, near the crest.

I'd been looking over my shoulder when it came. "God, I never realized you could see them."

"Well," McCarty said, "I guess you can. That one was perfect. I'm going to tell them fire for effect. Okay?"

I nodded, thinking about the way the shell had looked when it came in above us, black and small and moving very fast, faster than a jet even, and looking very low and close to us and then going out of sight, too fast to see as it passed us, hitting into the hill with the familiar crunch. I'd heard plenty of incoming; this was the first time I'd ever seen the shells. A short round, that was all we needed. Don't give us a short round. McCarty was on the radio now, telling them to fire for effect. He put the radio down and yelled to the marines around us.

"Stay low, the 105s are coming in."

Someone gave a halfhearted cowboy yell, a little cheer, but I lay there on my stomach flat against the upward slope of the hill, my helmet feeling wonderful, thinking how nice it would be if all of me could fit inside it. The first salvo of shells was on the way now, and there was a drawing-up feeling in the small of my back. I watched them over my shoulder, black and fast and low, three of them this time, and I could see all three. They shuttled in, very loud, to smash into the hillside above us. I could feel Yoke jerk under me. I thought maybe I should pray, and I started to, Hail Marys, but I never finished one, short as they were. I would start and then another three shells would come in over me and bang into the hill and shake me like a rat. My body would try to absorb the shock, and I forgot where I was in the prayer and had to start again. I stopped watching the shells come; it was too much watching them and worrying, and I just lay there flat as I could, my face in the dirt, shoulders hunched and my neck screwed down tight between them, trying to squeeze more of me into the helmet.

Shells came in like that for maybe three or four minutes. You couldn't really judge time; it had no meaning in a situation like that. Toward the end there was a short round, only one, and it was really short, falling below us, halfway down the hill. Dirt fell lightly on us, feeling wonderful, being only dirt and pebbles and not hot metal. Then the guns secured. I think that short one shook the gunners up, too, if their forward observers saw it. McCarty was on the radio. "Give us machine guns on the crest again. Now!"

The two guns resumed their chatter, typewriters gone mad, with McCarty shouting. "Keep their heads down, pour it on." He was looking around at the rest of us. Along the skirmish line individual marines were squeezing off single rounds now, the firing ragged compared to the disciplined bursts of the machine guns. McCarty looked around to me.

"I think we ought to go up there. How about it?"

"Hell, yeah, Stew. Let's take them." I was thinking about Jack Rowe's eye and the point man dead and the bloody marines coming down the path. Now that our shelling was over I wasn't even frightened, only sore and wanting very badly to go up and stand on top of this damned hill.

McCarty yelled orders to the marines within hearing. "On three we go," he shouted. "One, two . . ."

We were up and running, all of us, Wrabel next to me, running uphill but not feeling the grade or being winded or leg weary, just sprinting up. There were marines all around me. Some of the wounded must be coming with us, going up a second time. I didn't recognize anyone but Wrabel, but it didn't matter, we were attacking Yoke together, in daylight, assaulting a hill, and we were going to get there. I had the .45 out. It was silly, because you couldn't hit anything and I couldn't see a chink, but I remembered how few men actually fire in combat, how they seize up, and I thought I ought to be shooting the damned thing. Around me other marines were firing, their rifles and BARs at the hip as they ran. They couldn't be hitting anything either, but we'd be keeping their heads down, the chinks. I fired without aiming, just firing vaguely toward the crest of the hill. It felt good to be running and firing. I fired again. Around me there was shouting. I picked up the shout.

"No prisoners!" I yelled. "No prisoners! Kill 'em all!" That's what I was shouting, what others were shouting. Everyone took it up now, everyone near me anyway. It was stupid shouting stuff like that. My job was to get prisoners. Dead chinks didn't help anyone. But it just seemed to be the thing to shout at that moment, and since it felt good I kept shouting it. So did the others.

"No prisoners!"

When we reached the wire, I went right through it. I can't say just how, whether I dove over it, somersaulting, or vaulted it, or just got lucky and ran through a patch the 105s had cut, but I was through, kneeling on the hard scrabbly dirt of the hill looking up. Other marines were through, too. Now there was maybe twenty yards to go for the top. I could see what looked like the top of a bunker with a firing port cut into it dead ahead. I squeezed off one very carefully aimed shot, the first I'd taken slowly, aiming at the firing port. With a .45 even a twenty-yard shot was guesswork, sheer optimism, but dust was whipping up from the crest, all the way along, as if windswept. Everyone must be shooting now. I hoped it wasn't our machine guns, because we were going to be on that crest pretty soon. I was still carrying the two grenades and was momentarily taken with fear a chance shot might hit one of them and explode it against my chest. I pulled one out and then the other, lay one on the ground and pulled the pin and tossed the first. Before it exploded I had the second in the air. I had a good arm and they both made the crest, exploding with a satisfying crack.

I got up from my knees and started again. Twenty yards to go, nothing. The ground was gritty, dry, and it crunched under my boots as I moved. I looked around to see how many were standing, who was going to the top with me. Just a couple. I looked for Wrabel and then a grenade exploded very close. And another. Without willing it, I was lying on the hill now, looking toward the crest, that damned silly automatic in my right hand, and now I could see grenades in the air, as I'd seen the 105s, only these were bigger and slower and coming at me. One grenade seemed to be trailing something, tied up with rags. I couldn't understand that. A grenade went off right in front of me, stinging both hands and my face. Dirt, it was just dirt. Fragments of the grenade would have been hot. I didn't feel anything beyond the stinging, so I couldn't have been hit. I fired again. More grenades were in the air, more going off to both sides and above me. A burp gun ripped off a quick burst. I looked around. Marines sprawled like me on the slope just below the crest. Only Wrabel was standing, wrestling with another marine. He seemed to be taking the man's rifle away from him. I didn't understand that. Now Wrabel was using the rifle to fire uphill, still standing, but in a crouch. I wondered where Stew McCarty was and whether anyone had gotten to the top. Another grenade exploded in front of me, then one behind. I still didn't feel anything.

"Pull back," a voice came up from below. Sounded like McCarty. "Pull back, get out of here."

I stood, still facing the hill, and then turned and sprinted back toward the wire. This time I knew how I got past it, diving through the air to clear the apron and then rolling, tucked, when I landed. I spun back then to face the hill. Other marines were coming through the wire, carrying and helping other people. I fired off the last rounds in the .45, just covering, not hitting anything. Then I rolled to my side to shove in a fresh clip. Next to me a marine was lying prone but not firing. I edged over to him.

"What's the matter, you hit?"

"No, rifle jammed."

"Gimme." I took the M-l. The safety was on. I slipped it off and began to squeeze off single shots at the crest of Yoke. "This rifle's fine," I said, but the marine just lay there, not listening. Wrabel crawled to me.

"You see that guy up there, Mr. Brady? Wasn't shooting or nothing. I took his damn rifle. A corporal and he wasn't shooting." He joined me firing at the crest. Now McCarty crawled up to us.

"Well, the grenades stopped us," he said. "You hit?"

"No. You?"

"Not a bit, but if I land on this camera again I'm going to have broken goddamned ribs." He paused. "Well, where do we go from here?" For the moment, there was no firing.

I put down the rifle and looked at McCarty and then around me. Nearly every marine I could see was bloody, some of them really hurt, others, like me, just scratched up a bit. Some of the wounded were crawling down the hill, dragging themselves along, still with their weapons.

"Well?"

"Look, Stew, whatever you say. We can give her another shot, go up again, maybe try to get a squad around to the right and get in behind them. Only thing is, if we get anymore hit, who's going to get these people back home? Some of them are going to have to be carried. If we get more people hurt, won't be anyone to do it. That's what I think."

McCarty looked around, not excited and still looking relatively neat and clean, as regulars should. Then he nodded.

"Okay," McCarty said, "that's good enough for me. This isn't supposed to be a combat patrol anyway. We'll go down. But there's a BAR lying up there and I wanna get that."

"Sure, let's go." I hadn't been afraid since the last 105 shell had come in. It was very strange, being calm and not afraid, not even now. McCarty called for covering fire, and the two of us crawled uphill again. At the wire we stopped. Wrabel and a couple of others were there. McCarty nodded at them and started to wriggle through the wire, under the sagging strands, parting the wire carefully with his hands and moving on his back, squirming along but pretty fast. I squeezed off a round from the M-l, and the others took it up, a ragged tattoo of fire. Up above, a burp gun answered, but not aimed, nowhere near us. The chink was probably sitting on the floor of the bunker, firing blind through the port without ever getting his head up. McCarty was coming back now, with the BAR. He was a cool one. When he came through we all turned and started down the slope, two men at a time covering us, picking up men as we went. Sasso was there, bleeding from the arms and the chest but looking chipper.

"How is it?"

"Great, Mr. Brady, just shrapnails is all. Not bad." We went down to where I'd last seen Jack Rowe. The others who were still there, a corpsman and a couple of marines, they took extra rifles and let the wounded lean on them. I had two rifles now and a bandolier of cartridges I'd taken from somebody, the green cloth soaked with blood drying to a rust color, slung around my neck. There was no more firing. We caught up with Rowe on the floor of the valley, just below where Yoke began. He was lying there on the ground, looking very bad. Some people were coming toward us now from the MLR, stretcher parties. You couldn't land a chopper out here. I looked at my watch. Almost five o'clock. They'd gotten help out here pretty quick. The sun was hanging higher but still oversized, the way it looks in the morning, and it was going to be a fine day. When they got Rowe on a stretcher McCarty said, "Jim, do me a favor. Count heads and see we don't leave anyone out here, dead or alive."

I said sure and took Wrabel, and we counted off people and checked with squad leaders, the ones who were still moving. There were marines scattered all over the lower hillside and the flats at the foot of Yoke. Checking numbers meant getting off the paths and crossing paddies and little fields and cutting this way and that, and it was then I started being afraid again, not of the chinks, but thinking about mines, the way I used to be. It'd be a hell of a thing to do what we'd done this morning and then step on a mine. I took up prayer again and didn't stop until we finished the count. Long lines of men were moving across the flat now, in both directions, empty stretchers coming out, loaded ones going back. Overhead the 105s were flying again, hitting way up on Yoke and well back into the Chinese MLR, discouraging them from shelling us as we came out. I hustled along the line of men to catch up with Rowe's stretcher.

"How is he?"

A corpsman was giving him blood, holding the bottle and walking along beside. Rowe looked dead. They'd cleaned his face a bit, but his right eye looked gone, nothing there but a wound. I didn't look at his hands. No one answered my question, so I answered it myself, "He's okay," I said, "he'll make it. He's a Villanova wildcat, that boy. He'll make it, you'll see."

No one said anything, and I stopped talking, having the feeling I was making an ass of myself. The hell with it. I wasn't talking to them; I was talking in case Rowe could hear me.

I moved along the file of men, and then we stopped at the little knoll where the machine gunners had set up. McCarty was jotting something in a notebook. Later he figured out sixty-four of us had been on the patrol, with forty-eight actually going up Yoke, and thirty-two of us had been hit. I sat down, relishing the break as we picked up the machine gunners while the corpsmen fussed, bandaging wounds. Sasso sat there cross-legged, his shirt off. "I told you, Lieutenant, not bad."

"No stateside for you, Ace," someone said.

"Shit," Sasso said, laughing. Unless you were hit the way Rowe was, you felt pretty good, having gone through all that and being able to make jokes.

We were in through the MLR about eight. I hurried through the Dog Company position and down the other side of 212 to the CP. Colonel Gregory was waiting, and Nicholson, the S-3. They both shook hands with me.

"I'm sorry about that, Brady," the colonel said.

"Well, sir, nothing to worry about." I stopped and thought for an instant. "Anyway, there are chinks on Yoke. We found that out."

"How many do you figure?"

"Could be anything, platoon to a fire team. I'd say a squad. With plenty of grenades."

"Only a squad and they did this?"

"Yessir, they just sat there in the trench and tossed grenades downhill at us. They didn't do anything fancy, just rolled grenades down on us."

"We get any of them?"

"Colonel, I'd be a liar if I said yes. Maybe we hit a couple out of sheer luck, maybe the 105s got some. I'd say we must have gotten a few. But I couldn't swear to it, couldn't give you a count."

He put me on the phone to S-3 at Regiment, and I gave them the same report. The major I talked to sounded incredulous we'd taken all those casualties without giving him a single chink.

I stopped by the aid station, where they picked rock and dirt out of my hands and face and cleaned out some bad wire cuts on my right leg. I didn't even realize I had them. Too excited. When I took off my pants some grenade fragments fell out. Shrapnails. In January the snow had muffled the explosion that blew up Fitzgerald and me. I was starting to think of myself as fortunate. Back at the tent Mack shook my hand but didn't say much. The bloody bandolier was still slung around my neck, and I took it off and dropped it on the dirt floor next to the cot. I thought about trying to sleep for a while, but I was still too excited.

I don't know how anyone who hasn't been shot at up close in a real firefight can possibly understand how good you feel afterward. Men have been killed and hurt, the fight has been won or lost, but there is only the one truly significant fact: that you are still alive, you have not been killed. Later, I was sure, I would mourn the dead and the damaged. But not now. If you were not truly happy at a moment like this when you had just come down off the line walking, perhaps you never would be.

from The Proud Bastards

by E. Michael Helms

E. Michael Helms joined the USMC right out of high school, and served with the 2nd Battalion, 4th Marines (known in the Corps as "the Magnificent Bastards"). Helms arrived in Vietnam in 1967, and soon found himself in the thick of the action.

Quang Tri
Northern I CORPS
November-December 1967

"Hey man . . . youse scared?" The whispered, almost timid question comes out of the blackness from the rear of the dank bunker. Good question. I haven't really thought about it yet. Been too busy and fascinated with this whole scene to think about particulars. I better come up with some kind of an answer, though. This kid seems real jumpy. And it's my ass that'll be on the line when he takes his turn on watch. Don't want him getting *my* shit blown away before I've had time to figure out what the hell's going on here myself. Guess I'll lie a little bit:

"Naw, man. No reason to be scared here. This ain't the bush. Just keep your head down and your eyes and ears open. Charlie ain't likely to fuck with us here."

Damn, what an answer. Sounded real confident and assuring. Almost believe my own snow job. Probably close to being correct, though. The NVA and VC would have to be crazy to try a ground assault on this place. There's been some incoming from across the DMZ each day since I got here, and a few harassing mortar rounds at night. But a ground attack? No fuckin' way. They'd get greased before they ever got within five hundred meters of the wire. The firepower we've got here is unbelievable.

Another flare from the 81mm mortars section pops several hundred yards beyond the perimeter, bathing the darkness with its eerie orange glow as it sizzles and sways beneath the silk parachute. Somewhere in the distance to the northwest sporadic gunfire and the occasional boom of explosions interrupt the otherwise excessive quietness of the area.

I've been here at Dong Ha just below the DMZ for four days now, in-country for five. Work details during the day and perimeter duty at night while I wait for my outfit to come back off an operation. Been assigned to 2nd Battalion, 4th Marines. Also known as the "Magnificent Bastards." Supposed to be a good outfit, they've seen plenty of action in this war. Just came down from a place called Con Thien after a couple of months of heavy fighting. Lot of casualties, I heard. I'm anxious as hell to get to them. Hope I fit in OK. Those guys have seen a lot of shit and I'll be the FNG—fuckin' new guy—on the block. What the hell, though. They were *all* new guys once. A couple of months and a few firefights under my belt and I'll be an old salt teaching replacements the ropes myself.

"Where youse from?" Lampley, the nervous guy, is trying to make conversation again. He just got here this afternoon. Flew into Danang this morning, got processed and caught a quick flight up north, and here he is. He's still wearing stateside utilities and boots. Fresh out of boot camp and ITR. Just turned eighteen last month, he told me. Looks about twelve.

"Florida. How 'bout you?" It's early yet, and my watch, so I'll humor him. Besides, I know the lonely feeling of the first night.

"Pennsylvania, just outside Philly."

That accent! Thought I recognized it. Just like Corporal Mathis from the office me and Bentley were stuck in at Camp Lejeune.

Bentley. Damn, I'm gonna miss being with him. First time we've been separated since our bus arrived at Parris Island. Shit, I feel like a goddamn orphan or something. I drew 2/4 and he got 2/26. Bendix and Duvall are gone, too. I don't remember their outfits. Several guys from our old ITR unit got assigned to 2/4 with me, but none that I'm really close to. I'm sure gonna miss that son of a bitch Bentley. In a way I'm kinda glad though. It would be real tough if we were together and he got zapped and I had to watch him die. Shit. He probably feels the same way. I'm glad the fucker's gone. Won't know shit till this whole game's over with. Sure as hell hope he makes it.

A muffled pop, and the latest flare casts weird shadows that dance like ghosts amongst the layers of concertina wire strung in front of our position. Jesus! The hair on the back of my neck raises up as a cold shudder races down my spine. Looks like somebody's in the wire! Can't be. The cans would be rattling and the pop flares would be going off if anybody was trying to get through the wire, wouldn't they?

I turn my head away from the confusing landscape and shut my eyes for a second. I blink and look back. The infiltrating specters have vanished as the flare floats farther down the line. It's as easy as hell to get spooked here. I've got a lot to learn and get used to. That's about the tenth time in four nights that's happened. Conjuring up all kinds of strange shit. Gotta get a handle on this crap. I check the row of hand grenades lined neatly on the sandbag shelf before me. Gotta be ready. Next time it might not be my imagination crawling through the wire.

Lampley's finally calmed down enough to get some sleep. Hope he didn't see how scared I was a while ago. He thinks I'm an old hand at this. I haven't told him that I've been here less than a week. Must be the jungle boots and utilities I bought off that grunt in Okinawa the day before our flight to Danang. Slightly used and salty. Better than new. Makes me look like I've seen a little shit.

Low, crackling static sounds from the radio in our bunker as the command post calls for a situation report. I grab the hand-set and key it twice to indicate that everything is secure at our position. I strain my eyes at the luminous dial of the watch I borrowed from the sergeant in charge of the bunkers in this sector. 0300 hours. Halfway through my second two-hour watch. This shit gets boring after awhile. Beats the hell out of the work details I've been on, though. Burning shitters. About as low as you can go on the duty roster. I've spent the last three mornings carrying halved fifty-five-gallon drums sloshing full of shit and piss, pouring a layer of diesel fuel in 'em, light it up and watch the putrid mess burn. God, what a smell! Damn wind seems to keep changing and blows the foul fumes all over me no matter how much I try to avoid it. Permeates everything it touches. Glorious goddamn job. ("What did *you* do in the war, Daddy?" Chest swells with pride—"I burned shit, son.") Jesus . . .

"Wake up, wake up, wake up!"

"What the fu . . . what is it?" Lampley's got hold of my shoulder, shaking me awake. The whites of his eyes look big as saucers in the pitch blackness of the bunker.

"I think I see something. I'm sure I did!" Fast, excited voice, much too loud if there is something out there.

Aw, shit. Fucker sees a shadow and ruins the best Z's I've cut since I've been here. "Where at, Lampley?" My question betrays a tinge of disgust in my voice over my interrupted sleep.

"There, over there!" Shit, he's almost shouting now. My eyes follow his pointing finger beyond the wire about midway between us and the bunker to our left. Son of a bitch! Two small, darting figures about fifty yards beyond the concertina heading away from us! I grope in the darkness for the radio to report the movement and start to tell Lampley not to fire his rifle yet because the muzzle flash will give away our position but the little shit is already popping away with his M16. The gun team on our left two bunkers down is cutting loose and red tracers are streaking toward the place where the two gooks were. Jesus H. Christ! A tremendous explosion just blew fifty yards to our left front. The goddamn gooks must be blowing the wire!

The whole damn line is opening up now, firing from every bunker. More explosions to our left. They must be trying to knock out the gun team. Flares are popping everywhere and night has become brilliant day. I'm firing at shadows or gooks or something outside the wire to our left where the big explosion was. It doesn't matter now. They know where the bunkers are. Fuckin' B-40's probably gonna come crashing in and blow our shit away. Mortars are walking all over the area to our front outside the wire. I jam another magazine in my '16. Cease fire cease fire somebody's yelling cease fire.

We stare out at the weird scene. No incoming rounds now. Flares still going off all over keeping the whole base ablaze with amber glare. Weapons back on safety. Hearts still pumping wildly, strange high on massive adrenaline rush. Sergeant and assistant going from bunker to bunker checking for casualties and assessing the situation.

"Everything OK here?"

"Yeah," I answer, "anybody get hit?"

"Towns and his A-gunner caught some shrapnel from a rocket. They're OK. Keep your fuckin' eyes open and your heads down. Hundred percent alert till daylight." They head off in a low crouch for the next bunker.

Flares coming with less frequency now. Everything quiet again along the line. Almost back to normal. My temples have quit throbbing and my heart no longer threatens to explode within my chest. Man, that was something! Scary . . . exciting. Lampley stares across the bunker at me, an incredulous look on his face.

"I thought youse said we wouldn't get no ground attack here."

I stare back hard at him, and then break into a big grin. "How the fuck would I know? I've only been here six days."

From within the hollow belly of the C-130 Hercules the straining roar of the engines plays havoc with our eardrums as the camouflage-painted cargo plane finally reaches the apex of its steep ascent and begins to level off. For a while there I thought for sure this thing was gonna fall right on its ass and kill us all. Amazing the damned ugly thing can get off the ground at all, much less really fly. How the hell they could ever take off if this cargo deck was fully loaded is beyond me. Good thing this one is nearly empty. Just a few pallets of C-rations and crates of ammunition, and us six replacements for Echo Company.

Dykes is the only guy I know out of the bunch. All the others I know from our ITR unit have been assigned to the other companies in our battalion—Foxtrot, Golf, and Hotel. Dykes is eighteen, thin, with fat lips and a thick New Jersey accent. "Joisey," he calls it. I don't care for him too much. Much closer to a few of the other guys going to the different companies.

We're headed for a place near Quang Tri City where our company is providing security for a Seabee battalion while they construct a new airstrip and base. Word is that it's just far enough south of the DMZ to be out of artillery range. That'll be a pleasant change. Just the few rounds of that shit I experienced at Dong Ha is enough to convince me that one round is one round too many.

Crew chief wearing an olive drab flight suit and helmet walks nonchalantly to the rear of the plane where the cargo ramp stands half-ajar. I've been wondering about that. He idles over to the gap where one false step or slight jolt of turbulence could send him plummeting thousands of feet to an untimely demise. Stands there unconcernedly on the brink of eternity and fiddles with some buttons and switches mounted to the fuselage. No parachute. No safety line.

I squirm deeper into the webbing of my folding seat and grip the safety belt tightly with both hands, convinced now that this aircraft is faulty and the heavy ramp is going to fall completely off and take the rear part of the fuselage including me with it. Shit, if I'd wanted to fall out of a fuckin' airplane I'd have joined the goddamn army airborne. At least they could have provided a parachute. Finishes his piddling and ambles back up to the cockpit area.

The plane suddenly tilts forward and we begin a steep descent. Shit, I knew it! We're gonna crash! We can't possibly be landing yet; we only took off about five minutes ago. Crazy crew chief walking back toward us again, leaning forward against our dive. Looks totally unconcerned. I'm about to shit in my pants and he looks like he's out for a pleasant drive in the country. Maybe we're *not* going to crash. The hurtling hulk of the C-130 suddenly rights itself and seconds later a slight jolt and increased roaring of the engines signal our safe return to earth. Christ, I'm glad I didn't go into the airwing . . . I'd be a goddamn nervous wreck. . . .

We emerge from the bowels of the aircraft and are greeted by the chilling dampness of the early monsoon. Dark, shredded curtains of clouds reach down to mingle with the gray fogginess which envelops the bleak landscape. The low, sparsely vegetated sand dunes and flats are a sharp contrast to the red clay muck of Dong Ha. A fine mist quickly coats faces, hands, clothing, and equipment with a gentle wetness. A couple of hundred meters to the west of the sectioned metal airstrip a paved road runs north and south. Must be Highway One. Beyond the road a railroad track parallels it into the distance. To the east of the airstrip is a rather pretty and winding river. Several layers of coiled concertina wire have been strung around the entire area, marking a crude perimeter. At the north end of the runway heavy equipment rumbles as Seabees work to extend its length. In every direction scattered marines are busy filling sandbags to shore up hastily constructed bunkers and sleeping hooches.

A jeep comes speeding across the tarmac and skids to a sliding stop a few feet away. A tall, lanky marine hops out and grins. "Any of you guys for Echo?"

"Yeah, all of us."

"Jump in. I'm Corporal Sharpe, former grunt and now very short company clerk. Anybody here from California?"

Florida, Mississippi, New Jersey, New York, and two from Missouri. No Californians. Should've known he was from there by the way he drives. Must've been a former stunt driver in Hollywood.

We speed along down the runway toward a group of tents clustered in the distance. "You guys will like it here," he continues, talking loudly above the jeep's engine and the humming of the knobby tires on the metal surface. "Not much happening since we got here. Mostly just short patrols, ambushes, and LPs. Catch a few mortars and sniper rounds, but that's about it. Get to eat in the Seabee's mess hall once in a while. Number one fuckin' chow."

Jesus, he makes it sound like a damn picnic. Just some mortars and snipers. Nothing to worry about. Christ, as if you can't get wasted by a mortar or sniper. This guy must have really seen some shit. My curiosity has got the better of me. "Heard y'all were up at Con Thien a while back. How was that?"

His pleasant, almost exuberant expression suddenly goes blank. A hollow, faraway look replaces it. Silence for an awful moment. Jesus, I'm sorry I asked. Turns his head toward me. "Con Thien sucks."

I feel like a complete asshole. Way to go, Mikey. Real smart move, boy. How to win friends and influence people. . . .

We turn off the runway and down a sandy lane between rows of big heavy canvas tents. Sharpe pulls over and stops in front of a particularly large one whose sides are surrounded by a wall of stacked sandbags.

"Well, here we are. Company CP. I'll introduce you guys to the Top and he'll get you processed and assigned to your platoons."

Glad to see his mood has swung back to where it was before my stupid question. Curious again. "How long you got left on your tour, Corporal?"

Ear-to-ear shit-eating grin. "Two days and a wake-up, my friend. Two fucking days and a wake-up!" Lucky son of a bitch. . . .

Crack! The sudden and unexpected blast of a rifle from somewhere nearby across the river causes me to flinch and duck my head momentarily below the surface of the perimeter bunker where I'm standing watch. Lance Corporal Gray snickers in the darkness behind me.

"Relax. That's just some fuckin' rice farmer takin' pot shots in the dark. Does it every night. Must be his personal contribution to the 'cause.' Never hits anything. Nothin' to worry about."

Gray is my fireteam leader and assistant squad leader. Another short-timer. Been in-country almost ten months. Sandy-haired, thin twenty-year-old from Arkansas. Married. I like him. Southern "twang" when he talks makes me feel at home.

A flare pops high overhead and floats lazily across the river. No sign of the sniper. Relax, huh? OK. Shit. I guess after ten months of this shit I'll get used to it too. That little probe of the lines at Dong Ha a few nights ago has still got me on edge, I guess. How can these guys be so calm? I'm still nervous as hell.

Like that damn ambush our squad went on last night. We moved through the wire just after dark, heading downstream along the river. So damn dark you couldn't see shit. Everybody stuck a white plastic C-ration spoon in the back of their helmet's headband so we could see the guy in front of us. Don't know how in the hell the point knew where to go. I guess after awhile your eyes must adjust better to this darkness.

Stumbled along for about a half-mile or so and set up our ambush along a trail that follows the river. Laid there for about two hours I guess, and then I saw 'em. Several gooks coming our way, spread out between the trail and the riverbank. I was excited as hell. Thought my damn heart was gonna jump right out of my throat.

Picked out one of the figures and waited for the gun team to blow the ambush. And waited . . . And waited . . . Jesus Christ guys, they're gettin' awfully close. Shit, they're almost on top of us now. What the hell's the matter with you assholes. God, they must all be sleeping. Jesus, should I shoot? Better wait . . . Better blow it now or it may be too late. God, somebody fuckin' do *something!*

Flip my safety off and selector to full automatic. Aiming in. Gonna blow *that* fucker away anyway. Shit! Where the hell did he go? Hey, they're *all* gone! Just disappeared. There one second and gone the next. Damn. I *know* I saw 'em.

Look over at others in the squad. They're awake, staring into the darkness, looking bored. I almost blew the ambush on a bunch of conjured-up shadows. Came *so* fuckin' close! But they *looked* real. As real as the ones at Dong Ha, and I *know* for a fact they were real. God, will I ever get the hang of this shit? I better, before I really fuck up and get myself or somebody else killed. . . .

Standing shirtless atop our squad's hooch, stacking more sandbags on the top of our little palace. We "souvenired" us a section of that heavy metal runway from the Seabees for our roof. Adding all the sandbags we can get hold of on top hoping to make it as mortarproof as possible. Our area is just off the southern end of the airstrip on the river side and is a sitting duck if Charlie decides to throw a serious barrage at the runway.

Been here about a week now and starting to fit in. Starting to finally get it together somewhat. Haven't been fooled by any more shadows since that first ambush. Been on a couple of squad-size patrols. Listening posts every third night. Other nights we each pull two two-hour watches in the bunkers on the line. No action yet, other than a few widely scattered mortars and a few pot shots from our resident farmer-sniper.

Some guy I haven't seen before is coming from the platoon CP towards our hooch. Humming some sort of country-western song. Good. Must be another southerner.

"This second squad?" No southern drawl there.

"Yeah. Mike Helms, Pfc. Glad to meet you." I extend my hand.

"Charles Morton. Lance Corporal. Call me Chuck." Strong handshake and a friendly smile.

"Stow your gear inside, Chuck, and grab an E-tool and help Banks there fill some bags. We'll swap off later. . . ."

On watch again in one of the bunkers near the river. Morton cuttin' Zs on the soggy sand of the bunker's deck. He seems to be an all-right dude. Real happy-go-lucky attitude. Getting to like him a lot. Keeps trying to get me turned on to country music. Sings it all the time. Can't sing worth a shit, but sings it anyway. Wouldn't think a guy from Chicago would like that stuff. Him and Duvall would make a great duet. God, what a noise that would be. Probably make every water buffalo around here di-di.

Quick glance around the area from the light of one of the occasional flares. Nothing moving. Real quiet tonight. Sniper must have decided to take the night off. No mortars at all for two days. Been here a little over two weeks now. Got a few more new hands in the platoon. Feels good not being the FNG. Not an old salt yet by any means, but not the greenest either. Time for Morton's watch. I'm tired. Need to get some sleep. Big day tomorrow. First big operation. Big sweep through some forest area southwest of Quang Tri City. Probably be some real action. Excited and scared.

Morton takes the watch. I try to sleep, but toss and turn. Too damn quiet. Loud cracking of our pet sniper's rifle sounds somewhere down the line. A couple of flares pop and sizzle. That's more like it.

We awaken in the predawn darkness to a chilling drizzle. God, it's hard to believe that it can be so cold in this place. All the stories I ever heard about Vietnam were about how damn hot it was—one hundred twenty degrees in the shade and people dropping like flies with heat exhaustion and such shit. Guess that'll come later. For now I'm sandy, wet, and cold. Miserable. Banks just brewed up some of his infamous C-ration coffee. You have to stir it real quick or the vile shit dissolves your spoon. Feels good going down though. Gray declines in favor of some hot chocolate. Smart dude. His mama didn't raise no fool.

I choke down another mouthful of dry pound cake and check over my pack once more. Supposed to be gone for three or four days. Not much to pack. Got an extra skivvy shirt, two pairs of socks, and extra boxes of M16 rounds stuffed in the main compartment. In another pair of socks I've stuffed enough cans of C-rats for two or maybe three days, and have them lashed to the top and sides of my pack along with two 60mm mortar rounds. My poncho is rolled and tied to the bottom. Two canteens, bayonet, and a battle dressing hang from my web belt. (I've gotta scrounge up another canteen or two before the weather turns hot, I've been told.) Four fragmentation grenades are crammed in one pocket of my trousers, and two smoke grenades in another. Two bandoleers containing twenty full magazines of M16 ammo crisscross my chest, bandito-style. I carry a heavy can of M60 machine gun ammunition slung by a strap over my left shoulder, and my less-than-trusty M16 rifle in my right hand. All ready to go to war— if I can manage to walk with all this shit.

Midafternoon. Been humpin' for hours and have seen nothing. Warmed up some and the sun has tried to break through the clouds a couple of times. Still a light rain falling almost continuously. Crossed the river on the outskirts of Quang Tri City early this morning and headed southwest. Been following some half-assed excuse for a cart trail that roughly parallels the river since then. The company is strung out in a slow-moving column; fifteen-to twenty-meter intervals and staggered on both sides of the trail. Third platoon has the point now. We're in the middle of the column and first platoon has the rear. Thirty or forty meters to either side and near the front lone marines trudge through the tangled brush and occasional trees, providing security against the column being ambushed from the flanks. We pass by another ornate pagoda standing near the riverbank. Beautiful. Quang Tri seems to be a mixture of Buddhism and Catholicism. Seen a few Catholic churches as well as pagodas. Heavy French influence of the old days, I guess. Very pretty and tranquil setting. Hard to believe there's a war going on.

Deafening roar of an explosion. Ugly black cloud mushrooming up ahead on the right flank near the river. Evil whining of shrapnel and showers of dirt and debris everywhere. Smell of burnt powder hangs heavy in the thick air. I stare disbelieving from the ground where I've thrown myself at the body cartwheeling end over end . . . rising almost to treetop level . . . now slowly falling back to earth, disappearing again into the vortex of the volcano from which it spewed. Suspended animation . . . slow motion. Can't be real. Desperate cries of "corpsman up!" and shouts from platoon and squad leaders break the unnerving, ringing silence which has engulfed us. Trying to bring order to chaos and confusion. Gotta get a medevac in. Form a hasty perimeter around a clearing. Corporal Garcia leads our squad toward the river and we pass within a few feet of the blast area. See the body, or what's left of it. Jesus . . . it's Dykes, at least I think it is. The face is burned, but the fat lips . . . yeah, it's Dykes. There's only the upper torso . . . just one arm. Empty abdominal cavity and rib cage glaring hideously through shredded flak jacket and utility shirt. Eyes open in an unseeing stare. I tear my eyes away and hurry past, aghast. Can't shake the grisly scene. Feeling sick. Goddamn. Dykes . . . dead. Blown to shit. Christ. Muffled *wump wump wump* growing louder. Chopper approaching. Vintage CH-34 flying low over the river, landing in clearing amid yellow smoke and leaves from rotor wash. Wounded aboard. Lump that was Dykes aboard. Chopper lifts off, banks sharply to the right, and disappears around tree line–covered bend in the river. Saddle up and move out.

Dug in for the night atop some nameless, numbered hill. Two men to a hole. Morton hunkered down beneath his poncho against one side trying to sleep. Rain falling harder, tiny rivulets slowly turning the bottom of our foxhole into a quagmire. Shivering in sodden misery. Maybe I'll catch pneumonia or something and get out of this mess for awhile. Warm bed, clean sheets, hot chow. Little things taken for granted all my life. Not so fuckin' insignificant now. Never gonna take *shit* for granted, ever again.

Didn't eat tonight. Too tired I guess. Keep seeing Dykes—face black and staring up at the sky. Never did find his lower half. Just disintegrated I guess. Eighteen years old and gone forever. Gunny Townsend said he must've tripped a booby-trapped dud arty round, probably a one five five. Doesn't really matter what it was. It sure did a number on him. Blew him away *forever.* Having trouble with that sinking in. Eternity . . . hard concept to comprehend . . .

Must be close to noon now. Hope we stop soon. Been humpin'

along the river again all morning and my young ass has just about had it. The sun broke through about midmorning. Starting to finally dry out. Feels good. Boots are still soaked though, squishing water with every step. Feet sore. Hooked up with an ARVN unit early this morning. They're up ahead of the company and a little closer to the river. Good. Let them hit the shit first.

Sudden cracking and popping of rifles up ahead. Oh shit, here it is! Double-timing forward, gasping for breath now, more from excitement than exertion. Heavy fire coming from tree line just beyond a big cemetery about two hundred meters ahead. Jesus, firing intensifying quickly. Chattering machine guns and numerous explosions adding to the din. Don't sound like M60s—gotta be gook guns.

Another big burst of firing opens up from across the river to our right. Our platoon fans out and faces the river, sprinting for the better protection a slight rise in the ground offers ahead. Wicked hissing, snapping, and cracking; limbs, leaves, and splintered bark flying from bushes and trees catching rounds meant for us. Ten thousand infuriated hornets seeking to sting the life out of their victims. The ground shudders as incoming B-40 rockets scream and explode, sending geysers of wet earth and hot shrapnel in all directions. Streams of white-hot tracers flying back and forth across the river as our gun teams battle theirs in deadly duels. Hollow *POP* of M79 rounds from our grenadiers seeking targets in the bushes across the river. Lying prone and popping round after round at a couple of muzzle flashes I've detected in the thick entanglement of the far bank. Gettin' into this shit . . . not scared . . . firing away—get some!

"Awww . . . *Ouch!*" Black marine lying on my right grabbing the side of his neck with his left hand. Jesus, he must be wounded!

"What's the matter man? You hit?" Worried inquiry, looking for signs of blood spurting from beneath his clutching hand.

"Shit, no. Your goddamn hot brass is going down my collar and burning the shit outta me!"

"Sorry, man." I crawl ahead and to the left a few feet so my expended shell casings won't land on him. Resume firing.

The crescendo from the direction of the cemetery slacks off suddenly. Something's wrong . . . it sounds all one-sided. Shit! The goddamn ARVN are di-di'ng back this way. They race wild-eyed past us and across the road. Some of them drop into the slight gully of the roadbank and begin firing frantically over our heads in the general direction of the gooks. Others keep going and disappear into the trees beyond the road. Out-fuckin'-standing! Getting fired at from *three* directions now: the gooks from the cemetery, the gooks from across the river, and the chickenshit idiotic coward sons of bitches ARVN from our rear! Jesus fuckin' Christ, *now* I'm scared!

Behind me I see Captain Langston running with his radioman toward our forward platoon in the direction of the cemetery. A sudden sickening hollow *thunk!*, not unlike an overripe watermelon bursting open on hard ground, and the RTO (radio man) spills forward. The CO rolls him over and screams for a corpsman. Doc Poteat is trying to get to them, but the withering fire is too intense. From a few yards away I see frothy, pinkish blood bubble from the stricken grunt's chest with every labored breath. Bad shit . . . sucking chest wound.

Our 60mm mortar crews have finally set up and are giving the gooks across the river hell, walking bursts all over them. The firing abruptly ceases from that direction. Get some mortars! Doc is working on the wounded marine now and a medevac has been called. Heavy firing continues from the cemetery as our forward platoon continues to do battle with the gooks up there.

We're up and running in that direction, rounds still whizzing and snapping overhead. We gain the edge of the cemetery and spread out, taking cover behind the round earthen burial mounds of the Vietnamese departed. Corporal Garcia screams for me and Morton to cover Doc Hamm and another marine who are racing forward among the mounds for a wounded gunner. We pop up over either side of the raised circular grave firing furiously on full automatic. Cram the empty magazine into a pocket and quickly jam another in and keep firing. Gotta keep the gooks' heads down so Doc can do his thing.

A wall of green tracers flies at us from two directions at the far end of the graveyard. Crossfire! Down we go as great hunks of sod blasted from the mound shower us. Goddamn, that was close! Got our young asses zeroed in.

Time to vacate this position. We race frantically from opposite sides of the mound and dive headlong behind two others a little farther among the dead. Dark clouds have taken over control of the sky again and a cold rain begins to pelt us. Doc and the marine are dragging the wounded gunner back to safety. Garcia calls to us to help the A-gunner get the gun team's gear back. Can't leave it for the gooks I guess. Up and running. Tracers flying again. Evil green eyes searching to tear my body apart with their piercing stare.

I make a desperate dive behind another mound. Morton, where the fuck is Morton? Shit, hope he ain't hit. There he is, scrambling like a goddamn crab around the side of the mound where the A-gunner-turned-gunner is. One of our platoons has flanked the gooks and our mortars are working them over, big time. Return fire dying away, stopping. Gooks are hauling ass. Di-di, motherfuckers!

More medevacs to carry away our wounded. Nobody KIA. All that shit flying around for what seemed like hours and nobody dead. A miracle. Couple of guys real bad off, though. Doc Poteat says they might not make it. ARVN back up, milling around. Chattering and smiling those stupid smiles. Posing for pictures with gook bodies. Sons of bitches. Supposed to go in hot pursuit after the VC we just whipped. I hope they get their sorry worthless asses waxed.

It's been a few days now since Dykes bought it. Exactly how many I don't know. Real easy to lose track of time over here. The days just sort of seem to run together. I'm not really sure exactly what day of the week it is.

We're patrolling an area of beautiful rolling hills covered mostly by what looks to be harvestable hay. Scattered notches of various sizes dot the landscape here and there, and an occasional fencerow breaks the terrain. I guess this is the Vietnamese version of farm houses and barns and other outbuildings. Real pretty scenery. With just a little imagination you'd swear you were out huntin' quail on a cool gray autumn day somewhere in the southern United States.

To my left about fifteen or twenty meters away Lance Corporal Gabriel eases cautiously through the golden brown haygrass and pauses before the latest of several fences we've crossed since early morning. Thick, tangled bramble of vines and briars entwined amongst the strands of wire and encircling the posts. God, what a great place for rabbits! Bet I could hunt this row and kill my limit in a couple of hours. My mind snaps back to reality as Gabriel signals for me to come over to him. A ten-foot section of fence near where he is standing lies nearly flattened against a cushion of briars and brush. Looks like a good place to cross without ripping the shit out of our trousers on the barbed wire which tops the fence.

"Ya see dis shit?" he asks, lone yellowish front tooth flashing prominently against pink gums and thick dark lips.

"What shit?" I ask in return, seeing nothing out of the ordinary except an old dilapidated fence that's been pushed over.

"Dere, right *dere*," he says, kneeling down and pointing at the fence.

Jesus! A damn tripwire running inches above the downed fence and disappearing into thick undergrowth on either side. Barely visible. Christ, I would have probably walked right through it. Shit. "What's it leadin' to?" I ask, fighting the urge to turn and run screaming as far away as I can get.

"Damned if ah know, and ah shore as hell ain't 'bout to go fumblin' through dem bushes to find out. Go tell duh lieutenant what we got."

I hurry back down the column and meet Lieutenant Simpson already working his way up to the front of the platoon to see what the holdup is about. He looks the situation over and confers with Gabriel. Seems to be about as authoritative on this shit as I am. Asks Gabriel for a suggestion.

"Well, if it was me suh," slow, heavy, south Georgia drawl, "Ah'd blow duh shit outta duh muthafucka. Whole goddamn fenceline li'ble to be booby-trapped."

"Good idea, Gabriel. Do it." Lieutenant Simpson is green but he ain't stupid. More than willing to let experienced grunts handle tight and unfamiliar situations. Good sign in an officer.

Rest of the platoon falls back and takes cover. Gabriel pulls the pins of two frags and chunks them simultaneously into the brush on either end of the tripwire. "F'ah in da hole," he hollers as he hauls ass and jumps into the depression where I've taken cover about fifteen meters from the fence. Three quick explosions rent the air. Booby trap blown. The platoon passes safely through.

Gabriel has been breaking me in on walking point. Got moved to his fireteam in an effort to more evenly distribute the new guys with the salts. Black dude from Georgia. Kinda taken me under his wing like a mother hen and showing me the ropes. A real likeable guy. Starting to get real tight with him. He loves the kids that hang around the perimeter at Quang Tri. Always laughing and joking with 'em, and giving them cake and cookies and cigarettes from his C-rations. The kids all call him "numba one honcho." He's the first splib I've really been friends with since Johnnie Davies from my high school baseball team. That's what we call the blacks—"splibs." Hell, they call us "crackers" or "honkies." Nothing racial about it at all. No slurs intended or taken, either way. Only colors that mean shit in the bush are the green we wear and the red we bleed.

The concussion hurls me to the ground before I even hear the booming report. I shake my head trying to clear cobwebs and rid my ears of this terrible ringing. What the fuck happened? What am I doing down here? Oh shit, Gabriel! Fighting my way through the tangled brush trying to get to him. Gotta help him. Feeling woozy. Why won't this ringing stop?

Doc makes me sit down and checks me over. No blood. Can't think clearly. Bad ache and buzzing in my head. Voices sound far away and strange. I get up and walk to kneeling figures. Gabriel's covered with blood, utilities shredded. Writhing in agony, back and forth, back and forth.

"Mah ahm, mah ahm!" his voice is screaming. Not like Gabriel to scream and cry. Always laughs and smiles. Maybe I'm dreaming. I look closer to see his arm. It's *all* fucked up. Big chunks of meat torn away, grisly white bone sticking out in two odd directions, barely hanging together.

No, no, not Gabriel. He's my friend and he's gonna take care of me and teach me how to survive this shit.

Sitting down in the weeds again. Head is starting to clear. Chopper lifting off above whirlwind and disappearing beyond the gray horizon. Thinking how stupid and unfair all this is. I'm daydreaming about hunting rabbits and he finds the wire. Thirty minutes later he's all fucked up and I'm not even scratched. Hell, he was damn good on point . . . knew his shit. So much for experience. Looks like Lady Luck plays a big part in this game too.

I have officially been christened "Teapot." In one of those crazy moments where you'll do anything to relieve the boredom that sets in so often around here I sang the little nursery school jingle about a teapot for a couple of the guys in the squad. They got a big kick out of it and mentioned it to the lieutenant at a platoon meeting yesterday. Lieutenant Simpson "ordered" me to sing it for the entire platoon. I felt like an idiotic court jester or something but figured what the fuck—anything for the cause, and did it anyway.

Jesus, the guys ate it up. Belly laughs and applause. You talk about being hard up for entertainment. These people are desperate! Bob Hope I ain't, but I'm glad I did it anyway. Lance Corporal Porter liked it so much he started calling me "Teapot" and drew a real nice picture of a whistling kettle on the back of my flak jacket. Another sign of acceptance into the platoon. Been here only about a month but I don't feel like a new guy anymore.

from **Fortunate Son**

by **Lewis B. Puller, Jr.**

Lewis B. Puller, Jr., was the son of "Chesty" Puller—the most decorated Marine in history. Puller, Jr., joined the Marines and went to Vietnam in 1968. His memoir won the 1992 Pulitzer Prize for biography. He committed suicide in 1994.

Captain Woods devised an ambitious operation as a way to settle the score in the Riviera. He knew that it would be unacceptable from a political standpoint simply to level Viem Dong, the hamlet at the edge of the Riviera, a known Vietcong stronghold, from which we had been taking increasing amounts of hostile fire, but he also knew that our South Korean allies were free to operate without the political constraints that figured so heavily in all our planning. He therefore seized on the idea of a joint operation in which our company would be lifted at first light into the Riviera. We would then form a cordon around Viem Dong, and a South Korean company would sweep through the village and drive the unsuspecting enemy into our field of fire. Whatever else the Koreans did in the village was their own business, but with their reputation for brutality, we all knew that the village would be loath to support the Vietcong so openly in the future.

As Woods outlined the plan, in effect a cordon and search operation, for his platoon leaders and platoon sergeants a few days after our earlier conversation, I could see several of the men nod their heads and murmur approvingly. We could not be certain of engaging any of our enemies, of course, but our own risk was minimal. If our timing was right, the operation could turn out to be a turkey shoot. Beyond that we would be on the offensive for a change, and the morale boost to the troops would be of inestimable value. As I congratulated the skipper on his concept after our briefing and assured him that my men would do their part in its execution, I realized that my commander was savvy enough to use whatever resources were at hand.

The idea of a cordon and search was a fairly simple textbook maneuver with which any company commander would be familiar, but the expedient of using the Koreans to do our dirty work was the selling point of the operation that I knew convinced higher command to give Woods the green light. If we got our kills, we could take full credit, and if the ROKs became overzealous, we could plead our lack of control over an allied force. At any rate, the effect on Viem Dong was going to be devastating, and I felt ready for revenge as I hurried back to brief my squad leaders on the forthcoming activities.

The night before the operation was to take place the rain came down in great gusting sheets, and my men looked forward to remaining in their hooches and preparing for the next day. Instead we were given orders to commence a patrol so that our adversaries would not become suspicious because of our lack of activity. The men were not happy at the idea of trudging out to a meaningless ambush site, sitting in the rain for half an hour, and then returning to our starting point solely to satisfy the whim of some safe and dry intelligence expert, but as usual we grudgingly did as we were told. When we returned an hour and a half later, we were as wet as if we had sat all night in the squall outside, and instead of having a chance to get dried out, we were now going to march for another hour to the nearby army camp from which the operation would begin the next morning.

As we filed out of camp for the second time in the same evening, the men were grumbling loudly, and only the thought of the next day's payoff kept their complaints in bounds. We were cold and exhausted as we made our way through the wire into the base camp, and I could tell by the number of trip flares that the platoon set off (safely, since the other unit knew we were arriving) in clearing the wire that they were past the point of caring. Once inside, we were escorted to the helicopter pad from which we were to lift off in several hours. We settled down around its perimeter and huddled inside our ponchos as the rain pelted our helmets and hunched shoulders. The everyday tribulations of an infantryman were at best an ordeal, I recalled from some Basic School graffiti, and Turner and I shook our heads knowingly and tried to keep our cigarettes going in the rain. After I had made certain that my platoon was ready for the morning and that the squads understood the order of embarkation and their assignments once we deplaned, I slipped off for a last-minute briefing in the command center where the skipper had set up temporary shop.

It was dry inside the sandbagged bunker, and though not a coffee drinker, I gladly accepted a steaming mug and used its warmth to dry my chapped hands. We had gone over our operational plan in detail previously, and there were no last-minute changes; but the lieutenants listened attentively as Captain Woods retraced his five-paragraph order. Though it was not discussed, we were keenly aware that our men were outside in the rain while we had the luxury of hot coffee and a dry bunker, and our attentiveness was in part a reaction to the guilt we felt over our differing circumstances. Beyond that, however, the air was charged with the electricity common to the ritual of preparation for a kill, and the adrenaline pumping in our veins masked our weariness.

Somewhere in the background a radio cackled and sputtered. A World Series game was in progress. Mickey Lolich was on the mound for the Detroit Tigers, who were in the process of taking a seven-game series from the St. Louis Cardinals, in the culmination of a season that would assure baseball immortality for a young right-hander named Denny McLain, with his thirty-one games. Our minds, however, were on a different sort of contest.

When Woods finished his briefing and answered what few questions there were, we reluctantly made our way back to the helicopter pad to wait for the first signs of dawn. The rain had stopped by then, and most of the men were dozing fitfully and using their packs or helmets for pillows. An hour before liftoff I had Turner wake my sleeping marines, and we ate our C rations. By the time we had finished the mindless routine of heating, eating, and policing, the word came down that the choppers were on their way, and I smoked one last cigarette before assembling the men by squads in their staging area.

As soon as our chopper alighted, the men raced to its yawning tailgate and piled aboard. I made certain we all were accounted for before taking a seat beside the door gunner and giving the crew chief the thumbs-up. As we lifted off, I felt the familiar pull in the pit of my stomach caused by our rapid ascent, and when we leveled off, I relaxed my hold on the side of the craft and watched the blur of foliage passing just beneath us. The sky was streaked with the red of the rising sun, and I realized, as I watched its reflection on the glassy surface of the South China Sea, that at least for today the rain was finished. The pilot nosed down in a clearing between the beach and Viem Dong after only a few minutes aloft, and we scrambled down the gangway and fanned out to take up our positions as he reversed his direction and banked up into the sky.

I concentrated as best I could on making certain that the two squads to my left were on line and in position to hook up with the platoon adjacent to them, but in the confusion and noise from the other helicopters around us, control was almost impossible. The skipper's position was to be atop the high bluff to our right, overlooking Viem Dong. After I had gotten my men on line, my next assignment was to connect with his location. Watson followed closely in my tracks with the radio, but the two nearest men to us were at least twenty meters away on either side and for all intents and purposes out of hearing range. As we maneuvered, I scanned the area to my immediate front, which I had been neglecting in my effort to maintain platoon integrity.

Suddenly I saw a squad of green-uniformed North Vietnamese soldiers begin running out of the village and in my direction. They had apparently panicked when the helicopters began landing and were now probing for a way out of the noose we were drawing around them. As they advanced toward me, I was unable to get the attention of the marines near me, and it dawned on me, to my horror, that I was the only obstacle between them and freedom. I raised my rifle to my shoulder and attempted to draw a bead on the lead soldier; but my first bullet was off the mark, and when I pulled the trigger the second time, my rifle jammed. By now the North Vietnamese soldiers had spotted me, and several of them fired wildly in my direction until they abruptly altered their advance and veered off to my left. Standing alone with a malfunctioning weapon and seven enemy soldiers bearing down on me, I was at once seized by a fear that was palpable and all encompassing. My throat became as dry as parchment, and beads of perspiration popped out on my forehead before coursing down my face. I turned abruptly, with Watson in tow, and ran as fast as I could toward the safety of the bluffs above Viem Dong, where the company headquarters party was to be located.

A narrow trail led up the hill to the headquarters group, and as I approached, it never occurred to me that the thirty meters between my course and the commanders' position had not been secured. I knew only that the firepower advantage of the NVA squad I had just encountered would be neutralized if I could reach the men milling at the crest of the hill. With only a few meters left to cover in my flight, a thunderous boom suddenly rent the air, and I was propelled upward with the acrid smell of cordite in my nostrils.

When I landed a few feet up the trail from the booby-trapped howitzer round that I had detonated, I felt as if I had been airborne forever. Colors and sound became muted, and although there was now a beehive of activity around me, all movement seemed to me to be in slow motion. I thought initially that the loss of my glasses in the explosion accounted for my blurred vision, and I had no idea that the pink mist that engulfed me had been caused by the vaporization of most of my right and left legs. As shock began to numb my body, I could see through a haze of pain that my right thumb and little finger were missing, as was most of my left hand, and I could smell the charred flesh, which extended from my right wrist upward to the elbow. I knew that I had finished serving my time in the hell of Vietnam.

As I drifted in and out of consciousness, I felt elated at the prospect of relinquishing my command and going home to my wife and unborn child. I did not understand why Watson, who was the first man to reach me, kept screaming, "Pray, Lieutenant, for God's sake, pray." I could not see the jagged shards of flesh and bone that had only moments before been my legs, and I did not realize until much later that I had been forever set apart from the rest of humanity.

For the next hour a frantic group of marines awaited the medevac chopper that was my only hope of deliverance and worked at keeping me alive. Doc Ellis knelt beside my broken body and with his thumbs kept my life from pouring out into the sand, until a tourniquet fashioned from a web belt was tied around my left stump and a towel was pressed tightly into the hole where my right thigh had joined my torso. My watch and rifle were destroyed by the blast and my flak jacket was in tatters; but I did manage to turn my undamaged maps and command of the platoon over to Corporal Turner during one of my lucid intervals. I also gave explicit orders to all the marines and corpsmen hovering around me that my wife was not to be told of my injuries until after the baby was born. There was, of course, no possibility of compliance with my command, but the marines ministering to me assured me that my wishes would be honored.

Because we were on a company-size operation, there were six corpsmen in the immediate area around Viem Dong, and each of them carried a supply of blood expanders, which were designed to stabilize blood pressure until whole blood could be administered. As word spread of my injuries, each of the company's corpsmen passed his expanders to Doc Ellis, who used up the last of them while my men slapped at my face, tried to get me to drink water, and held cigarettes to my lips in an attempt to keep me awake. When the chopper finally arrived, I was placed on a stretcher and gently carried to its entrance, where a helmeted crew chief and medevac surgeon helped me aboard. Someone had located my left boot which still contained its bloody foot and that, too, was placed on the stretcher with me.

As the chopper began its race toward the triage of the naval support hospital in Da Nang, I was only moments from death, but I remember thinking clearly before losing consciousness that I was going to make it. I never again saw the third platoon of Golf Company, a remarkable group of young men with whom I had had the most intense male relationships of my life, and I felt guilty for years that I had abandoned them before our work was finished. I was to feel even worse that I was glad to be leaving them and that, in my mind, I had spent my last healthy moments in Vietnam running from the enemy. I came to feel that I had failed to prove myself worthy of my father's name, and broken in spirit as well as body, I was going to have to run a different gauntlet.

In the naval support hospital triage in Da Nang, located just down the road from the Seabee compound where I had feasted on frozen strawberries and ice cream only a few days earlier, the remainder of my clothes were cut away, massive transfusions were started directly into my jugular vein, and my severed foot was discarded. On arrival, my blood pressure had failed to register, but once it was restored and I was stabilized, I was wheeled into the operating room, where my left stump was debrided and left open, and the femoral artery, which was all that remained of my right leg, was clamped shut. The procedure was fairly simple because there was so little left to work with. I remember thinking, before I succumbed to the anesthesia, how clean and shiny the tiles in the operating room appeared, how cold the room was, and how worried the eyes all seemed above the green masks of the doctors and nurses who labored over me.

When I regained consciousness, I was in a clean bed with white sheets. An assortment of tubes carried liquids to and from my body, and when I reached up to remove the annoying one affixed to my nose, I found that I could not do so because both my hands were wrapped in bandages the size of boxing gloves. I understood the reason for my bandaged hands because I had seen my right hand with its missing thumb and little finger earlier, and I also knew that my left hand now retained only a thumb and half a forefinger. The word *prehensile* no longer applied to me. I did not yet know or knew only vaguely that I had lost my right leg at the torso and that only a six-inch stump remained of my left thigh. In addition to the damage to my extremities, I had lost massive portions of both buttocks, my scrotum had been split, I had sustained a dislocated shoulder and a ruptured eardrum, and smaller wounds from shell fragments peppered the remainder of my body. Only my face had been spared. It remarkably contained only one small blue line across my nose from a powder burn.

Back in the United States, where the attention of most Americans was occupied with the outcome of the World Series, the assistant commandant of the Marine Corps, General Lewis Walt, who had been one of my father's company commanders in World War II, called Saluda, Virginia, with the news of my wounding and followed up his conversation by coming down from Washington. A young marine officer was dispatched to Fort Belvoir to break the news to my wife. There was no one home at the Todd quarters when he arrived, but he alarmed neighbors, who alerted my father-in-law as soon as he returned home. He called and through official army channels was able to ascertain roughly what had happened.

Communications from both the army and Marine Corps were badly garbled in the first days after my wounding. My wife was at first told that I had lost only one leg and later that I had lost one leg below the knee and one above the knee. When she got the first message, she went straight to her father's pantry, poured a double shot of bourbon, and tossed it off in one motion. Already furious that she had been the last to receive the news, she spent a sleepless night after Walter Cronkite reported my injury on the "CBS Evening News." The next morning she traveled to Saluda to be with my parents. By the time she arrived, they had received a more accurate assessment of my injuries, and my wife was soon to discover that if I survived, as was doubtful, I would do so with "a bilateral above the knee/hip disarticulation." Numb with fear and exhaustion and seven months' pregnant, she took solace from the only male Puller who was still capable of standing on his own two feet.

Sometime later that week, before I was medevacked to Yokosuka, Japan, in the first stage of a painful journey home, a marine general and old family friend, Tommy Tompkins, made a special visit to my bedside to pin a Silver Star and Purple Heart on the pillow cradling my head. For the photo opportunity that accompanied the presentation and reading of my citation, the tube was removed from my nose and the photographer was careful to frame his shots of me from the waist up. Even in my delirious state I did not feel that I had earned a Silver Star, and I expressed my reservations repeatedly to Colonel Tom McKenney, another old family friend who spent most of those first few critical days in Da Nang at my bedside. There was no such reservation about my eligibility for the Purple Heart, and while my first one may have been cheap, the second award could hardly have been paid for more dearly.

While I was still in Da Nang, a parade of young officers who had been my peers in Basic School made the obligatory trek to the hospital to see me, and the concern on each of their faces so alarmed me that I finally requested and was given a bottle of whiskey to help them through the experience. For my part, I was becoming dependent on massive injections of morphine to quell the phantom pain in my missing limbs and postpone the inevitable acceptance of my loss, so my visitors were forced to drink alone. Mike Downs, my future brother-in-law, who was on his way back to the States, rerouted his homeward path to spend a few minutes with me, and he told me years later that he had resigned himself to never seeing me alive again after he had completed his visit.

For the most part the medical personnel who attended me while I was in Da Nang, as well as those who treated me in Yokosuka, were dedicated professionals who worked tirelessly every day in a world of blood and gore that would have broken men and women of lesser stature. There were also Red Cross volunteers who spent hours at my side as I began, through a narcotic netherworld, to assimilate the magnitude of my physical loss. Several of these "doughnut dollies," as they were affectionately labeled, helped me with letters to my wife that I do not remember dictating but that she saved, along with all the other letters I had written as a virile young platoon leader, the youthful optimism of a newlywed just separated from his bride contrasting with the stark terror of a shattered war casualty who had as yet no frame of reference for a life without legs.

There was one exception to the caring individuals who nurtured me in those first days as I clung precariously to life, whom I was told about by Tom McKenney a year after I had returned to the States. A young doctor who objected generally to American involvement in the war, and specifically to the fact that he had been drafted, entered the triage shortly after I was carried in and began taking pictures of me. It was assumed that he was documenting the effects of trauma on newly wounded combatants, so no effort was made to stop him until later in the week, when he announced to some of his colleagues that he had gotten some great pictures of the Puller kid that he was going to use in antiwar lectures after rotating. His pictures were confiscated immediately. I have often wondered if he was ever able to separate his views on the war from his Hippocratic obligation toward the warriors who were fighting it.

My journey home was begun against the best medical advice, but because my father, who was himself in poor health, had begun talking about flying to Japan to meet me, a decision was made to send me home early. In Yokosuka I developed a stress ulcer as a result of the shock of being wounded, and two-thirds of my stomach had to be removed. The pain was excruciating, and I was not expected to survive the operation, which exposed a second ulcer once the surgeons got inside. In my debilitated state the second ulcer was considered inoperable, but remarkably it stopped bleeding on its own, and I was again stabilized.

When we got under way again, I was assigned a nurse whose sole duty was to be available in case the exposed femoral artery in my right side ruptured.

A day later my plane set down at Andrews Air Force Base outside Washington, DC. I had, in keeping with the parable of the Spartan soldier, returned on my shield. My temperature was 105 degrees, and I had not had a dressing change since leaving Japan. I was transferred to the base hospital near the terminal, where my wife and family had gathered and had begun steeling themselves to meet me.

There were no brass bands to greet me, no rousing renditions of "Stars and Stripes Forever," and no politicians to offer their support for a job well done. I was home, though, back in the United States after a splendid overseas tour that had not quite reached its third month. And I had avoided, for whatever reason, the fate of those casualties who were returning home in aluminum boxes.

from Images from the Otherland
by Kenneth P. Sympson

Kenneth Sympson served in Vietnam during 1965 and 1966 as a USMC artillery officer. Some 20 years later, while recovering from surgery for non-Hodgkin's lymphoma, he began work on a memoir of his military service.

The Landing Zone

If I remember correctly, there was a special descriptive name for the strategy that was used on Operation Texas. I've since forgotten the name, but here are the essentials of how the scheme was intended to work.

Intelligence indicated that enemy troops were located in a certain area of a province. We didn't know their exact position, so we tested a spot, say a village that was north of where they were most likely to be. We dropped a unit of marines in there and had them fan out east to west and then head south. A short while later, we landed another unit to the south of the first, and, likewise, had them spread out and sweep south. If the first unit made no contact, we shortly pulled them out, leap-frogged the second unit, and landed them farther south to continue the process. Thus it went until we made contact or finished sweeping the designated area.

You could cover a large region fairly quickly, and if a unit made contact, you would be in position to land additional troops promptly around the point of contact, thus encircling the enemy. So that's the way Operation Texas started. That was the strategy as explained to us in briefings prior to the operation. *

We were in pursuit again of the 1st Viet Cong Regiment. One company had landed and had come under immediate attack. They were taking small arms and machine-gun fire from an enemy hidden in the trees of a small village, and they were having a difficult time securing the landing zone for the remainder of the battalion. Air support had been called in, and the village was soon being hit hard by marine A-4 Skyhawk jets and UH-1E gunships. The men of the battalion continued to land into the hot LZ.

My liaison team and I were with the battalion commander, Lieutenant Colonel P. X. Kelley, as he accompanied the next of his companies to our target. The landing zone was in a field just outside and to the west of the village. The village was called Phuong Dinh. The buildings of Phuong Dinh were barely visible from the air as we came in; it seemed mostly a patch of high, dense trees, an island of vegetation in an otherwise fairly clear space of open and generally flat land. The place was already smoking from the bombardment and rocket fire from the marine aircraft.

As we approached the LZ, we had a clear view of the troops who had already landed and were receiving and returning fire. We could see them below as they deployed, spreading out, moving quickly, then dropping to the ground as they sought toeholds of cover to protect

---

*I must admit that my quite distinct memories regarding our initial strategy toward locating the 1st VC Regiment collide with history. After reviewing the account of the battle in *U.S. Marines in Vietnam, an Expanding War, 1966*, Jack Shulimson, History and Museums Division, Headquarters, U.S. Marine Corps, Washington, D.C., 1982, it seems clear that I misunderstood or misremembered parts of the pre-battle briefing. The historical account from the initial landing outside the village until the operation's end, however, is closely aligned with my own memory of the events.

themselves from enemy fire. There was very little in the LZ to protect the troops and nothing to shield the helicopters. The UH-34 transports were spending as little time as they could on the ground.

It seemed that the strategy had worked, and we had made our contact with elements of the 1st Viet Cong Regiment.

A Company Is Trapped

The enemy was in Phuong Dinh, and they seemed most unhappy about us approaching their nest. By now we had three companies on the ground positioning themselves to assault the village. The company on the left would maneuver into a location on the high ground just north of the village. Two companies, one behind the other, were preparing to attack straight on. To soften the defenses further, Lieutenant Colonel Kelley had requested additional artillery fire on the village. When the artillery bombardment ended, the enemy weapons seemed silenced. The ground attack began.

Echo Company had spread out, and the men of the unit approached the tree line at the edge of the village. There was a trench there and the marines were preparing to cross it to enter the village. The enemy would sometimes run away in the face of a large force, melting into the cover of the jungle or into hiding holes and tunnels, deferring battle until it could be waged on their own terms. Was that to happen today? After all that pre-attack bombardment, had they decided to leave while they had a route out of the area?

Today they chose to stay. And if they were hurt by the air and artillery preparation, their wounds were not yet serious. The Viet Cong had set up machine guns—.50 caliber I believe—at either end of the trench. They had waited for the right moment, then opened fire, deadly enfilade down the line of marines. Abruptly, it turned into a macabre nightmare of small arms and machine-gun fire, grenades thrown at close range across the trench in either direction. One platoon fought its way through the first line of the village defense, only to be stopped by a second. Men were trapped in the trench and on either side of it. Scant protective cover was available. They could not cross the trench alive, and to retreat from the village meant leaving what protection they had to expose themselves in an open field.

We didn't have a clear picture of what was going on. Echo Company seemed trapped, but in the fury of the fire fight, we were unable to communicate readily with our men in the wood line. The battalion commander was using a radio frequency designated for infantry communications, and the men at the battalion command post seemed to be working to communicate with the commanding officer of the lead company of marines. We had our own frequency which we used for artillery-related traffic; I should have been able to get briefed by my FO on the artillery network about the status at the front line.

The FO assigned to Echo Company on the right flank wasn't an officer; we must have run out of them. I think he was a corporal who was actually the team radioman—the senior enlisted man on the team, who had been given the temporary assignment as FO. He and his FO team were supposed to be up near the CO of the infantry company, the unit pinned down near the village.

I tried contacting my FO on the radio. I tried repeatedly, anxiously, and never got a response. He could not have been over 100 meters away. Our equipment had been working fine before we left: we had fresh batteries, we performed radio transmission checks, we did everything possible to prepare. I couldn't understand why I couldn't raise him, and if I couldn't talk to him, I couldn't find out the status of his company. And I had no way to determine what could be done to help.

The weapons fire continued unabated along the trench and in the wood line on the southwest edge of the village. Staccato bursts from the VC .50-caliber machine guns and the cracks of grenades rose from the background of small arms fire, of crisp orders (in English and Vietnamese), of cries of pain. I kept trying to make radio contact with my FO, yelling into the handset. What the hell was wrong with him and why didn't he answer? Precious time was passing, and I was getting more and more furious at him.

Amid the barely contained chaos, new helicopters started to arrive in the LZ. They were not bringing troops in; they were there to start taking them out. We had begun to evacuate our casualties.

Suddenly I understood: it was then that I saw my FO. Four marines were trotting, crouched over, toward the medical evacuation helicopter; they were holding tightly to the corners of a poncho and the burden they carried was my FO. I had been mad as hell at him and he was dead; he was a sack of meat on green plastic. I do not remember the man's name, and I still cannot form an image of his face.

You are no longer an individual when your foothold on survival is so tenuous, and when your own fate is so inextricably bound to the fate of a group. The hurt and anguish inflicted on others becomes palpable in your own being.

The Few Good Men
I remember observing enemy troops in an exposed section of the Phuong Dinh fortifications. They had just seen us as we were moving up to the slight rise that was to become our observation post. And I remember the looks on their faces when they realized what we were about to do. I watched them through my binoculars as they tried to take us out with rifle fire. And they watched us as we did what we were scripted to do.

I just cannot remember the names of the people on my liaison team, other than Bauerman. But I remember they all came with me without a word when I told Lieutenant Colonel Kelley that I had to go forward to call in fire on the village. They certainly knew they would be sitting ducks. They were young, but they had seen a lot during their time in-country and they were not stupid. They knew what was happening around them, and they knew the many ways it could turn out. And they realized that the Viet Cong, about 50 meters or so away, were aware of what we were about to do—the tell-tale radio antenna and binoculars gave us away.

The men of the liaison team, younger than me, some perhaps too young to be served beer in a California bar, stayed there with me until it was over. And when it was over, the ground around us was covered with errant shrapnel from the artillery rounds that landed on and about the people who had tried to kill us before we killed them. Small jagged pieces of fractured metal were everywhere, just everywhere. They were already rusted in the short interval between when a round would explode and when the pieces of its casing would strike the ground.

We were blessed then and somehow kept from harm.

Rain of Terror

I'm not sure today exactly why I reacted as I did, but I surely had to do something to help the marines who were still trapped. I had the power. I had four artillery batteries on call: two 155mm and two 105mm howitzer batteries. And I was a terribly good FO. This was real, and I could not stand on the side while others died.

I told the battalion CO that I wanted to take the artillery liaison team up to call in fire on the village so that we could extract our remaining troops. He approved, and Bauerman and two radio operators followed me to a slight rise about 50 meters from the trench.

The village was densely treed. This was a bit of a problem, since the trees probably would cause some premature detonations of the shells; but the trees also would provide a measure of protection to us from some of the shrapnel. We were alone, perhaps 40 meters out in front of the battalion command post. The observation post gave us an excellent view of the village, of the trench line, and of the company of fellow marines locked in combat a short distance off to our right.

I contacted the 155mm howitzer battery several miles away and called in the first adjusting rounds on the village. They were firing almost due south and the village was directly east of us. Fortunately, there would be minimal dispersion of the rounds in our direction.[*] I

---

[*]Dispersion has to do with the consistency of fire of a particular weapon. Several rounds from the same howitzer, fired at the same settings with identical ammunition, will impact within a certain pattern in the target area. With a howitzer or a gun, during standard low-angle fire, the dispersion pattern is oval shaped with the long axis of the oval oriented along the flight path of the round. The least dispersion or probability for error, then, would be to the left or right of the flight path. Thus our location at the time of the fire mission minimized the danger and allowed the greatest precision in adjusting the fire close to our own position.

adjusted the fire to a point inside the village and called for fire for effect, all six guns in the battery firing as one on the target. I then carefully adjusted the fire, moving it closer to the trench, then back and forth along the edge of the village. The 155mm howitzer was very accurate and could fire very consistently on a target.

After the initial shelling along the village side of the trench, I called up a battery of 105mm howitzers and started to adjust their weapons on the village. Before long I had 24 howitzers firing. Shells from 105mm and 155mm howitzers were now slamming into the hamlet in a continuous barrage, with the weapons firing as fast as the men at each artillery piece could reload, check the settings on their sights, and pull the lanyards. The men at each of the batteries knew where we were, knew how close we were to the target and what could happen if they were not as accurate as we prayed they would be.

I blanketed the village with standard high explosive shells. I switched one battery to white phosphorus shells and spread their fire and smoke the length of the target area. My goal was to create a cloud of smoke to provide at least a small amount of cover to the men of Echo Company as they tried to extricate themselves. And to get past the trees and perhaps into the tunnels and bunkers, I used some delayed-fuse shells to give the rounds additional time to continue past the point of initial impact before exploding.

A rain of metal poured from the sky above Phuong Dinh.

We seemed attached to some anchor in time. There was motion, things changed, but we didn't appear to be traveling a straight time line. We were oscillating around as if we were riding a plumb bob on a string, suspended, making circles and ellipses in time. There was no progress; it was just happening, and the damned thing would not be over, wouldn't go away. I think I lost track of what I was supposed to do there. The idea was to modify the flow of battle so that our forward troops could withdraw to safety. But for me, this had become the wrath of God, and I was His messenger.

Hours and thousands of artillery rounds later, the place was dead and it gave up its hold on our troops.

That night we dug in on an open field just south of where we had originally landed. Our perimeter was set perhaps 100 meters from the trench and the lines of fortifications that had protected the village. There were some sounds, some Vietnamese chatter, some movement in there, but we were not interested enough to investigate. We were badly hurt, hunkered down in defensive positions and hoping that we had damaged the Viet Cong unit enough to keep them from us that night. It appeared that we had stepped into a larger nest of hornets than we had anticipated, and our greatest concern was that they would regroup and attack us in the night.

Several times during the night I called in volleys of artillery fire on the village, paying little attention to where the shells actually fell. It was hard to miss the village after all the practice that afternoon.

As a punctuation to the fire that day, I requested a TOT, a Time On Target mission. A TOT requires the coordinated fire-for-effect from two or more artillery batteries. There is no adjustment phase. The batteries involved are given the time at which all rounds are to explode on a common target. There is no warning to the enemy at the target site; he suddenly has 12 to perhaps 48 or more artillery shells exploding in his lap.

Taking into account the characteristics of their weapons, the shells to be fired and the distance from the guns to the target, each battery calculates the time at which they must fire their guns so that all the rounds strike the target at the specified time.

I don't recall now how many batteries were to be involved in the TOT that night; it could have been as many as four. Each battery was to fire a single volley—six rounds—in a fire-for-effect. The TOT was set at midnight; the fire direction centers for all of the batteries would have synchronized their time earlier that evening.

The word had been passed to the men of 2/4 that a TOT was scheduled. As the designated time approached, you could almost feel the marines readying themselves to hear and to see the fireworks. These things are exciting, and this one was to occur very close by. When the time arrived, for a bare instant you could hear the whistling of the shells; then they slammed into the target nearly together and the village erupted. Then silence.

The next morning we probed the place again. No response. And we moved into the village. The network of tunnels didn't seem bothered much by the pounding of artillery fire—I should have done a better job on them. The trees were still upright but torn and ragged. Otherwise, there wasn't much left standing above ground. The embankments, the grass of the village, the huts—everything was shredded. Bodies and parts of bodies were everywhere. We found 146 Viet Cong; somebody told me they all had shrapnel wounds.

Sliced and diced.

Sorry 'bout that.

No Longer an Outsider

Many of the men who came to Vietnam with 2/4 had unit memorabilia—pins and such. Maybe they bought these things in the post exchange in Okinawa. Anyway, they were not for sale in Vietnam. Sometime shortly after Operation Texas, a man from 2/4 gave me his Zippo cigarette lighter. On the front of it was the raised emblem of the 2d Battalion, 4th Marines, with the inscription "Second to None—The Magnificent Bastards." It's one of my most prized possessions, though I haven't used it as a lighter for probably 20 years. It now rests in a plastic bag in my desk drawer, always there for me for times like these when I can take it out, look at the brightly enameled crest and reminisce about being part of that proud family. A proud family caught in bad times and doing the best it could to survive.

Sudden Death

Everyone has probably experienced one of those special times, those so-called defining moments, when you arrive at a cusp. When everything is so different that you cannot help but see some special part of yourself. Not to say that what you see is good or bad; it could cover a spread of aspects of yourself, some of which may reflect in a positive way, others that may be quite negative. But when you spin from the cusp, you are not the person who entered it.

Operation Texas was one of those times for me. A pity perhaps that I did not realize that until only recently.

Texas was the opportunity of a lifetime for a forward observer, the chance to fire what could have been one of the most technically challenging and one of the most dangerous missions of the war. The enemy was very close, very well dug in. They had the advantage of us, having pinned down our lead company within hand grenade range of their first line of defense. The requirements for precision in calling in the fire, in adjusting it, and in executing the mission at the battery were extraordinary. We didn't have computerized tools in those days. We had hand-held compasses and maps of dubious accuracy. We had only ourselves and our now-primitive weapons to depend upon.

And, of course, there were probably other ways to skin that cat. We could have continued on the ground either to fight our way across the trench and into the village or to fight our way out of range. We could have used more air strikes.

I didn't think these were acceptable. I knew artillery could do severe damage to the enemy; I was an artilleryman, after all. But to call the mission meant moving forward to a highly exposed rise, where the target area would be in perfect view. I knew I could do it. I was scared of dying there, but there was no one else. There was simply no choice.

So I told the battalion commanding officer what I wanted to do, and he gave me his approval. My artillery liaison team and I went forward and began our work.

Twenty-six years later, former Commandant of the Marine Corps and retired General P. X. Kelley visited Rochester to help promote the effort to raise funds for the construction of a local memorial to the veterans of the Vietnam War. A luncheon was scheduled with several local marine officers. Following that, he was to go to the proposed site of the memorial for a press opportunity.

When I learned of the visit, I contacted the organizer and asked if he could arrange for me to meet the general. I explained to him that I had served as Lieutenant Colonel P. X. Kelley's artillery liaison officer for several months in Vietnam. In particular, I served with him on Operation Texas. The arrangements were made, and I was invited to the luncheon.

As the day grew closer, there was little else I could think of than seeing P. X. Kelley again. My last image of him was toward the end of the fire mission on Phuong Dinh. For a moment, I had turned around to look back at the battalion command post. Just then, Lieutenant Colonel Kelley, alone and in the open, was walking up to the observation post. He was about five meters from me when I yelled to him, "Get the fuck out of here!" (I didn't ask him if he remembered that.)

As the time of the luncheon approached, I began to get nervous. I had never met again or talked to anyone I had served with in Vietnam, and I was about to have lunch with the former CO of the Magnificent Bastards. I had no idea what I might do.

The luncheon was at the home of a former marine officer. Also invited were several other former officers and the current commanding officer and executive officer of the 8th Tank Battalion. The 8th Tanks are a marine reserve unit headquartered in Rochester. I knew none of them, and I was uneasy about the affair.

When I arrived, the host told me that he served the same years as I had, and we discovered that we were, in fact, classmates in the Basic Officers Course in Quantico in 1963. Amazing. For so long I had felt as if I were the sole member of the community to have served in Vietnam, and now I'm finding soulmates popping up everywhere.

I'm now a little more relaxed. My host leads me in to meet the general. It was a strange and wonderful moment seeing him again. With the exception of a few more pounds, he looked no different from the way I remembered him from 1966.

"How are you, Ken?" the general asked in a low voice.

"Fine, sir. How are you?" I replied.

"No, I mean, how *are* you?" he repeated in a more intense way.

I thought at first that we were exchanging pleasantries. Nobody ever gives a shit how you feel when they greet you with a "How are you?" But then I realized that he wanted to know and that he really cared. That he wanted to know if I had come back to the world. The thought that that was his intent spread a chill up my spine, and my voice broke.

"I'm OK, sir."

I am more and more troubled by the meaning to me and others of what occurred on March 21,1966. It was the day of Operation Texas. By then, there seemed little new to learn; it had become a repetitive job. All this had begun to be so commonplace that I stopped bothering to carry my camera; there was no longer anything unusual to record. So as fate would have it, the most memorable moments of my life were etched forever that day only in my mind.

My fascination with that day has grown over the past few years from nothing to daily introspection. The men of 2/4, the sounds of war, the fields outside the village, the shrapnel fragments all over the ground. The tree line to our right along the village fortifications where Echo Company, 2nd Battalion, 4th Marines was locked in close combat with the enemy. The faces of the Viet Cong that I saw through my binoculars as I fired artillery on their position at the edge of the village. They were looking at me. I cannot forget seeing their eyes.

There is some evidence that I killed over a hundred and fifty people. Most of them on that sunny Monday afternoon of March 21, 1966. The others went one at a time, a few at a time. And they didn't die quickly and easily; they were savagely ripped and torn to death by the concussion and the fire and the jagged disintegration of shell casings.

How many did I never see at all, either living or dead? How many were victims of harassment and interdiction missions that I ordered to be fired blindly at night? How many more were wounded but escaped, only to suffer and die later from their injuries? How many more were mutilated and went home not whole? Was the curious peasant a VC scout who presented a real threat or was I overcome by paranoia? Where did that 8" round from the cruiser land—the first one I fired that just missed the top of the mountain and continued on another mile or so? Was anyone there when it exploded?

My wife tells me that I had no choice in what happened, that I did what I had to do at the time. I think she is correct. These are the things that wars are about, and there is nothing at all special here in that regard. She tells me that I should forget it and go on. It's history.

But I don't believe I can forget. Though it is history, it is part of me. More than that, it shaped and shaded much of the person I am today—physically, emotionally. So I think I must remember it all, but that I must somehow seek to encapsulate it within a context which lets me see that it is not part of the present. And it is not part of the future.

There is a family portrait on my desk in front of me. My wife and I, our three daughters, our dog, Charlie. Everyone is smiling pleasantly, even Charlie. When I look at that photograph, I think how much I love them, and I think how much different things could have been had I lost one of those many flips of the coin some 28 years ago.

I cannot resolve if what I did was right or wrong. I don't see that such things can be morally ambiguous. The nuns in grade school told me that to kill is to commit a mortal sin. There is no caveat in the Ten Commandments on that issue; it doesn't say it is acceptable to kill in order to protect life or in retribution for life taken.

If I recall correctly, the Xaverian Brothers, who taught me at Saint Joseph's Preparatory School, were the first to introduce me to the notion of the end not justifying the means. What simplistic horseshit. How can the answer be so simple, so clean and pure, when the problem is so complex and foul?

Several months ago I read a short article in the local newspaper regarding Pope John Paul's latest encyclical *Veritatis Splendor*, or *The Splendor of Truth*. The article said that the pope made a distinction in the encyclical between evil acts and those who commit them. Having more and more difficulty rationalizing the murder of warfare, particularly that for which I was responsible, I grabbed at the possibility of finding in the pope's writings a reasoned argument that would somehow leave me innocent. That would hold still that the dying was evil, that the killing was evil, but that the perpetrator, due to the circumstances of war, the immediate danger, a drive for self-preservation, whatever, could be excused of murder, could be held guiltless in the eyes of God.

So I sought the pope's writings; I hadn't concerned myself with such things since high school, when I was trying to unravel the mysteries of free will. Unable to find the encyclical locally (oddly, the archdiocese of Rochester seemed rather unaware of the document), I finally found a distribution point in Washington, D.C.

When the *The Splendor of Truth* arrived, I pounced on it. I read it cover to cover, quickly, looking for what I had hoped it would contain. But as I read, I grew more and more frustrated—there was no absolution. I must have misinterpreted what the article in the newspaper said, or perhaps the reporter had gotten something wrong from his source for the piece. What I found in the pope's writing was the precise opposite of what I had sought.

Twice more I read the pope's words. Twice more I was condemned by them. What had occurred 28 years ago—what was happening in my mind right now—was intrinsically evil, was against the natural law. My acts could not be made less than evil for any reason—not the circumstances surrounding the events, not any anticipated relative good. It seems I have been left again with insufficient guidance, and I am still adrift seeking a safe channel through the evil I have seen and the evil I have done.

Might I have found the answers had I talked through what I had seen and done, explored my reactions and feelings, instead of avoiding them?

Am I a better person for the experience or am I worse? If I am a better person than I otherwise would have been, can that possibly be worth the price? Is it necessary to see and feel and smell death to appreciate life? Is it necessary to kill to realize the finality of that? I don't know how to tell. I don't know. I will never know, will I?

How sad.

What a shame.

Sorry 'bout that.

It is now late evening in Rochester. It is March 20 here. In the village of Phuong Dinh in the south of Vietnam it is late morning on March 21. We have engaged the Viet Cong again and so many will not walk away from here.

from # Keeping Faith
by Frank Schaeffer
and John Schaeffer

*Novelist Frank Schaeffer was shocked when his son John
joined the USMC. Father and son's joint memoir (written in
alternating voices) describes their struggles to adapt to
their respective roles in the Marines' extended family. John
takes up the story near the end of his training on Parris
island.*

During our last days on the island, as Marines, we were no longer
smoked or pitted. From our uniforms to our language and
bearing, we were, however, held to a higher standard by ourselves and our DIs. You could not walk out of the squadbay
without a DI hovering over you, tugging at your uniform, straightening
it, looking over your boots, or upbraiding you for not living up to his
expectations.

"Is that how you want to walk out of here, son?"

"Sir?"

"I just wasted three months of my life!"

"Sir?"

"Look at your gig line! Blouse *aligned* to belt buckle, buckle *to*
trousers!"

"Yes, sir!"

This harassment did not pose a problem for us. We had already settled into Marine habits, and one of those habits is grooming. We Marines wear shirt stays in our dress uniforms (long elastic garters that fasten onto our socks, run under our trousers and clip onto our shirt tails) to keep our perfectly pressed Bravo and Charlie (khaki) shirts taut. We starch and press our cammies. The dress blue uniform has many features that stopped making sense to other services in the eighteenth century and has earned the Marines plenty of mockery from the Army, Navy, and Air Force in the form of epithets, "seagoing bellhops," and the like.

Everything in the Corps related to our uniforms is regulated from the number of creases up the back of our blouse (three) to the required distance between the buckle of our trousers to the bottom of our tie (one inch). A Marine standing tall in his or her dress blues is the product of a group effort. Each Marine acts as other Marines' full-length mirror. This grooming goes on among Marines of all ranks, as well as between Marines and their officers and NCOs. It makes perfect sense to us. Discipline starts in the small things.

> last days on the island
> end of a life
> whatever you want to call it
> tour Leatherneck Square?
> why would you want to see
> the dust I sat in?

The morning of the last Thursday on the Island, Family Day, the whole of Bravo Company went on the Mot Run (motivation run). The four hundred graduating Marines of Bravo Company ran past all the other battalions and rang the big brass bells that hang in front of each battalion office. (There are four training battalions on PI.) The run was about four miles or so at a very fast pace. It was another cool windy day with light rain. No one got tired or was short of breath. We were too happy to be running in what amounted to our victory lap to feel anything but joy.

We had seen others do the Mot Run every week and yet had never believed it would be a reality for us until the day it happened. This was not training but celebration. It was one of the events that we had been looking forward to through all of boot camp.

After the run we changed into "Charlies" (green trousers and short sleeve khaki shirt), and prepared to meet our families. Parents, friends, and relatives were allowed to spend six hours with their new Marine on Parris Island Depot and see a little bit of what their sons have gone through. On the Thursday of Family Day, families were given more or less free rein.

Having my parents on the Island was one of the most uncomfortable and surreal experiences of my life. They were from a different world that had nothing to do with the Marine Corps. I had gone through boot camp picturing them where they belonged, in the garden, at the kitchen table, at their beloved Metropolitan Museum of Art in New York, walking under the oaks and hickory trees on their favorite path to the nearby bird reserve. *Never*, in my wildest imaginings, did I picture them strolling the sandy paths of Parris Island.

I did not want to return to their world. I had truly adapted to boot camp life and was afraid of leaving. I had a hard time not calling Dad, "Sir," and Mom, "Ma'am." I did not introduce them to my DIs. I tried to prevent our worlds mixing as much as possible. I feared what would happen when I would graduate and return to the civilian world.

The high point of our reunion was when we met up with Reyes on the rifle range. Seeing Reyes with his mother and sisters somehow made the weirdness of seeing my parents become a little more normal. He looked as if he was having as strange a time as I was. His family was standing in a silent knot around him, as my parents were around me.

Reyes's mom handed me my promised BK Broiler, and my parents gave Reyes his slice of pizza. Then we all stood around looking awkwardly at each other and smiling. Reyes and I were almost too shy to speak to each other in front of our families. We were still Recruit Reyes and Recruit Schaeffer to each other and here we were with people who thought of us as Juan and John. His family congratulated me, and my parents congratulated Reyes. Then we all stood smiling.

"They good boys," said Reyes's mom.

"Yes," said my mother.

"We are proud of them," mumbled Dad.

"*Sí*," said Reyes's mom and smiled.

"Now they can eat," said my mother.

Reyes's mother looked confused. My mother pointed to her mouth and smiled. Reyes's mom nodded and grinned and patted Reyes's flat stomach. In the distance the rifles on the range began to pop. A platoon of recruits marched past to their outdoor hut where they were about to undergo their Grass Week instruction on sighting their weapons.

Reyes's mother hardly spoke any English, and his little sisters were shy and wide eyed and dressed in bright pale pink and blue dresses as if they were going to a birthday party. (Reyes's father was unable to get a day off work.) I was waiting for someone to yell at me for just standing around. It would have almost been a relief to have a DI run over and get in my face.

Now that Reyes and I had the food we'd longed for, we felt silly. Reyes had never had this strange egg pizza. My parents and his were from the opposite ends of the earth and life. Reyes and I weren't even hungry. We'd gorged ourselves silly since the Crucible. We ate our food together self-consciously while our parents watched each bite go down.

I returned to the squadbay that night and crawled into my rack for the last time. All our "trash" (uniforms and personal belongings) was packed and the squadbay was stripped and bare of everything but our seabags, hanging bags, and the uniforms we'd be wearing at the graduation. As I closed my eyes I realized that the platoon had not prayed together that night. Now for the first time, just as I was about to leave, I understood that the squadbay and Parris Island was my sanctuary and the only place I was truly comfortable. I felt frightened and sad.

• • •

Genie and I arrived on Parris Island laden with egg pizza, a cake, and other assorted treats. The whole way to the Island I was in the grip of an ecstasy of anticipation and nervousness. It was my first time on a Marine base, and I felt every inch the ragged "nasty civilian." None of my clothes seemed to fit. My hair felt too long even though I'd just gotten it cut. The polish on my shoes was dull. I hoped my limp would be mistaken for a war wound.

When at last we were on the long causeway that leads onto the Island, I was struck that, for a place that loomed so large, formidable, and complex in my imagination, the geography was simple and beautiful. Gray choppy water, marsh (much like our own north of Boston), patches of close-cropped lawn, graceful Cyprus trees bearded with Spanish moss, and a picnic area flashed by as our car, windows down, filled with the sweet tangy scent of sap.

At the guard post I fumbled—sweaty hands—for the papers John had sent us. The young Marine guard never asked for them and merely waved us through, along with hundreds of other cars arriving for the Thursday ritual of Family Day.

After passing several one-story brick buildings we were directed into a large parking lot just beyond the sparse hard-topped parade deck and Iwo Jima memorial. Following the instructions John forwarded to us, we went to the visitor center and signed in. It was a thrill to find John's name on the 1st RTBN roster under Platoon 1093. My ears were ringing and I was a little out of breath.

Suddenly John was there. He was in uniform walking toward us over the parade deck. It was the first time I'd seen him wearing anything but civilian clothes. It was the first time I'd seen him in three months. It seemed as if it had been a year.

John appeared nervous and tongue-tied. Genie and I hugged his gaunt body and he hugged us. In the next ten minutes, as we slowly walked up the sidewalk back toward the visitor center, we must have reached out and touched John a hundred times. He was so thin.

"Congratulations, John. You're a Marine!" I said.

Genie nodded and her eyes filled with tears as she hugged him.

"Yes," said John.

"We're so proud of you!" I said.

"Thanks."

"What would you like to do? We have pizza," said Genie.

"Great."

"Do you get to show us around?" I asked.

"We have six hours of liberty but we can't leave the Island until after graduation tomorrow. Do you want to see my squadbay?"

To see John in uniform was a shock. To sense that he was at home in this strange place and nervous at our presence was a surprise. How had we become unfamiliar to our son? To feel this new thing, this layer, this uniform that had come between us was unsettling. The fact that John was subject to rules that separated him from us, "We have six hours of liberty but can't leave PI," made me feel queasy, as if I was glimpsing John through some thick glass wall that let me see him but cut me off.

As John glanced over our heads at other Marines (also awkwardly accompanying their parents), nodded, called out a name now and then, saluted officers, received the greetings of other uniformed stern young men or barked out an authoritative, "Stay motivated, recruit!" I felt as if my son was suddenly beyond my reach. Certainly John had been governed by the rules of others before, at schools, on teams and such. Those rules were ones I could countermand. If a school did something I did not like, I could take my children out. Now my authority had been usurped by something bigger and much more frightening than schoolteachers.

John kept trying to walk in step with us as he glanced unhappily at our undisciplined feet treading every which way on the sandy cracked concrete pavement. Finally John asked Genie and me to *please* walk in step, that he was feeling strange. Could we please keep step with him? He asked this with a laugh and joked that he felt that if he walked out of step, someone would yell at him. We all laughed but I could see from John's nervous glance at our free-form feet that he was sincerely perturbed by the whiff of anarchy we'd brought with us.

I could not help but study John's face. He looked toughened and more vulnerable all at once. The grime of the hard nights and days of the Crucible were still worked deeply into the skin of his large hands (so deeply that for weeks after no amount of washing would make him clean).

"It's the dirt we've been crawling in and the camo paint. The Crucible finished off my hands. I tried to bleach them but nothing works."

John smiled. His close-cropped "high and tight" haircut left pale skin exposed above the tan line where his cover had protected his scalp for three months of sun-baked, outdoor marching, drilling, and exercises. His "high and tight" made his angular face appear practically hawklike.

As he tried to guide us, John got lost several times. After about the fifth wrong turn, he explained that he had never seen PI from the inside of a car. There were whole parts of the Island he'd never visited. Moreover he had never been allowed to look away from whatever path he was on. Other than the trails and roads he had marched down, John really did not know the Island or how to get anywhere. In the end we gave up driving and walked.

"I don't know how to get to the chapel from here. We'll have to go back to the squadbay. I know how to march there from my squadbay . . ."

The scale seemed wrong to John. PI is really a small place but the DIs made PI as big as they wanted by taking the circuitous path or marching in circles through the woods. John constantly expressed surprise at how close each location we visited was to the next. He overestimated distances from one area to another and thought some places we asked to see, like the rifle range, were miles away when they were really only a few hundred yards from where we were standing. It was as if he had been lost inside a maze for months and had just stepped into the daylight to learn that the "endless" twists and turns he had been wandering were actually all in a space the size of his yard.

John kept muttering, "I didn't know *this* was here!" or "You mean you can get to the food court by just walking across *this* street? Wow!"

I knew John had suffered. I could see hardship stamped in his drawn face, skin tight over bone. I knew that tens of thousands of young men and women like him had passed through PI. Yet here it was, a small sandy place, barely more than a gritty little bump above the wetlands with a few palm trees and cypresses, so simple, stark, and worn around the edges that it looked shabby as an overused baseball diamond. Even the neat rows of yellow footprints on the pavement outside the receiving center were small looking.

John showed me the actual set of footprints he'd stood on the night he arrived on the Island. Somehow he remembered which ones they were. There was a tense smile on his face as he pointed them out. Moments later we took pictures of him standing under the inscription over the receiving center doors, "Through These Portals Pass Prospects for America's Finest Fighting Force."

All the memorials to the battles and fallen heroes were so small, nothing more than humble painted boards or simple white waist-high concrete posts with the names of battles in plain black letters painted onto them. I caught glimpses of platoons of new recruits as they were beginning the long journey my son had just completed. They were scared and pale looking and being marched from place to place, DIs hovering over them, badgering, yelling, hounding, running up and down the line, advising, correcting, screaming like a bunch of unhinged, overprotective, and bizarrely severe mothers. "They're going easy on them because you're watching. You ought to see them when there are no parents around," said John.

John's experience of the Island had not included such areas as the PX or the food court, both locations he wanted to visit in the worst way, as if they were longed-for mythical destinations of surpassing beauty. Once we got to the store, a seedy PX-supermarket loaded with all the crap, the glitzy boom boxes, shit jewelry, and other nonnecessities the military pushes on underpaid Marines, John touched everything he saw. It was as if he'd just stepped off a boat from the old Soviet Union and had never seen the consumer wonders of an American store before. He was so disoriented that for the first time an inkling of the truth of just how intense his training must have been dawned on me.

John could not have been suffering more thoroughly from sensory deprivation if he'd just been released from a cell in the gulag. As for Genie and me, we were happy enough to load up on Marine T-shirts and other kitsch memorabilia. My favorite was a shirt John bought me. It featured a drawing of a big heron swallowing a little frog. The frog was already halfway down the huge bird's throat. He was desperately reaching back out of the bird's beak and grasping the bird's neck. The tiny frog was choking the huge bird while being swallowed. Stenciled on the frog's ass were the initials, "USMC." The slogan on the T-shirt read, *"Never give up!"*

In his squadbay, John showed us his rack, the punishment quarter-deck where he'd done push-ups until muscle failure dropped him face down into a pool of sweat, and the sandpit where he'd had his "heart thrashed" until he vomited. He showed us the showers—"thirty second showers during the first weeks we kind of had to run through without stopping"—the gear locker, the nooks, and crannies of his Spartan world. He showed us the brass drain he'd adopted as his cleaning project, how it was shined up, how he could look over the marsh to the water, ships, and lights of the town beyond.

By the end of the afternoon John started to talk in sentences of more than a few words. When he did begin to speak, it was like listening to the slightly garbled playback from some faulty electronic device. We got bits and pieces, descriptions in the past tense mixed in with the present tense. When I happened to walk on a certain painted area on the quarterdeck in front of the DIs door, John hurried forward and urgently whispered, "Dad! You *can't* step there!" Then he looked bewildered for a moment, smiled, and said, "Oh, I guess *you're* allowed. I guess they can't smoke parents. Boy, if I ever did that I'd be pitted for hours."

"But, John," I said, "now you're a Marine you can stand here too."

"Are you nuts? The DI is just over there!" hissed John.

I didn't argue. There were still teachers who would have given me sweaty palms if I'd seen them thirty-five years later. I understood.

We drove down to a picnic area near the entrance to the Island from the causeway and sat under the cypresses. John ate more of his pizza. He ate with less gusto than I'd expected. He explained that his stomach had shrunk again during the Crucible.

When I said that I hoped there was not too much pepper, John laughed, "*Pepper?* I eat anything now! Remember how I didn't like cheese, except on pizza? Well, I eat it now. I was licking plates during the first weeks and sucking the last drops of catsup out of packets and asking for other recruits' apple cores. The pepper's no problem . . ."

As we strolled the Island after our picnic we saw raw recruits being issued equipment and confident recruits, halfway through training, marching up to weapons battalion to vibrant cadences that sounded like the offstage chorus of an opera punctuated by the rasping shouts of the gravel-voiced DIs. My favorite moments were when the recruits shouted their responses in unison, "Sir, yes SIR!" as they marched past.

Knowing that my son was one of them, knowing what they were enduring as mirrored in his gaunt face, seeing the furious dedication of the DIs was a deeply moving experience. I watched several platoons march past through the glimmer of tears.

I felt small, an alien to all the selflessness around me. I knew I was unworthy to be standing so effortlessly, so casually, on ground into which so many millions of gallons of sweat had soaked.

What had I ever done for my country that made me worthy to be defended by these young men and women and these selfless DIs? I was standing on the footprints of forgotten men who went forth from this place and laid down their lives so that I could go to my town hall without fear, speak my piece. They had gone forth to protect my right to take Genie for a wife, because we freely chose each other, to have Frank for a friend, to defend a way of life where Frank and I could disagree and still work together, even be best friends . . .

The ascetic spirit radiating from the DIs reminded me of the monks I'd met on the Holy Mountain of Athos in Greece when I traveled in pilgrimage to the fantastical cliff-dwelling monastery of Simonopetra. (The DIs and monks would have been mightily surprised to hear this!)

Perched high above the Aegean Sea in that grim and beautiful eleventh-century stone fortress, I briefly lived with monks who, now, seemed to me to be somehow related to the DIs I was watching.

The monks and DIs seemed to both be searching for the same thing: the will to overcome the flesh for a higher purpose. One thing was certain, they were motivated not by greed but by love.

• • •

> the night before graduation
> I have one fire watch to go
> Marines are ironing uniforms
> in the shining lights from the head to be ready,
> squared away
> to leave this place,
> get the hell off the island,
> homesick once they leave

Many did not make it. Fifty or more recruits who had started with Bravo Company were dropped, hurt, sent home, or recycled. Twelve were dropped from our platoon alone.

I did not sleep well the night before graduation. We woke at 0430 to move out of the barracks and prepare it for the next platoon. We started by breaking down all the racks, sweeping and swabbing the decks, cleaning everything that we could think of and reach. Our uniforms had been ready since the night before.

As we moved all of our belongings onto the grass outside of the barracks—so that we could leave as soon as possible after graduation— one of our DIs said, "We don't want to see any of your ugly faces ever again, and if I see any of you in the fleet I'm gonna beat your ass!" In DI speak this was an affectionate farewell. (However, there were a few members of the platoon—"turds"—he really might beat if he ran across them.)

We formed up in front of the barracks before the beginning of the

graduation ceremony, then marched to the road that led onto the wide
concrete parade deck the size of a very large parking lot. We stood at
attention off to one side on an access road platoon by platoon. Six platoons (one company) were graduating that day. In the distance we
could see the parents already beginning to file into the stands—a sea
of red T-shirts, red caps, and sweats. (Red was Bravo Company's color.)
The stands held about two thousand people. It seemed a long wait
before we received the order to march the few hundred yards onto the
parade deck.

We had seen so many other platoons cross this place every Friday.
We had never imagined crossing it ourselves. Our mantra had been
chow-to-chow, Sunday-to-Sunday. Finally the last minutes on the
Island were ticking away.

It was freezing, and we were in our blue "Deltas" (khaki short sleeve
shirts, blue trousers, and cover). We were cold, but none of us shivered.
We marched. Four hundred pairs of "corframs" (shiny patent leather
dress shoes) struck the deck together. Our bodies were solid feeling
and warmed with pride and the discipline instilled through countless
hours of what had once seemed like "pointless exercises" and painful
punishments.

We felt the pride shining down on us from the beaming faces of our
families. We had a sense of true accomplishment. We were United
States Marines on the parade deck of Parris Island.

• • •

The sky was slate-gray. It was cold. I left Genie sitting alone on the
stands overlooking the parade deck. We were among the first parents
to arrive, and I went to get her a coffee. We had been fighting. We had
almost lost our way to PI in the dark that morning and had argued
about who had missed the way. Once I got back from the food court,
we huddled together against the stiff breeze.

For a long time nothing happened as other parents began to arrive.
Then we heard the platoons singing cadence as they began to form up

outside their squadbays in the distance. Before we could see them, their voices floated to us on the chill wind. I squeezed Genie's hand.

I took a deep breath. I was happy. John was graduating! He had made it through boot camp!

Then came the parade and the saccharine upbeat canned speech sounding like something the Disney writers might have come up with for a new USMC ride about "your Marines." But nothing could cheapen the fact that there, on the parade deck, was the small red guidon snapping in the wind displaying the number 1093. Third man marching from the front, top of the row, was a tall Marine, my son, in step with the rest.

I wiped my eyes and looked around. It occurred to me that this was the first time I'd ever been in an integrated crowd of this size dedicated to one purpose and of one mind. I had lived and worked in Africa for a year with a mixed-race movie crew. I'd been in plenty of ball parks, concerts, and mixed-race events. I had black, Hispanic, and Asian friends. This was different. The parents and Marines on PI that morning were not only of many races but were representative of many economic classes as well, from the very poorest who had arrived by bus or crammed onto the back of pickups to one or two parents who wore expensive suits and cashmere overcoats.

A toothless Mexican grandfather stood across from me, so drunk his embarrassed family was doing their best to prop him up. We were white and Native American. We were Hispanic and African American and Asian. We were old ex-Marines wearing the scars of battle, or at least baseball caps emblazoned with battles' names. We were southern white crackers from Nashville and pierced skinheads from New Jersey and black kids from Cleveland wearing ghetto rags and big white ex-cons of no fixed address with ham-hock forearms defaced by jailhouse tattoos. We were fat mothers poured into bulging sweats and we were thin twelve-year old little sisters with big hair in minuscule skirts and skimpy tank tops, coatless and shivering in the steady cold wind.

I heard many languages. Families full of brown babies, squat wide mothers, and dark-skinned weather-beaten grandfathers were speaking

Spanish. The aluminum stands groaned under the weight of large southern white tribes, their video camera–toting women painted gaudy, hair exploding in haloes of blond above huge bosoms, the guts of their men hanging over American eagle belt buckles.

A Native American with turquoise and silver braided into his long white ponytail was sitting silent behind Genie next to a stocky Romanian family, none of whom spoke English and who, even in the frigid morning breeze, exuded a miasma of garlic as they yelled and waved small American flags at their Marine, and blocked the view so that the pale, quiet, well-dressed family from Maine, sitting behind them, had to step out onto the stairs to see their Marine out on the deck.

None of the Marines looked our way no matter how much we waved or hollered their names. "Eyes front," they stood at attention, trouser legs flapping in the steady cold wind. I fell into a reverie.

The platitudes my educated North Shore friends mouthed about "racial harmony" and economic and "gender diversity" were nothing compared with the common purpose uniting the parents gathered in the stands to honor our Marines. In Georgetown, when I had visited Francis I always noticed that the African American students seemed to sit in their own corner of the dining hall, roomed with each other, and kept to themselves, as did the whites and other "ethnic groupings." I glanced around at the other civilians on the stands. We were strangers but our Marine sons were brothers.

In the fleet our Marines would room together as they had in boot camp, drink together, work together; southern crackers, wasps, blacks, whites, Arabs, and Asians, united by a high purpose: the defense of our country and loyalty to the Corps. (Somehow I doubted that anyone from Georgetown or NYU would be coming down to Parris Island any time soon to learn what an authentic multiracial, economically diverse culture looked like!)

We were cheering and rushing out of the packed stands and embracing our sons, brothers, sisters, cousins, and each other. (Two months later when I attended Jane's graduation the same scene was repeated with two hundred female graduating Marines and their proud and joyful and mostly poor and lower middle-class families.) Then we were packing up and hauling John's seabag and his canvas hanging bag to the rented car. John's last words on Parris Island were, "Stay motivated!" spoken out the car window to three new and frightened looking recruits who glanced at him in awe, said, "Yes, sir!" and hurried on.

We took John back to the hotel where we would spend the night. The first thing John did was change into the civilian clothes we'd brought with us. When he stripped off his socks I was horrified at the state of his feet. They stank of putrid cheese and were raw with huge filthy blisters. Strips of flesh were hanging off them. John explained, "There's been no time since the Crucible to go to a doctor."

I washed out John's socks. I reeled from the stench of the infection and marveled at the willpower it must have taken to stay with his platoon and graduate. The big toe of his left foot was a swollen, twisted lump three times its normal size and bent to the side. I rubbed his feet with antibiotic cream and bandaged them. John seemed oblivious to the pain and muttered to me to stop making such a "fuss" and that, "A lot of the guys' feet are in the same shape. It's no big deal."

"They let you march on *this*?" I exclaimed, pointing to his misshapen toe.

"Are you crazy?" asked John. "I didn't tell them. I might have been recycled! You should have seen Yates. He had such bad stress fractures we had to carry him the last day of the Crucible so he could finish with us. But he made it. He's a Marine."

John's socks and underwear could not have been more grubby if he'd been living in a coal mine. John protested that he'd done all his laundry the day before, but that "after a while the sweat and dirt never really washes out."

An hour later Genie, John, and I strolled through the lovely streets and shady flagstone squares of Savannah. We spent a glorious day as John, having gone from tongue-tied silence to torrential loquaciousness, regaled us with boot camp stories. "It's just so strange, it's just *soooo* strange to be out here!" John kept saying.

• • •

this place makes
no sense, people slouch,
doors close in front of
old women, people are fat!
I hate the rudeness, the chaos,
sleeping in is heaven, watching
the sunrise every day
can get tedious
sunrise will forever have
a touch of violence now.

from Growing Up Empty
by Loretta Schwartz-Nobel

Loretta Schwartz-Nobel's 2002 book about hunger in America includes a chapter on military workers. She found evidence that many young Marines don't earn enough money to feed their families.

The first time Carol called, it was the end of August. She asked me to stop by but didn't say she and her baby were hungry. When I got to her house, I found the eighteen-month-old trying to eat from the garbage pail in the kitchen. Carol was too weak to get out of bed. Her husband had been in the field for ten days and they'd been completely out of food for three."

Lisa Joels, the founder of HELP (Helping Enlisted Lives Prosper), was talking to me as we drove toward the base commissary at Quantico, a Marine training center in Dumfrees, Virginia.

"Carol called again at the end of September," Lisa added. "She asked how to get a free Thanksgiving turkey. I said, 'Hey, I'll be happy to tell you but Thanksgiving is two months away. Do you have any food in the house right now?' There was a long pause before Carol said, 'No.' It's really very hard for a lot of military families to admit that they have nothing to eat at the end of each month so they hint around at it and wait for me to ask."

Lisa pulled into the base commissary parking lot and turned off the engine.

"These kids bought so heavily into the idea that the military would take care of them that now they think it's their fault and they feel ashamed. They think that they must be doing something wrong. They aren't, though. They just run out of food and food stamps every month like all the other poor families in America."

Military pay varies. Lisa explained, "It varies by rank, marital status, and length of service. At the bottom of the scale in 2000, a newly enlisted, single Marine earned $887.70 a month before taxes, with a housing allowance of about $215 a month. If he was married, his salary stayed the same but his housing allowance went up to roughly $385 a month. It's just not enough."

We began walking down the aisles of the commissary and now, as Lisa spoke, she piled bread, cheese, drumsticks, potatoes, spaghetti, bananas, peanut butter and jelly into a cart.

"This stuff should last them until the next food stamps arrive," she said as she stood back and looked at the food in the cart. "I think I've got it down to a science."

"How can you afford to buy people food?" I asked, once we were back in the car and driving toward Carol's house.

Lisa shrugged. "My husband's an E-7 with eighteen years behind him. There are two of us working and we only have one kid. We're also very careful but I think I'm blessed. The more I give, the more it seems to come back to me, contributions, office equipment, furniture, you name it. I started this organization after I went to Philadelphia and listened to Colin Powell speak at the President's Summit on Volunteerism. He said, 'Go out and help a neighbor. The hardest thing you'll ever do is hold a stranger's hand.' It was at a vulnerable time in my own life and his words really got to me.

"My son has cancer and he had just gone into remission. I felt so grateful that I wanted to give something back. I'd heard that a lot of enlisted families were having a hard time but I'd never explored it. This time was different, I felt energized and determined. As soon as I got back home, I began driving around the base and knocking on the doors of all the new families. First, I introduced myself, then I asked them how they were doing and if they needed anything. It didn't take long. When I got about four houses into it, I found a girl living in a totally empty house. She didn't tell me anything was wrong, she just seemed really glad that someone had stopped by to welcome her. She invited me in. As soon as I got inside, I said, 'Hey. Where's your furniture?' She said, 'We don't have any.' I said, 'Where's your car?' She said, 'We don't have one.' I said, 'Where do you sleep?' She pointed to a sleeping bag crumpled up in the middle of the floor. Then I asked if she and the baby had enough food to eat. First, she nodded yes, then her eyes filled up with tears. I was dumbfounded. I came home and I said to my husband, 'My God, Barron. You're not going to believe this but, honest to God, I just found these people right down the road from us who have absolutely nothing. She's sixteen years old with a four-month-old baby. Her eighteen-year-old husband was too proud to say, 'I have no bed. I have no food. I have nothing.' "

Lisa shook her head sadly then said, "Since starting HELP in 1997, I've found more than fifteen hundred families at this base alone in situations that were just as bad or worse."

My own husband had served in the military. He'd been taken straight from a neurosurgical residency and placed aboard a submarine as the medical officer during the Vietnam War. When I called him that night and told him what I'd learned from Lisa Joels, he couldn't believe it either.

The next morning, we parked the car in a relatively run-down area of the base reserved exclusively for enlisted families and walked up a brown dirt path where modest, 1950s style attached brick houses stood in small clusters. Lisa knocked on the door of one of them. A young, sharp-featured boy of about twenty-one dressed in tall black boots and military fatigues opened the door partway. He peeked around the edge then stepped outside and quickly closed the door behind him. He had obviously been waiting for us and didn't want us to come in. The first thing I saw were his eyes. Although they were an unusual shade of pale blue, it wasn't the color that struck me most. It was the impenetrable flatness, the hardness and the distrust.

"Thanks," he said, reaching for a bag of the groceries. He was clearly uncomfortable when Lisa opened the door and whisked past him carrying the packages. I glanced inside then took a breath before walking in behind her. Despite what I had been told, I still wasn't expecting to see this level of chaos and poverty in a military home. There was nothing in the living room besides what looked like about a week's trash that the baby had spilled and was crawling around in. Lisa stepped around the trash and walked directly into the kitchen, then opened the refrigerator. Except for some red liquid that had congealed on the shelves and one slice of unwrapped bread, it was completely empty.

"Carol stresses out," Alex said apologetically as he saw us taking in the scene. "She's been having a really hard time coping lately and I haven't been around to help. I've been working ninety-six-hour shifts. I'm away four days at a time training lieutenants in the field. I've been doing it for three years now. I'm away from home so much that I can't even get a second job to help make ends meet like a lot of the other guys do. I really want to take better care of my family," Alex added, as he saw me watching the baby. She was trying to eat one of the empty McDonalds wrappers that was on the floor. I bent down and picked her up, then opened the loaf of bread Lisa brought and asked if it was all right to let her have a slice.

"Yeah. Sure," he said as the baby grabbed it.

She crammed it into her mouth, devoured it and began crying for more. Alex handed her another, ate one himself, then suggested that we'd probably be more comfortable sitting outside on the stoop.

"I'm sorry the place is such a mess," he said, apologizing again. "Carol lost a baby a few weeks ago, and she hasn't been herself since."

"She did?" Lisa said, spinning around. "What was the problem?"

"I don't know," Alex answered. "I wasn't here.

"But I'll tell you one thing I do know," he added, once we were all outside on the stoop. "From the time I was fourteen, I raised two sisters alone and ran a hundred-acre farm in Kentucky. I worked eight to twelve hours a day on that farm and I went to school in between. Then I took another job on the weekends that paid four dollars and fifty cents an hour. It was hard, very hard, but it was a lot easier than this is." He lit a cigarette and looked at me. "I knew marriage wasn't going to be easy, but I love my wife and I wanted to marry her. The way the Marine Corps made it sound, they were going to help take care of us, they made me think we'd have everything we needed." He squeezed his eyes shut for a minute as if they burned then opened them again. "They've done exactly the opposite. They've torn this marriage apart. They never said you'll get no food allowance for your family. They never said you'll need food stamps and WIC and you still won't have enough. They never said we're going to take you away from your wife and kids nine months out of twelve. They never said the Marine Corps is no place for a family, period . . . but they knew it, they knew it all the time."

In the old Marine Corps, there was a rule that an enlisted man could not be married without his commanding officer's permission. He had to be an E-4 and have two years of service before he was even eligible to bring his wife and family with him. In those days everyone said, "If the military wanted you to have a wife they would have issued you one in your duffel bag."

The young men objected because it went against their hope of being able to get married and take care of their families the way they thought a real man would. That was the main reason many of them joined the corps in the first place.

Even today, most people think that if a family is in the military they get free medical care, free dental care, and free housing. They assume it because, directly or indirectly, they have been led to believe it. Although they have usually not been lied to, they have not been told the whole truth either. Most do not realize that there is no food allowance for wives or children. The housing is free only if it is available. If the family wants a dental plan, they have to pay for it because it is only free for the soldier, and even the soldier has copays for fillings and extractions. Nor is the term "free medical care" entirely accurate. Some things are covered, others are not. If a family is stressed by lack of money and food, for example, and needs non-emergency mental health care in order to cope, they too have a copay. If they are too poor to afford food and clothing and if it costs twenty dollars every time they go in to talk about it, it stands to reason that they are not going to have very many visits.

Theoretically, the commissary saves families lots of money because it lowers the prices of the items that are being sold by about 30 percent, but in fact, here too the truth is more complex. Since the commissary never has specials, only standard markdowns, it is often actually more expensive than clipping coupons and buying specials at the regular supermarkets. While the Post Exchange has wonderful prices on the clothing it discounts, it carries mostly expensive brands, even for children. So, in the end, it is sometimes considerably more expensive to shop there than at Wal-Mart, Kmart or other less expensive stores.

Under federally established poverty guidelines, the first three military ranks, E-1 through E-3, are eligible for food stamps unless they have assets worth more than four thousand dollars, in which case they are disqualified. But, even with food stamps, a lot of military families have the same problems as Alex and Carol. Toward the end of the month, all the food they purchased with their food stamps has been eaten. Their paychecks have been spent and their refrigerators are empty. There might be a bottle of catsup or mustard and maybe some WIC milk, but many families will be completely out of food. Others will be eating ramen noodles three times a day because they can get ten packs for a dollar at the base commissary and because their next payday is often still a week or more away.

Junior enlisted families also usually end up losing their telephones. That's often because they've made so many desperate long-distance calls home for help and money that they can't pay the phone bill. Pacific Bell and many other phone companies require a payment of three times the highest bill just to get a disconnected phone turned back on. So, once they lose their phones, that's it. Most of these families will never be able to get them back again, at least not during that tour of duty.

As a result, these young men and women often find themselves more deeply isolated than they have ever been. They are often hundreds, even thousands of miles from home without the support systems or the life skills necessary to deal with hunger, poverty, separations and other difficult conditions.

"The only group that's ever helped us since we came here is yours," Alex said, turning to Lisa. "Navy Relief only drove us deeper into debt. Do you know what I have to do? I have to make a monthly contribution to my platoon for parties and trips that I never take because I'm always in the field. It comes out of my paycheck. The contribution isn't exactly mandatory, but I've been told in so many words that if I don't make it, there are plenty of shit details they can put me on." Alex's mouth twisted slightly and his nostrils flared, then he spit over the edge of the wrought-iron rail onto the brown grass. "Most people here are like me. They joined the Marine Corps to get away from something. They wanted structure because they never had it at home, they thought they were tough enough to handle it because they'd already gone through a hard life, but they were wrong. Nothing prepares you for this. I was angry when I came here. I still have a scar between my eyes where my mother punched me with a fistful of rings when I was five. My mother always beat me and my grandmother stabbed me in the hand." Alex laughed a hard, bitter laugh then tossed his head. "My family put the 'D' in dysfunctional. I think I was searching for my father when I came here, a lot of us probably are. Have you seen those recruiting ads?" Alex asked as a bitter smile crept across his face. "The ones that show a father with his arm around his son and the father is saying, 'He's not just my son, he's my hero.' Well that's the military playing on our need for approval. They act like our families will suddenly love us now and respect us."

"Yes, I've seen the ads," I said, surprised by his openness and his understanding of why young men like him are especially vulnerable.

"But my father was different," Alex added as his expression softened. "He was gentle and I was very close to him. He died a week before my sixth birthday and I can still remember standing at my bedroom window looking up at the sky and the stars and thinking that my father was up there floating around somewhere. I was praying—just praying—to St. Mary that he would come back home to me." His eyes clouded over then filled up. He looked away so I wouldn't see. "I've cried two times in my life, just two," he said, regaining control. "One was for my father, the other was for my grandfather. After my father died, my grandfather was the only one who was there for me. He had been in the Marines too, the old corps. That's one of the reasons I joined, I came here looking for a better life. I was hoping I could change things, turn my luck around, but I ended up with more rules, more punishments and more poverty than ever and I still had no sense that I was valued.

"I was after a dream. One of my teachers in school used to call it the American dream but that dream turned into a nightmare. Now, I feel like I'm in a goddamn prison with every other weekend off." Alex waved to another Marine who was walking up the path, then he stepped on his cigarette and ground it into the earth until every strand of tobacco was buried, until the thin white paper had turned brown and disappeared in the dirt.

"When I finally get home for my big weekend off, I still can't relax because I have to worry about feeding my baby daughter and feeding my wife. For myself, it doesn't matter," he added, raising his shoulders and puffing up his chest a little. "I can last four days without food if I have water. I've lived with so little for so long that I've got my body trained, but my wife and my baby need to eat. I know my kid is growing up without enough food and I don't know what the hell it's going to do to her. I'm scared to death she'll be stunted or retarded or something."

"How often do you run out?" I asked.

"At the end of every month for sure," Alex answered, pensively, "but to be honest with you, sometimes it's a lot more often than that. Even when we do have food, we usually don't have enough."

"Hey, Carol. How ya doin'?" Lisa called as a young woman walked up the path. She was rail thin and sallow. Her jeans and T-shirt hung loosely on her frail body. As soon as Alex saw her his face lit up.

"Hi, baby," he said gently. "How'd it go?"

Carol shook her head as if to say no. "I've been trying to get a job," she explained to me after we'd been introduced. "But we don't have a vehicle and most of the jobs around here require that. Actually, we do have one, but it's been missing second gear ever since we bought it, and we can't afford to fix it. We can't even get down to the food stamp office to recertify for the stamps."

"That's how it usually goes," Lisa whispered, pulling me aside while Alex handed Carol the baby. "One problem compounds another for these young enlisted families. They're still paying three hundred four dollars a month for a car that's been sitting there broken for over a year."

"It's a 1994 with seventy-six thousand miles," Alex said, overhearing Lisa. "We owe about thirty-five hundred dollars on it, and if we don't keep up the payments, well lose both the car and our credit." Carol walked into the house and came out with a piece of the cheese. "Thanks for the food, Lisa," she said as she handed it to the baby.

"Boy, she's really hungry," Lisa observed. "When's the last time that baby ate?"

Carol started to say something then she looked at Alex and stopped. They both seemed uncomfortable, as if they thought an admission of hunger might incriminate them or discredit them as parents. Maybe they were afraid, as Lisa mentioned later, that the baby might be taken from them by the authorities.

"My job is to be a big tough man," Alex said, breaking the silence. "But the only way I can feed my wife and kid is to send them back to her mother's house or call you." Then Alex spat on the ground again. "Maybe they think that's OK. Maybe they believe that a hungry soldier is an angry soldier and an angry soldier is a good killer and for them, maybe that's the bottom line. All I know is that I've been in the field three hundred of the last three hundred sixty-five days. I was hurt out there, hurt bad enough so I needed surgery. After the operation, I wasn't supposed to be out of bed for two full weeks. They gave me five days off and then sent me back. They were doing war games. The doctor told me not to lift more than ten pounds or stand more than thirty minutes. They knew that, but I was out there standing five hours at a time and lifting sixty or seventy pounds. I'm testing ballistic plates that are supposed to protect people from live rounds but sometimes they don't work. That's how me and two other guys got hurt.

"I've put in three years, and I've only got shit to show for it." Alex looked at my notepad. He smiled then stood back and looked a little surprised. "You really are taking me down word for word." He paced for a minute, as if he was thinking over the risks and possible consequences, then said, "Hell. I don't care what you write. I don't give a damn. Why should I? I'm getting out of here soon. My dream of a good life here is dead. I'm a short-timer now, so I don't have to follow the rules anymore.

"Besides," he said rhetorically, "how much worse can it get? As soon as I see someone trying to jerk me or my friends around, I speak up. They make excuses that I'm in the field all the time because of my expertise, but the truth is I'm out there because I stood up for another Marine."

The baby tugged at Alex's bootlaces then reached up his leg for the rest of him. Alex smiled a broad, beautiful smile that didn't match the anger flashing in his eyes just a moment before, then he picked her up and kissed her forehead.

"When I finished boot camp, I was the proudest soldier in the world. I loved the fact that I was a Marine. It was second only to my marriage and the birth of my daughter. They didn't tell us it would be like this. When we finally hit payday, the first thing we do is run to the commissary because we're so damn hungry all the time."

"The baby always has food," Carol interrupted, looking uneasy again. Then, as if she sensed that we might not believe her, she added, "We make sure we have enough for her even if it's only ramen noodles."

The Marine
by Mike Sager

Mike Sager profiled Marine Lieutenant Colonel Robert O. Sinclair for the December 2001 Esquire.

Dragon Six is Oscar Mike, on the move to link up with Bandit. Foot mobile along Axis Kim, he is leading a detachment of ten U.S. Marines across a stretch of desert scrub in the notional, oil-rich nation of Blueland. He walks at a steady rate of three klicks per hour, three kilometers, muscle memory after twenty-three years of similar forced humps through the toolies, his small powerful body canted slightly forward, his ankles and knees a little sore, his dusty black Danner combat boots, size 8, crunching over branches and rocks and coarse sand.

His pale-blue eyes are bloodshot from lack of sleep. His face is camouflaged with stripes and splotches of greasepaint—green, brown, and black to match his woodland-style utilities, fifty-six dollars a set, worn in the field without skivvies underneath, a personal wardrobe preference known as going commando. Atop his Kevlar helmet rides a pair of goggles sheathed in an old sock. Around his neck hangs a heavy pair of rubberized binoculars. From his left hip dangles an olive-drab pouch. With every step, the pouch swings and hits his thigh, adding another faint, percussive thunk to the quiet symphony of his gear, the total weight of which is not taught and seldom discussed. Inside the pouch is a gas mask for NBC attacks—nuclear, biological, or chemical weapons. Following an attack, when field gauges show the air to be safe once again for breathing, regulations call for the senior marine to choose one man to remove his mask and hood. After ten minutes, if the man shows no ill effects, the rest of the marines can begin removing theirs.

The temperature is 82 degrees. The air is thick and humid. Sounds of distant fire travel on the wan breeze: the boom and rumble of artillery, the pop and crackle of small arms. He is leading his men in a northwesterly direction, headed for an unimproved road designated Phase Line Rich. There, he will rendezvous with Bravo Company, radio call sign Bandit, one of five companies under his command, nearly nine hundred men, armed with weapons ranging from M16A2 rifles to Humvee-mounted TOW missile launchers. In his gloved right hand he carries a map case fashioned from cardboard and duct tape—the cardboard scavenged from a box of MREs, meals ready-to-eat, high-tech field rations that cook themselves when water is added. Clipped to the map case is a rainbow assortment of felt-tip pens, the colors oddly garish against the setting. His 9mm Beretta side arm is worn just beneath his right chest, high on his abdomen. The holster is secured onto his H harness, a pair of mesh suspenders anchored to the war belt around his waist—which itself holds magazine pouches with spare ammo and twin canteens. Altogether, this load-bearing apparatus is known as deuce gear, as in U.S. Government Form No. 782, the receipt a marine was once required to sign upon issuance. These days, the corps is computerized.

Near his left clavicle, also secured to his H harness—which is worn atop his flak vest—is another small pouch. Inside he keeps his

Leatherman utility tool, his government-issue New Testament, a bag of Skittles left over from an MRE, and a tin of Copenhagen snuff, a medium-sized dip of which is evident at this moment in the bulge of his bottom lip, oddly pink in contrast to his thick camo makeup, and in the bottom lips of most of the men in his detachment, a forward-command element known as the Jump. They march slue-footed in a double-file formation through California sage and coyote bush and fennel, the smell pungent and spicy, like something roasting in a gourmet oven, each man silent and serious, deliberate in movement, eyes tracking left and right, as trained, each man taking a moment now and then, without breaking stride, to purse his lips and spit a stream of brownish liquid onto the ground, the varied styles of their expectorations somehow befitting, a metaphor for each personality, a metaphor, seemingly, for the Marine Corps itself: a tribe of like minds in different bodies, a range of shapes and sizes and colors, all wearing the same haircut and uniform, all hewing to the same standards and customs, yet still a collection of individuals, each with his own particular style of spitting tobacco juice, each with his own particular life to give for his country.

In the center of his flak vest—hot and heavy, designed to stop shrapnel but not bullets or knives—is a metal pin about the size of a dime, his insignia of rank, a silver oak leaf. Ever since he was young, growing up on the outskirts of Seattle, the second of four sons born to a department-store manager and a missionary's daughter, Robert O. Sinclair always wanted to be a marine. Now, at age forty, he has reached the rank of lieutenant colonel. He has what many consider to be the ultimate job for an infantry officer in the corps, the command of his own battalion, in this case BN One-Four—the 1st Battalion, 4th Marine Regiment. A proud unit with a distinguished history, the One-Four saw its first action in 1916, during the Banana Wars in the Dominican Republic. In the late twenties, the 4th Marines became known as the China Regiment when it was sent to Shanghai to protect American interests. During World War II, the One-Four was part of a larger force that surrendered to the Japanese at Corregidor. Its colors were burned; the survivors became POWs, forced to endure the infamous Bataan Death March. Re-formed two years later, the unit avenged itself in the first wave of landings on Guam. It has since fought in Vietnam, Desert Storm, and Somalia.

Come January, Sinclair and the One-Four—expanded to include tanks, artillery, amphibious and light armored vehicles, engineers, and 350 additional troops—will ship out on three Navy amphibious assault vessels as the 13th MEU (SOC), Marine Expeditionary Unit (Special Operations Capable), bound for the western Pacific and the Persian Gulf, ready for immediate action, fully equipped to wage combat for fifteen days without resupply or reinforcement, a unit precisely suited to a war against terrorism. "We specialize in conducting raids," says Sinclair. "We're tailor-made for special ops. We're trained to get in, hit a target, kill the enemy, and friggin' pull back to our ships again. We can go by helo. We can infiltrate by land. We can go ashore conventionally. We can put together anything. We're ready to do whatever it takes."

At the moment, in marine lingo, it is twenty-four sixteen thirty uniform May zero one, 4:30 in the afternoon on May 24, 2001, well before the prospect of going to war suddenly became real and imminent this fall. It is the fourth day of something called the Battalion FEX—a field exercise, on-the-job training for Sinclair and his marines. Truth be told, this is the first chance Sinclair has ever had to take his entire battalion out for a spin. Eight months ago, he had a lower rank and a different job in another unit somewhere else. Eight months ago, 90 percent of the men in his battalion were somewhere else; a good percentage of them had only recently graduated from high school.

All told, between the time he took the flag of the One-Four—a dragon wrapped around a dagger on a blue diamond; the motto: Whatever It Takes—and the day this January or sooner when he and his men and all their equipment steam out of San Diego Harbor— wives and families and a brass band left behind on the dock—Sinclair will have had only eighteen months to build from scratch a crack fighting force, trained for every contingency from humanitarian aid to

police action to strategic guerrilla raids to full-scale invasion. He has
seven more months to get the bugs out. There is much to be done.

And so it is that Bob Sinclair is Oscar Mike across a stretch of desert
scrub in the notional country of Blueland, which is actually in the state
of California at Camp Pendleton, the largest amphibious training base
in the world, spread across 125,000 rugged and breathtaking acres
along the Pacific coastline. In ten mikes or so, ten minutes, over the next
rise, Sinclair will link up with Bandit, the main effort in this five-phase
operation. From there, Sinclair will lead his marines into the mountains,
toward a BP, a battle position, high atop a steep, no-name hill. At zero
four hundred hours, with the pop and arc of a white double-star-burst
flare, the battle will commence: a non-supported, nonilluminated
night attack against the invading enemy forces of Orangeland, dug in
at a critical crossroads, eyes on the Jesara oil fields.

Or that is the plan, anyway. Like the bubbas say: A plan is only good
until the first shot is fired. Sometimes not even until then.

At Phase Line Rich, Sinclair and his men take cover in a stand of high
weeds. The four young grunts who form his security element—a corporal and three privates, pimples showing through camo paint—
employ along a tight circular perimeter. They assume prone positions
on the deck, in the rocky sand, cheeks resting against the stocks of their
weapons, three M16A2 rifles and an M249 SAW, Squad Automatic
Weapon, a 5.56mm light machine gun with a removable bipod.

The ground is riddled with gopher mounds, busy with ants, bugs,
and small lizards. Three types of rattlesnakes inhabit the area, along
with scorpions, coyotes, roadrunners, and mountain lions. Overhead,
against a backdrop of rugged mountains and gray sky, a red-tailed
hawk backpedals its wings, suspended in flight, talons flexed, fixing a
target far below.

Sinclair sits with his legs crossed Indian-style. A fly buzzes around
his head; bees alight upon the intricate yellow flowers of the black
mustard weeds. Filled to capacity, his assault pack and his ass pack
form a backrest, a comfortable pillow on which to lounge. Inside the

packs, among other items, he keeps a roll of toilet paper; extra socks; reserve tins of Copenhagen; map templates; his NVGs, night-vision goggles; his CamelBak, a one-gallon water reservoir with a long drinking tube attached; and his MOPP suit and booties, Mission Oriented Protective Posture, marine lingo for the overclothes worn with the gas mask in case of NBC attack.

Five feet six inches tall, Sinclair has a quick, high-pitched giggle and bulging biceps, a Marine Corps tattoo on each shoulder. He is, in the words of one of his officers, "a good human being who's able to be a taskmaster." He has a pretty wife, his second, and a baby son and partial custody of his eleven-year-old stepson. They live among civilians on a cul-de-sac in a cookie-cutter subdivision about thirty minutes from the base, a black Isuzu Trooper and a black Volvo station wagon parked side by side in the driveway. He loves fishing, prays before eating his MREs in the field.

Though Sinclair was once lampooned in a skit as the Angry Little Man, he is known to his marines as a teacher and a father figure. Above all, he is known as a bubba, a fellow grunt. Unlike most marine officers, Sinclair joined the corps right out of high school. He spent the summer in boot camp in San Diego, then went off to Western Washington University. Following graduation (he majored in political science), upon completion of his basic officers' training, Sinclair was asked to list three career choices. He wrote infantry three times. He was chewed out by his CO for disobeying orders—if the Marine Corps says three choices, it damn well means three—but it was worth it to him to make the point.

At twenty-two, as a lieutenant, Sinclair became a rifle platoon commander. At twenty-nine, as a captain, he was a company commander in an infantry battalion similar to the One-Four and saw action in Somalia and Rwanda. In his early thirties, as a major, he served time as both a key member of a general's staff and as the director of the Infantry Officer Course in Quantico, Virginia. Today, as CO of the One-Four, he is known for his attention to detail, his almost wonkish expertise in battlefield tactics and techniques. Important also is his reputation for pushing down power to the NCOs, for delegating authority to the noncommissioned officers, the sergeants and the corporals, an essential managerial concept in this bottom-heavy organization. The smallest of all the services—about 170,000 compared with the Army's 480,000 (800,000 including reserves)—the Marines also have the lowest officer-to-enlisted ratio, one-to-nine, compared with the Army's one-to-five. More than half of the corps is composed of the three lowest pay grades—lance corporals, Pfc.'s, and privates. Every year, more than 30 percent of the enlisted ranks muster out and return to civilian life. Discounting career officers and NCOs, that means a complete recycling of bodies about every three years.

Now, as Sinclair sits in the weeds near Phase Line Rich, dark clouds gather ominously over the mountains. "Guess we're in for a nice little hike," he says, flashing his trademark smile, toothy and overlarge.

"Yes, sir!" sings out Sergeant Major, sitting to his right. John Hamby, forty, is the ranking noncommissioned officer in the One-Four, the most senior of all the enlisted, though still junior to the greenest second lieutenant. A good ol' boy from Georgia with a booming gravel voice, he is always at Sinclair's side, offering advice and support, implementing orders, watchdogging the interests of his men. Asked about his favorite marine memories, he thinks a moment, names three: the day, at age twenty-nine, that he received his high school diploma, the 4.0 valedictorian of his class; the day his father pinned his sergeant major chevrons to his collar; the day, when he was stationed in Vienna as an embassy guard, that his son was born by emergency C-section.

"Those peaks behind Basilone Road are gonna be a ball buster," Sinclair says. "Holy Moses!"

"Been there many times," Sergeant Major says. He spits a stream of brownish liquid into the weeds. "Character builder, sir."

"It won't be as steep as yesterday, but it's a lot friggin' higher," Sinclair says, his flat northwestern accent flavored with a bit of southern drawl, affected to a greater or lesser extent by most marine officers, no matter what their regional origins—homage, perhaps, to the antebellum notion of the southern gentleman, upon whom the patriotic ideal of a young American military leader was modeled. He spits a stream of juice, then kicks some dirt over the wet spot on the ground, covering it up.

"You would think there'd be a limit as to how much character you can build, sir. But I ain't reached it yet."

"Oo-rah, Sergeant Major."

"Ain't that right, Colon?" Sergeant Major cuffs the shoulder of the nervous young radio operator sitting behind Sinclair, nearly knocking him over. Pfc. Mike Colon is twenty years old, a slight youth just this side of pretty: five feet four with long curly lashes. The twelve-pound radio he's carrying—a one nineteen foxtrot SINCGARS, a single-channel ground-and-airborne radio system—fits with some difficulty into his assault pack. The ten-foot whip-style antenna makes balance difficult. Thirty minutes into the hump, he has already slapped Sinclair on the helmet several times with the thick rod of rubber-coated steel.

Born in Puerto Rico, raised in the ghetto of Holyoke, Massachusetts, Colon speaks English with the singsong rhythms of his home island. Both of his earlobes are pierced, a remnant of his days with the Latin Kings. Six months ago, Colon was breaking rocks with a ten-pound sledge in the CCU, the Correctional Custody Unit at Camp Pendleton, busted down to private for drinking in the barracks. It was his third offense; the Old Man could have run him out of the corps. But Sinclair prides himself on being able to judge his marines, to see into their souls. As he likes to say: "You can't friggin' command from behind a damn desk." In battle, you have to know what to expect from your men. That's the whole reason they practice everything so many times. That's the whole reason he's out here on the Jump rather than back in the rear, commanding from a camp chair in the relative comfort of the COC, the Combat Operations Center, a big black tent with a generator, lights, computers, and a banquet-sized coffee urn.

Sinclair saw something in Colon, and Colon responded: He was down but he never dropped his pack, as the bubbas say. Now he has found himself assigned as the Old Man's radio operator. He darts a look at Sergeant Major. Privilege in the Marine Corps is often a two-edged sword. Had he not been so honored by this assignment, he'd be back at the COC himself, pulling radio watch. He aims a stream of brownish juice toward the ground. A little bit dribbles down his chin, onto his flak vest. "A definite character builder, Sergeant Major."

Sinclair twists around, flashes Colon his smile. "There ya go, stud," he sings encouragingly.

"Here comes Bandit right now," announces the OpsO, the operations officer, indicating the lead element of Bravo Company, coming around a bend double file.

Major Minter Bailey Ralston IV—Uncle Minty to his friends—is Dragon Three to Sinclair's Dragon Six. He plans and coordinates all battalion movements in the field. Thirty-two years old, a strapping six feet two, he's a graduate of the Virginia Military Institute. Since 1856, every Minter Bailey Ralston before him had been a pharmacist. Growing up in the tiny town of Westin, West Virginia, the only boy of four children, he set his sights early on the Marines. "John Wayne and comic books took me to the dark side at a very early age," he says.

Blond and blue-eyed, with circles under his eyes, Ralston was up all last night on the laptop computer in the COC, pecking out Battalion Frag Order zero one tach four, the detailed, six-page battle plan for tonight's movement. Grimacing, he pops two large pills without water. Three weeks ago, he underwent surgery on his right calf muscle. He is not yet cleared for exercise of any kind.

Sitting next to Major Ralston is the FSC, the fire-support coordinator, Major Randy Page. Six feet four with green eyes, thirty-four years old, Page hails from Wagon Wheel, New Mexico, population fifty. His job is coordinating artillery and other weapons fire to support the grunts on the ground. Married with no kids, a foreign-film buff, a self-professed computer geek, Page loves being in the field. His favorite marine moment is a snapshot: "You're in the rain, you're on a knee, and everyone's just miserable. And you just kinda look around and it feels like—you feel like crap because you're cold or hot or wet or whatever—but it just feels good."

Now Page hoists himself off the deck. He scans the horizon, taking a deep draft of the spicy air. "Looks like that fog is comin' in a little early, sir."

"Roger that, Major Page," Sinclair says, grunting a bit as he rises, as men of a certain age begin to do.

"On your feet, marines," growls Sergeant Major. He kicks playfully at the boot of Lance Corporal Joseph Gray, the other radio operator on the Jump. Gray has been dragging lately. He's newly married to a very young Cuban girl. There are troubles at home, a baby on the way. Sergeant Major reaches down and offers Gray a helping hand. "Move it, Devil Dog," he barks.

After a long, steep climb—the last bit a 70-degree slope through sharp thistles—Dragon Jump and Bandit are in place on the summit of No Name Hill, looking down upon Battalion Objectives Four and Five. Huddled together in the pitch-dark, Sinclair and his men are totally assed out. They sit in rocky sand, on a firebreak cut across the topographical crest of the hill. A cloud bank has settled over them. Visibility is nil; their NVGs, which use ambient light, are inoperable. It is cold and wet and quiet, the silence broken only by the beep and crackle of the SINCGARS radios.

The time is zero one thirty hours. According to intelligence, there is a company-minus, about 150 men, of Orangeland forces dug in around the two key crossroads in the valley below, just to the northeast of No Name Hill, fifteen hundred meters away as the crow flies. Scout/sniper reports have the enemy armed with AK-47 rifles, light and medium machine guns, and 82mm mortars. Based upon documents taken from the body of a notionally dead officer (members of the One-Four's H&S company, headquarters and service, are playing the role of the enemy), there is reason to believe that the Orangeland forces, members of the dictator's elite Revolutionary Guard, will attempt to hold their positions at all costs.

Though the original frag order tasked Bravo Company as the main effort of the attack, it has become clear that the plan is no longer viable. Not apparent on the contour map was the fact that the north-east face of No Name Hill is a sheer cliff. There is no way Sinclair is going to order a company of green marines down the side without rap-pelling systems. Likewise, the firebreak is useless as an avenue of approach; cut by giant bulldozers, one hundred feet wide, that piece of terrain is completely exposed—the face sloping down gradually onto the objective like a ski run.

Because they're here to learn how to think on the fly, Sinclair has ordered Ralston to recast the attack, a laborious process that began with Ralston—owing to the blackout conditions in effect—lying for a time beneath his rain poncho, his red-lensed flashlight in one hand, a pen in the other, writing up formal orders for the new attack, composing sentences such as: o/o ATK TO DESTROY EN VIC BN OBJ 4. Once com-pleted, the orders were disseminated via radio down the chain of com-mand. Upon receiving his orders, each marine made a few notes for himself in his olive-drab journal, part of his required gear.

The new play goes like this: Charlie Company, down in the valley, formerly the supporting effort, becomes the main effort in the attack. It will move across the desert floor, around the bottom of No Name Hill, then turn left in a bent-L formation. Upon seeing the signal flare—a green double star burst—it will attack the enemy's flank. Bravo Company will remain on No Name Hill in a support-by-fire position. In addition, Sinclair has called up the CAAT platoon, the Combined Anti-Armor Team, a motorized unit comprising Humvee-mounted .50-caliber machine guns and wire-guided TOW missile launchers.

While Charlie Company moves into its new position—difficult in the dark without NVGs, foot mobile at the excruciatingly slow rate of five hundred meters an hour through the difficult terrain—Sinclair and his men hunker down on the firebreak atop No Name Hill, a dark circle of faceless shadows enveloped in a fine, cold mist.

Lounging against his assault pack, Sinclair's camies beneath his flak vest are sopping with sweat. He's cold and tired, and his knees ache. He's "dawggone friggin' miserable"; he's happy as he can be. This is what he signed up for. He's glad he chose to go out on the Jump tonight, down and dirty with the men, the more miserable the better, commanding with his eyes instead of a radio handset. There's a purity to being in the field. It helps you keep your edge. It helps you keep your sense of perspective. You learn not to take your lifestyle and your freedoms for granted. You learn not to care so much about what year the wine was bottled, what brand of clothing you wear, all that horse-shit that people think is oh-so-civilized. Being out here, you learn to appreciate the simple things, like just how great it is to sit on a toilet to take a dump.

Over the years, Sinclair has endured conditions much worse than these. He's been in the desert in Kuwait, 130 degrees. He's looked into the eyes of starving infants in Somalia. He's rescued civilians from the American embassy in Rwanda. And he's seen men die; he's written impotent letters home to inconsolable mothers after a firefight with Somali thugs in pickup trucks. It's bad out here tonight on No Name Hill, but it's not so bad. In real-world time, he's a thirty-minute drive from home. Come tomorrow evening, he'll be in his living room with Jessie for their fifth wedding anniversary—the first such celebration he's ever been able to attend.

"I read the other day that gas prices have gone up 149 percent in the last year," Sinclair says, trying to pass the time.

"The cost of living here has gotten to be more expensive than Hawaii," says Page, seated to Sinclair's left. His words come out a little slurry. He chides himself for not sleeping last night. He shakes his head, trying to rid the cobwebs.

"Guess there's no chance we're gettin' a raise anytime soon," Ralston says. Though no one can see it, he has his boot off, an instant ice pack on his badly swollen calf. He missed the last big exercise because of his surgery—if you can't do your job, the Marines will replace you. Someday Ralston would like to be in Sinclair's boots; this is too good a billet to let go because of a little pain. Or that's what he thought. Now the calf is throbbing. Could I be happy as a civilian? he asks him-self, only half kidding.

"The president has already submitted his supplemental budget this year, so we're looking at zero three at the earliest for any kind of COLA," Sinclair says, meaning cost-of-living adjustment, his wonkish side still apparent through his own physical exhaustion. Oddly missing from his encyclopedia of knowledge is the exact amount of his salary. For that information, you must see Jessie. He draws $72,000 a year, plus an additional $1,700 a month for food and housing.

"That's just peachy," Sergeant Major says. He pulls down about $45,000 a year, plus $1,500 a month for food and housing. "Maybe I'll trade in my car and get a beat-up old Volkswagen. Put the wife on the street corner."

"We won't quote you on that, Sergeant Major," Sinclair says.

"Definitely not," says Page.

"Even I don't go that far," Sergeant Major says. His voice softens, grows sentimental, like a guy talking to the bartender late at night. "There ain't none like her. She's mine. We have our times, but it wouldn't be no fun if there wasn't a little challenge."

"Damn," says Ralston. "The wind's kickin' up."

"I'm kinda hoping that stink is you and not me," Sergeant Major drawls. "You know it's time to take a shower when you can smell your own ass."

"Jeez-Louise, Sergeant Major!" Sinclair says. "Thanks for sharin'."

At zero three fifty atop No Name Hill, the rain has subsided; the clouds remain.

Sinclair and his men are on their feet now, helmeted shadows milling between two Humvees. Parked on the firebreak, on the crest of the hill, each of the four-wheel-drive vehicles is fitted with a TOW missile launcher and an infrared sight. In a few minutes, when the liquid nitrogen in the mechanism reaches a temperature of $^-318$ degrees, Sinclair will be able to look through a rubber-capped eyepiece and see the heat signatures of his otherwise-invisible foes, tiny red human forms in the valley far below. Mounted to turrets atop the roofs of the vehicles, the TOW sights emit a loudish ticking noise, a strangely familiar sound, like the timer on a heat lamp in a hotel bathroom.

"Spare a dip, Sergeant Major?"

"Sorry, Major Page, I'm plum out."

"What about you, OpsO?"

"I was just gonna ask you."

"Well, isn't this a fine damn thing," Sergeant Major says. He pauses a beat, thinking. A few days ago, back at Camp Horno—the One-Four's compound at Pendleton—Sergeant Major needed a sleeping bag for a reporter to take on the FEX. Informed by supply that the battalion was fresh out of sleeping bags, Sergeant Major ordered the lance corporal on the other end of the line to shit a sleeping bag posthaste. The bag was delivered in ten minutes.

Now, five days into the FEX, twelve hours into this movement, what Sergeant Major needs—what they all need—is a good whack of nicotine. He turns to Sinclair. "What about you, sir?"

Sinclair pulls off his right glove with his teeth, reaches into the pouch secured over the left side of his chest. He takes out his tin of Copenhagen, opens it. "A few dregs," he says, disappointed. Then he brightens. "Criminy! Check my assault pack!"

Sinclair turns his back and Sergeant Major unzips him, rummages carefully through his gear. Though entirely offhand, it is an intimate act. He comes out with a fresh tin. "You ain't been holdin' out on us now, sir, have you?"

"Pass it around, by all means!"

"An officer and a gentleman," Sergeant Major declares.

"Anything for my marines," Sinclair says. He looks around the loose circle of his men, the faceless shadowy figures so distinctly recognizable, even in the murky gloom. In boot camp there are no walls between the shitters in the latrine—that's how close you get to the other guys. And when you have to lead them, when your word is literally their command, well . . . it's hard to find a way to express it. Eight months into his tenure as the CO of the One-Four, Sinclair finds himself stepping back every now and then and thinking, Dawggone, I still can't believe I have this authority! You go through the years, gaining experience, working hard, moving up. And then one day you're the

Old Man. But you still feel like you; you're the same as always—a little bit afraid of fucking up. It makes you want to be careful. Not cautious, just more careful to consider things from every imaginable side. Bottom line is a most awesome fact: He has lives in his hands.

When he looks at one of his marines, Sinclair doesn't care what age or color he is, what MOS or billet he occupies. He doesn't care if he's a wrench turner down in the motor pool or one of his company commanders. If he didn't need that man in the One-Four, the Marine Corps wouldn't have assigned him. Every truck driver hauling water and chow to the grunts in the field; the comm guys running wire and maintaining the nets; the eighteen-year-old rifleman toting a 60mm mortar launcher over his shoulders, sucking on his water tube like a pacifier as he humps up a hill—they're all important to him as a commander. They all need to know that Sinclair's thinking, Hey, stud, I know that job may not seem fun or exciting, but I need your skills to make this whole thing work.

"So what do we do now?" asks Sergeant Major. He takes a pinch and passes it on. He's feeling better already.

"We could fight this little battle," says Ralston.

"I make it zero three fifty-nine," says Page, taking the tin from Ralston.

"I know," Sinclair says. He rubs his hands together greedily. "Who can we meritoriously promote?"

"Excellent idea, sir!" Sergeant Major says.

"How about Rivers?" suggests Page.

"He's ready?" asks Sinclair.

"Definitely, sir."

"What do you think, Colon?"

"Definitely, sir," says the radio operator, taking a dip, passing the tin.

"All right, good to go," Sinclair says, inserting his own pinch of dip between lip and gum. He steps up onto the fat tire of the Humvee, swings himself into the turret. "We'll just take care of business here," he calls down from his perch, "and then—"

Now there comes the distinct explosive pop of a flare, and everyone turns to see. A green double star burst, lovely and bright and sparkling, it floats down toward earth on its invisible parachute, as languid as an autumn leaf falling from a tree, illuminating the target below in surreal shades of magnesium green.

Down in the valley, Charlie Company opens fire. There is the crackle of small arms shooting blank rounds, clusters of bright muzzle flashes against the dark, the loud cacophony of voices that accompanies a firefight—men on both sides shouting orders and epithets as the battle is waged at close quarters.

Atop No Name Hill, fore and aft of the vehicles, platoons from Bravo Company are set along different elevations of the firebreak. As this is only an exercise, the budget for the FEX is limited. The men of Bravo Company have been told not to expend their blank rounds. They have humped ten difficult miles in the last twelve hours to get into position for this attack, through fields of cactus and thistles, up steep slopes and through ravines, weighted with myriad weapon systems and gear. They have shivered in their own sweat in the fine, cold rain, faces in the sand with the insects and the weeds, fighting boredom, dehydration, fatigue. They have done everything the Old Man has asked, and they have done it without question or excuse or complaint. On order, they open fire.

"Bang bang bang bang BANG!" they shout into the darkness, two hundred strong, every shape and color, all wearing the same haircuts and uniforms, their voices echoing across the valley, a shit-storm of simulated plunging fire raining down death upon Orangeland's elite Revolutionary Guard: "Bang bang bang bang BANG!"

By zero seven thirty, the enemy has been vanquished.

Dragon Jump and Bandit have humped down the firebreak, consolidated with Charlie Company. Together, they occupy Battalion Objectives Four and Five.

It is cool and overcast. The two key crossroads are little more than dirt trails etched through the valley. Sinclair and his men mill about. No

Name Hill looms above them, impossibly high from this vantage point, a scrubby, humpbacked ridge stippled with boulders, the firebreak running like a raw scar over the crest. Colon and Gray and the other enlisted are circled up, passing a rumpled menthol cigarette that Colon has found in his pack. Sinclair and Sergeant Major lean against a Humvee, shooting the shit with the battalion XO, the executive officer, Major Rich Weede. Thirty-seven years old, a graduate of VMI, Weede is Dragon Five to Sinclair's Dragon Six, responsible for many of the nuts-and-bolts issues of command. Since 1935, there has continuously been a Weede on active duty in the Marine Corps. His grandfather retired as a lieutenant general. His father retired as a colonel. His brother is a captain.

Sinclair has logged only about six hours of sleep over the last five days. His eyelids are sprung like window shades. His smile seems plastered onto his face. His knees feel disjointed, as if he's walking on eggshells. He feels thready and insubstantial, oddly gelatinous, a little queasy, as if he's treading water in a vitreous sea of adrenaline and dopamine, nicotine, and excess stomach acid. Now the drifting conversation has turned toward a mutual friend of Weede and Sinclair's, a retired officer.

"So he's got a beer distributorship?" Sinclair asks, his voice tight and forced.

"Every day he's gettin' invitations to fuckin' golf tournaments," Weede says, breaking out a couple of cheroot cigars.

"That's like the time I met this guy through my father-in-law," says Sergeant Major, accepting a cheroot, taking a bite. "He flies me down to Texas to play golf at his country club, and we played a round, and then he takes me over to his warehouse. He tells me how he's having problems with his employees, how he can't get them motivated. And then he says, 'Your father-in-law seems to think you're pretty good at that shit. You want a job? I'll make it well worth your while.' "

"I'd a friggin' asked how well," Sinclair says, taking a bite of his cheroot, working it down to his gum.

"That's like Gunner Montoya," Weede says, blowing a smoke ring. "He said he told the guy, 'I'm a marine gunner, I don't know a friggin' thing about this business.' And the guy tells him, 'You're a marine, you can manage this shit, trust me.' "

"The salary kicks up to a hundred grand after a year," Sergeant Major says. "He put in his papers this month."

"I can't even fathom that kinda money," Sinclair says. He looks off toward No Name Hill, shaking his head.

OpsO Ralston limps over, and Weede offers him a cheroot. "Time to head back to the barn, sir," Ralston says to Sinclair. It's a three-hour hump back to Camp Horno.

"We goin' up Sheepshit Hill, sir?" asks Sergeant Major.

"Only the best for my Devil Dogs!" Sinclair sings.

"They'll be back by this afternoon and too tired to bitch," drawls Sergeant Major. "Then they'll get up tomorrow all sore and thinking, Fuuuuuuuck! But come Sunday, their tune'll change. It'll be: That wasn't shit!"

"Twenty-four hours from now they'll be bragging about how tough it was," Sinclair says. He spits a stream, kicks some dirt over the wet spot.

"You know," Sergeant Major says. "I didn't sign up for infantry. I was gonna be a mechanic."

"Well, I did. All I ever wanted to be was a grunt."

"Then I guess all your dreams have come true, sir."

"Oo-rah, Sergeant Major."

On a sunny Sunday afternoon a few weeks later, Sinclair is sitting beneath a striped umbrella on the patio behind his house. He is barefoot, dressed in a tank top and surfer shorts. His face and neck are deeply tanned; his shoulders and legs are milky white. Even on his day off, he sports a fresh shave. In his mind, he's never off duty; he's a marine every hour of every day. He doesn't even go to Home Depot without shaving first. He has his whitewall-style haircut trimmed weekly, seven dollars a pop.

Sinclair was up early today, ripping out the roots of a tree in the front yard that had begun to encroach upon the sidewalk. For a tool he used an old bolo knife he bought in the Philippines when he was a second lieutenant. A short machete made from dense steel, the thing hasn't been sharpened in twenty years and it's still the best dawggone piece of cuttin' gear he's got. Now that the tree roots have been vanquished, Sinclair needs to repipe the irrigation in that area. Not to mention all the other chores. His tidy two-story house, decorated in earth tones, is filled with projects not yet completed: a partially painted wall, a set of dining-room chairs only half reupholstered. An epic list maker, he has yellow Post-its everywhere at home and at work. He's got a lot to do before January.

At home, Jessie is the idea guy; the Old Man is the grunt. When he comes through the front door, he always says, "Just tell me what to do. I don't want to make any decisions." Jessie and Bob met on a blind date eight years ago. He was a captain then, a company commander; her sister was dating his radio operator. They went to a Japanese restaurant. When he returned home that night, Bob looked in the mirror and told himself he had found the woman he was going to marry. Two days after their date, Jessie came down with the flu. Bob drove an hour to bring her some medicine. "I could tell right then he was a keeper," she says.

Jessie sees Bob as being tough in his professional life, yet very tender in his personal life. He is honest and sincere, a mature man with a lot of integrity, very different from other men, a grownup in every way. When she was laid up in the hospital before their son, Seth, was born, he took off work and camped out in the room with her for an entire week. Five years into their marriage, he still refers to her as "my bride."

Soon after they began dating, Bob went off on a six-month deployment. Jessie sent him care packages filled with Gummi Bears and pistachio nuts. They wrote letters every day. She didn't know where he was, exactly. Somewhere out on a ship. Bob is an awesome letter writer. He would write about what he did that day and how he was feeling about stuff. And then there were the romantic parts. Those were her favorite.

One night when he was on the float, Jessie's phone rang. It was Bob. "I just wanted to tell you I love you," he said casually, and Jessie thought, Uh-oh, I don't like the sound of this. Before he hung up, he mentioned that she should watch CNN the next day. Sure enough, there were the Marines, evacuating civilians from the embassy in Rwanda.

Following his deployment, Bob was transferred to Quantico, Virginia, for three years. The couple maintained a long-distance relationship, getting married along the way, holding their reception at the Japanese restaurant where they'd had their first date. Though she doesn't want to say it in so many words, Jessie is not looking forward to this deployment. Bob's been home now for a long stretch. She's used to having him around. He's funny, he's good company, he has sexy arms and a nice smile. He doesn't mind doing the vacuuming. He thinks everything she cooks is delicious. And though he's not much into television—not even sports—he's happy to sit with her and watch her shows: *Friends, Ed, The West Wing, ER, Malcolm in the Middle*. When he goes away, it's always hardest in the beginning. Then she bucks up and gets in the groove; she just kind of goes about her business. In time, she even starts to enjoy being on her own—pretty much, anyway. It's funny, but having Bob gone so much has taught her just how secure a person she really is. In that way, the Marine Corps has been good for her as well.

This time the float will be a little different for the Sinclairs. They'll have e-mail. And because he's the battalion commander and she's the Key Volunteer Adviser—informally in charge of overseeing all the dependents—he'll be calling her by telephone weekly.

The biggest difference, of course, is Seth, eighteen months old, a towhead like his mom. The first time Bob left for two weeks in the field, he came home and Seth wouldn't go to him. You could see it really crushed Bob. And now he'll be gone six months. He's seen kids hide from their dads when they return from a float; he's seen kids cower in fear. And Luke, her son by her first marriage, has grown close to Bob as well. Luke likes to tell the story of how Bob took him fishing for the first time. Luke caught a catfish that was this long. Actually, Bob helped. "But he told everyone I caught it myself," Luke says proudly.

With everyone out of the house for a while, Sinclair is taking some time to reflect, a little reluctantly, on his career. He rocks back and forth gently in his chair. "This is probably going to sound like propaganda," he says, taking the opportunity, in his family's absence, to indulge himself in a dip, "but my primary motivation for being a marine is that I love this country. I feel that being born in this country is a privilege. Right, wrong, or indifferent, this is still the greatest country in the world. All you have to do is travel to figure that one out. I thank the good Lord that we have a lot of great men and women in this country who feel the same way as I feel, who are willing to make that ultimate sacrifice for what they believe in. None of us wants to die. But we know if we have to, it's for the greatest reasons.

"I have to admit that becoming a dad, especially this late in life, has completely changed me. When you're younger, it was like, Okay, if you die, you can leave your parents behind, or your brothers. That would be sad, but you know, you can kind of accept that. Once you get married, you're kinda like, Hmmm. But you can justify that, too. The wife's an adult, she's intelligent, she's beautiful, she can get on with life. But then all of a sudden you've got that child. I never understood it until Seth was born and lying there in the hospital weighing two pounds, not knowing whether he was going to live or die. And I just looked at him and said, 'This is a life that we've created and that I'm responsible for.' His entire hand could grab around the knuckle of my little finger when he squeezed."

He rocks in his chair; he is a man who is seldom at rest, who wakes up at full speed and doesn't stop until he shuts his eyes, whereupon he falls instantly into a deep, untroubled sleep, as he did on the couch after the FEX, on the night of his anniversary. At least he made it through dinner.

Birds sing in the trees. A lawn mower drones, echoing through the cul-de-sac. The grass in his backyard is lush and green; the fence line is planted with riotous bougainvillea, rich shades of red and purple and pink. An old dog naps at his feet. A small fountain gurgles at the back corner of the lot. "I know this float is going to be tough," Sinclair says.

"But it's like anything else. We'll get on that ship, we'll do what we have to do, and then we'll come back, and life will continue to move on. That'll be six months you can never make up, but what we do as marines is that important. Nobody wrenches your arm to sign that contract. These men do this on their own. They all know the risks. That's why leading them is just an honor beyond belief.

"I am loyal to the corps, but my family is more important to me. If you take it in order, I'd say it's God, country, family, and then way down at number four on the list is the Marine Corps. That's not insulting the corps; it's just that the bottom line is that someday the corps is gonna kick every one of us out. Even the commandant of the Marine Corps is gonna retire, and they're gonna say, 'Thank you very much for all your years of service, General, but it's time to move on.' They're gonna do the same to me. They always say we're here to train our own replacements. There will always be plenty of great people to take my place. But my family will always be there for me. I mean, I'll probably be up for colonel soon. But with our family situation—the fact that, you know, Jessie can't leave the state to share custody of Luke . . ." His voice trails off. "I'd hate to leave the corps, but I can't leave my family and become a geographical bachelor again."

He spits a stream of brownish juice onto the lawn. "The bottom line comes down to this: It's hard to put into words. It's more like a feeling. You feel it, and you know it's right. It's like trying to explain morals or religion or love. The Marine Corps exists to fight and win America's battles, to help keep our country free. It sounds corny, I suppose. But like they say, somebody's got to do it. I guess one of those somebodies is me."

September 2001: Sinclair is at his desk at Camp Horno. There is a heightened security aboard the base, but training continues as normal. Sinclair's deuce gear and his flak vest and his helmet lie in a heap in the corner of the small room. His M9 side arm, holstered, is atop his desk.

On September 11, upon waking to the horrific news from the East Coast, Sinclair called his XO, Major Weede, and told him he was going to stay put for a while and watch the events unfold on television. He felt a need to be home with his family. He also knew he didn't have to hurry to the base; it takes a long time to plan military action, Sinclair points out. The Japanese bombed Pearl Harbor on December 7, 1941. The first ground offensive by U.S. forces against the Japanese didn't occur until August 7, 1942, when the 1st Marine Division—the division that includes Sinclair's One-Four—invaded Guadalcanal.

Come January, however, or whenever Sinclair and his 13th MEU (SOC) steam out into the WestPac, things will probably be much different. The kind of campaign they're talking about is the kind the One-Four has been trained to undertake. With the threat of war, perhaps a sustained one, Bob and Jessie Sinclair must put their worries about career and future and geographical bachelorhood aside. There is no doubt about the order of his priorities at a time like this.

"It's one of those things where you train your whole life for something you hope you never actually have to execute. But I think there's something primal about each one of us marines. If we're at war, you want to be in the operating forces. You don't want to be sitting on the sidelines. This is what we do. This is what we're trained for.

"The initial thing I felt, seeing that plane fly into the tower, seeing the pictures of the Pentagon, was absolute anger. You realize that your country has been attacked. That is a deep, deep wound, a sharp slap to the face. You wanna strike back. But at the same time you have to keep your head. You know that you've got this whole system in place. There are politicians and diplomats. In a way, you're angry deep down inside your gut, but you're also in realization that, okay, there are people who are much smarter than me, and they are in charge, and I completely trust their leadership. As a member of the military, I'm here to support and implement whatever decision they make.

"Like the president said, 'Get ready.' Well, we are ready. This battalion is ready right now. We'll do what needs to be done."

from **Jarhead**

by Anthony Swofford

Anthony Swofford served as a lance corporal in a USMC scout/sniper platoon during the first Gulf War. He published his memoir in 2003.

his is war, I think. I'm walking through what my father and his father walked through—the epic results of American bombing, American might. The filth is on my boots. I am one of a few thousand people who will walk this valley today. I am history making. Whether I live or die, the United States will win this war. I know that the United States will win any war it fights, against any country. If colonialism weren't out of style, I'm sure we'd take over the entire Middle East, not only safeguard the oil reserves, but take the oil reserves: *We are here to announce that you no longer own your country, thank you for your cooperation, more details will follow.*

Our rucks are heavy with equipment and ammunition but even heavier with the burdens of history, and each step we take, the burdens increase.

The sky is a dead gray from the oil fires billowing to the north. We hump and hump and look at one another with blank, amazed faces. Is this what we've done? What will I tell my mother?

Troy says to me, "I feel sorry for these poor bastards. They didn't have a chance."

We stop for a water break. A few feet behind me a bombed jeep sits on the road. A corpse is at the wheel, sitting erect, looking serious, seeming almost to squint at the devastation, the corpse's face not unlike our faces—what has happened? Bombs, bombs, big bombs and small bombs, all of them filled with explosives meant to kill you! On either side of the jeep, more corpses, two near me, one not, all belly to the desert, as if they were running from the bomb—as if running would've helped. The back sides of the corpses are charred and decaying, the bottom halves buried in the sand, the sand wind-smeared like cake icing against the bodies, and I wonder if the bottom halves of the men are still living, buried by the mirage, unaware that death lurks above. Maybe the men are screaming into the earth, living their half lives, hoping to be heard. What would they tell me? *Run.*

I assume the men were screaming before the A-10 or A-6 dropped its bombs. But maybe they were on their way to Kuwait City for supplies, and it was evening and the men neither saw nor heard the plane that dropped on them. Perhaps one of the men was telling a dirty joke or repeating a rumor he'd heard about the major's wife. But they must have been screaming. I hear them now.

We continue walking. Cortes is having trouble. He's complaining, asking how much farther until we get there, is it over yet, where are the trucks? He still doesn't understand that this is war, not boot camp. As a recruit you can cry about your blisters and occasionally convince a sergeant that even though you are a worthless malingerer and you need a truck to carry you the rest of the way this time, you'll make the next hump. I want to say to Cortes, "This might be the last hump you're ever on, you might die soon. Don't you want to hump hard and long and make all of us proud of you for finally carrying yourself?" But I know that inverse logic could just as easily be applied, and probably is being applied, by Cortes: "This might be my last hump ever, I might die soon, so why not ask for a truck? I'd rather take a ride to my death than be forced to walk my way there." I will not be surprised if Cortes sits down during the next water break and refuses to continue.

My body is sore. My feet are burning, though I will not blister because, as though my feet were made for the Marine Corps grunts, I never do; in the past I have walked forty miles straight without a blister. But my shoulders feel as though fires have been lit on them. My crotch is sweaty and rancid and bleeding. I can feel sand working into the wound. My knees are sore and my back and even my toes hurt, but I will not stop until I'm told to. The sniper rifle, fourteen pounds, is heavy in my fists. I think of the M16 broken down in my ruck, 7.78 pounds, and I again run through a gear manifest in my head, making sure that everything in my ruck is absolutely necessary. Along the road jarheads have discarded pairs of boots and socks and cammies, porn magazines they didn't throw away before, when ordered to, a white-gas stove, a shaving-gear bag. Jettison it if it will not save you.

We stop for chow. I eat the powdered cocoa and dehydrated pears from my MRE and give the main meal, spaghetti, to Dettmann. I put my crackers in my cargo pocket, saving them for later when I will need salt. We are in a slight draw, and I walk up the rise in order to shit in private.

On the other side of the rise, bodies and vehicles are everywhere. The wind blows. I assume this is what remains of an Iraqi convoy that had stopped for the night. Twelve vehicles—eight troop carriers and four supply trucks—are in a circle. Men are gathered dead around what must have been their morning or evening fire. This is disturbing, not knowing what meal they were eating. I am looking at an exhibit in a war museum. But there are no curators, no docents, no benefactors with their names chiseled into marble. The benefactors wish to remain anonymous.

Two large bomb depressions on either side of the circle of vehicles look like the marks a fist would make in a block of clay. A few men are dead in the cabs of the trucks, and the hatch of one troop carrier is open, bodies on bodies inside it. The men around the fire are bent forward at the waist, sitting dead on large steel ammunition boxes. The corpses are badly burned and decaying, and when the wind shifts up the rise, I smell and taste their death, like a moist rotten sponge shoved into my mouth. I vomit into my mouth. I swish the vomit around before expelling it, as though it will cover the stink and taste of the dead men. I walk toward the fire circle. There is one vacant ammunition box, the dead man felled to the side. I pull my crackers from my pocket. I spit into the fire hole and join the circle of the dead. I open my crackers. So close to it, on top of it, I barely notice the hollow smell of death. The fire looks to be many days old, sand and windswept. Six tin coffee cups sit among the remains of the fire. The men's boots are cooked to their feet. The man to my right has no head. To my left, the man's head is between his legs, and his arms hang at his sides like the burnt flags of defeated countries. The insects of the dead are swarming. Though I can make out no insignia, I imagine that the man across from me commanded the unit, and that when the bombs landed, he was in the middle of issuing a patrol order, *Tomorrow we will kick some American ass.*

It would be silly to speak, but I'd like to. I want to ask the dead men their names and identification numbers and tell them this will soon end. They must have questions for me. But the distance between the living and the dead is too immense to breach. I could bend at the waist, close my eyes, and try to join these men in their tight dead circle, but I am not yet one of them. I must not close my eyes.

The sand surrounding me is smoky and charred. I feel as though I've entered the mirage. The dead Iraqis are poor company, but the presence of so much death reminds me that I'm alive, whatever awaits me to the north. I realize I may never again be so alive. I can see everything and nothing—this moment with the dead men has made my past worth living and my future, always uncertain, now has value.

Over the rise I hear the call to get on the road. I hear my name, two syllables. Troy is calling, and now Johnny, and Troy again. I throw my crackers into the gray fire pit. I try, but I cannot speak. I taste my cocoa-and-pears vomit.

I join my platoon on the other side.

We hump until past dark and form a combat bivouac within about two hundred yards of ten burning oil wells. The flames shoot a hundred feet into the air, fiery arms groping after a disinterested God. We can also hear the fires, and they sound like the echoes from extinct beasts bellowing to reenter the living world. We can feel the heat. We begin to dig individual prone shelters—shallow, gravelike pits, effective protection against small arms and artillery.

Kuehn is especially aggravated by the fires and the constant petrol rain. He asks Johnny if we can use ponchos to build a lean-to of some sort, or if he can sleep under a five-ton. Johnny refuses both requests, and Kuehn begins to scream, he tries to speak, but he's making no sense, flipping out, speaking a lost language of fear.

Kuehn is a large man, and Johnny is small, even gentle, but Johnny grasps Kuehn's shoulders and shakes him, yelling, "Wake up, Kuehn, come back to me. Come back to us. This is war, baby this is your war."

Kuehn laughs. "Goddamn, you know I'm here to fight. I just want to get the hell out of this oil." He collapses into the desert. I throw my poncho over him, and I dig his shallow shelter and coax him in.

The oil fires burn and moan all night. The petrol rain falls, and *Gas* is called two or three times, and finally I fall asleep with my gas mask on, a good way to die, but I don't.

The next morning I awake with my gas mask stuck to my face. I peel the mask away, and despite the fires, the morning air is fresh and cool against my skin. Because the moisture inside the mask may have tainted my filters, I replace them.

Johnny and I are attached to Fox Company in order to take part in 3/7's assault on Ahmed Al Jaber Airfield. The remainder of our battalion is supposed to rendezvous with trucks or troop carriers and join the attack in progress. Johnny and I drive with Fox Company in five-tons. The grunts aren't supposed to like us, and they don't. The goodwill that the Golf Company sergeant showed us is many days in the past. We jump on the truck and the grunts eye our rifles with suspicion and disdain, unconvinced that our weapons and our training are superior to theirs. I consider their weapons to be rather filthy and the men themselves are filthy, and of course I'm filthy too, but my weapon is clean, and I cannot see myself.

I've missed riding five-tons, something I haven't done since joining STA Platoon because we use Humvees. The big, hulky trucks offer an expansive view of the desert, and the same destruction I saw yesterday from ground level is spread out for me in a 360-degree panorama. Death is everywhere at once. The shells of troop carriers and tanks burn, flames rising from the vehicles in a profane tribute to the dead men. Bodies litter the desert as though the men were in a great crowd, chanting with fists raised as they waited for their deaths. Everyone on the five-ton shares the same view, but none of us has anything to say to the others. It's as though we want to keep the carnage to ourselves.

As we drive in the tactical convoy toward the airfield, we occasionally pass a POW internment area, nothing more than a few-hundred-foot circle of concertina wire, and in the center a mass of surrendered men, constrained with plastic thumb cuffs. Marines walk the perimeter with M16s. We drive close enough to the wire so that I see the faces of the POWs, and the men look at us and smile. Occasionally an embarrassing scene of thanks unfolds as a detainee is processed, the detainee kneeling in front of his once enemy and now jailor, weeping and hugging the marine's legs. I suspect the performances are equal parts genuine and dramatic, men genuinely happy at the prospect of not dying and smart enough to please their fierce and potentially deadly jailors with an act of supplication.

It's easier to surrender than to accept surrender. The men who surrender do so with blind faith in the good hearts and justice of the men and the system they surrender to. They are faithful and faith is somewhat easy. Those who accept the surrendering men must follow the rules of justice. This requires not faith, but labor and discipline.

I feel more compassion for the dead Iraqi soldiers I witnessed yesterday than I do for these men, alive and waving the propaganda pamphlets with vigor and a smile as they await processing. These live men were my enemy just before surrendering, while the dead men are quite simply dead. Moments before surrendering, these incarcerated men might have tried to kill me, so until very recently they were capable of receiving my bullets. The dead men have been incapable of killing me for days or weeks or at least hours and so I would not have shot them. When I'd considered my enemy in the past, I'd been able to imagine them as men similar to me, similarly caught in a trap of their own making, but now that I see these men breathing and within arm's reach, witness them smiling and supplicating and wanting to be my friend, *my friend,* even as I am on my way to kill their fellow soldiers, I no longer care for the men or their safety or the cessation of combat. The enemy are caught in an unfortunate catch-22, in that I care for them as men and fellow unfortunates as long as they are not within riflesight or they're busy being dead, but as soon as I see them living, I wish to turn upon them my years of training and suffering, and I want to perform some of the despicable acts I've learned over the prior few years, such as trigger-killing them from one thousand yards distant, or gouging their hearts with my sharp bayonet.

We dismount the trucks two klicks from the airfield. The lieutenant we've been assigned to doesn't know how to use snipers, so Johnny advises him. This problem is common—grunt officers know a sniper might be a good thing to have on the battlefield, but what can they do with the sniper and that fancy rifle? The lieutenant's dilemma is understandable, because he must first decide how to deploy his own grunts. Johnny and I want to be as far away from the grunts as possible. Grunts get antsy and kill the wrong people, just like tankers. Johnny points out a nearby rise to the lieutenant and tells him we'll be there and gives him our freq and our call name.

The lieutenant asks, "What will you do, Corporal?"

Johnny says, "Sir, we will call in air and arty if you need it, and we'll tell you what we see, if anything. We will eliminate targets of opportunity. Sir, we will save you if you need saving."

We hitch a ride nearer the rise with two combat engineers. They're in a Humvee with enough C4 in the back to blow a hole the size of

Mecca in anything. The engineers are proud of the work they did at the minefield, as they should be, and they are prepared to detonate a path all the way to Baghdad. The driver has written, on the back of his Kevlar helmet, COMBAT ENGINEERS BLOW YOUR MIND.

Johnny and I dig a shallow hide and settle in for the afternoon. The air control tower is our main target of interest. I read it at eight hundred yards and Johnny agrees. Distance estimation cannot be taught. You can show a marine a target and tell him that it's five hundred yards from him, but unless that five hundred yards is felt, he'll believe you but he'll never know for sure how you came up with that figure; he'll believe you but he won't know. He'll say, I have no idea how you figured that out, it looks like five thousand yards to me, or fifty. He can stare all day at that target and never understand. And another marine, you can tell him that it's five hundred yards away and he'll say, I knew that. This is the marine you want next to you, the marine who understands distance.

We prepare both weapons in the hide, Johnny behind the .50 and me behind the M40A1. That .50 is so damn heavy, and Johnny humped it twenty miles yesterday, that I want him to shoot it as payoff for his labor. We're above the grunts, northeast of the airfield, and we wait for the battle to unfold. The wind has shifted so that the entire area is blanketed with the thick, dark smoke from the burning wells. Occasional brown pockets of lucidity are available, and they offer a scene of devastation, the landing strip pocked with bomb depressions and disabled vehicles and corpses. The grunts from Fox Company dig their temporary shelters to the south of us. The sporadic radio traffic tells me that to our northwest the other marine task forces are engaged in tank battles and occasional firefights with foot infantry.

A recon platoon is situated south of the airfield and 3/7 is entrenched to the east. The Iraqis at the airfield sporadically fire artillery, with their usual lack of precision. *Gas* is called twice and we put our masks on, but by now it has become a chore rather than a lifesaving necessity. I know that within minutes the all-clear will be announced, and I wonder if it isn't the same prick calling *Gas* every time, just for the fun of it.

Enemy soldiers are moving inside the air control tower. An argument is occurring between two commanders. They point at each other's face and gesture toward the enemy troops, us, and I'm sure one man wants to fight and die and the other man wants to not fight and not die. The men scuffle, and their troops pull them apart.

I request permission to take shots. The men in the tower are perfect targets. The windows are blown out of the tower, and the men are standing, and I know that I can make a headshot. Johnny has already called the dope for the shot. He thinks I can take two people out in succession, the commander who wants to fight and one of his lieutenants. He thinks that the remaining men in the tower will surrender plus however many men are under that command, perhaps the entire defensive posture at the airfield.

The Fox CO tells me over their freq, *Negative, Sierra Tango One— break. Negative on permission to shoot—break. If their buddies next to them—break—start taking rounds in the head—break—they won't surrender, copy.*

I reply, *Roger, roger.* I want to say, *Fuck you, sir, copy.*

I know the opposite of the captain's assertion is true, that when you're sitting in a tower and your neighbor's head becomes a gushing wound, his new wound will be the proper motivation for retrieving the white towel and the propaganda pamphlets from your ruck.

I can't help but assume that certain commanders, at the company level, don't want to use us because they know that two snipers with two of the finest rifles in the world and a few hundred rounds between them will in a short time inflict severe and debilitating havoc on the enemy, causing the entire airfield to surrender. The captains want some war, and they must know that the possibilities are dwindling. The captains want war just as badly as we do. And also, the same as us, the captains want no war, but here it is, and when you're a captain with a company to command and two snipers want to take a dozen easy shots and try to call it a day, of course you tell them no, because you are a captain and you have a company of infantry and what you need is some war ink spilled on your Service Record Book.

The combat engineers blow two breaches in the eastern fence line, and as the dark oil-fire smoke gets darker, and the sky blackens like midnight even though it's only seventeen hundred, the infantry assault companies enter the airfield and we watch. We watch the grunts moving like mules, we watch the smoke, and we hear the resulting confusion, over the freq. The infantry take more rocket and artillery rounds, and it sounds as though a few grunts have shot one another, that one fire team rounded a corner of a building and shot up their buddies, because they couldn't see to know that the movement they heard came from their own platoon. *Gas* is called again, and again we put our masks on, but we don't believe.

At the fence line nearest us, a platoon of Iraqis appears, waving white towels and smiling. There's no one there to accept them, and the men push themselves against the fence, as rioters might at a soccer match, but the soccer match is behind the men and what they are looking for is nowhere to be found. The men sit and stretch out in the sand, as though the war is over.

No one has called Johnny and me for many hours. The airfield assault continues and the fence-line platoon of surrendering Iraqis remains, some of the men smoking casually and eating canned rations. Because I'm angry and frustrated over being forgotten and ignored, I tell Johnny I want to shoot one of the Iraqis, and I spend half an hour hopping from head to head with my crosshairs, yelling, *Bang, bang, you're a dead fucking Iraqi.*

We hear medevac requests over the freq, and mortars are called in to support the grunts, and in a few more hours the assault is over and I've remained a spectator.

The rest of our battalion and platoon arrive at the secure airfield at 2200. The oil fires have decreased visibility and rendered our night-vision devices worthless, and the commanders have made the smart realization that marines who can't see can't fight, or they end up fighting the wrong people, each other, and there has been enough of that already. We sleep amidst an occasional volley of friendly and enemy artillery and again more calls of *Gas*. The only real excitement occurs when the first call of gas comes and Cortes's team is in their Humvee, playing poker. Cortes can't find his gas mask, and he jumps from the vehicle and runs in circles, screaming that he's going to die, and we tell him to stop running and to stop screaming and especially to stop breathing so that he can share a mask with someone until they find his. Finally, Dickerson tackles him and forces his gas mask over Cortes's face, if for nothing else to quiet him. Welty finds Cortes's mask, on the floor of the vehicle, right in front of Cortes's poker seat. Perhaps Cortes has been dreaming for days, putting his mask on and taking it off in somnambulistic splendor, only to be rudely awakened and shocked by this last call of *Gas gas gas!* Cortes has slept through so many training cycles and firewatch duties, there's no reason he wasn't sleeping the war away.

The gas calls continue throughout the night, and because we have nothing better to do, we continue to don and clear.

Though we've been running over the enemy or allowing them to surrender by the hundreds, our final destination is Kuwait City and the commanders insist that the fight for the city will be long and vicious, a protracted house-clearing mission costing many thousands of casualties and much heartache and countless widows and sad mothers of America.

The morning after we bivouac at the airfield, Johnny and I are deployed via Humvee to a hide. Our position is in a corridor about twenty klicks north of the airfield (and the rest of the battalion) and ten klicks west of the Burqan oil fields. Another STA team is ten klicks south of us. Our mission is to call for fire on armor or troops in our area and to snipe officers if they present themselves for such treatment. We spend the day dialing theater-wide freqs and listening to jarheads and army doggies getting a little bit of fight at various other locations.

Most of these engagements are either armor to armor, air to armor, or artillery and air dropped on the occasional holdout of enemy infantry. Johnny and I talk about what has kept those enemy soldiers fighting, and we decide that it's probably the same thing keeping us in the fight—pride, bravery, stupidity, fear. As we talk throughout the day and listen to the war unfold on the radio and watch the movement of U.S. troops across massive swaths of desert that until just hours before had been controlled by the Iraqi army, we think the war is ending. We sit and watch and listen, and in the silent stretches between our talking I feel not like a brave and proud and stupid man, but a lucky man, who showed up at the war a boy, with enough training to keep him just ahead of the battle and enough sense to keep him somewhat detached, because the war has been mine to fight but not mine to win or lose, and I know that none of the rewards of victory will come my way, because there are no rewards, not on the field of battle, not for the man who fights the battle—the rewards accrue in places like Washington, D.C., and Riyadh and Houston and Manhattan, south of 125th Street, and Kuwait City.

The fighting man receives tokens—medals, ribbons, badges, promotions, combat pay, abrogation of taxes, a billet to Airborne School—worthless bits of nothing, as valuable as smoke.

Johnny and I listen to the war drone on until all of our batteries die.

The next morning we are supposed to be extracted by Humvee, but the vehicle never shows, and at 0700 we begin patrolling on foot toward what should be the new battalion CP coordinates. We are concerned over the absence of our extraction team, and then, as though to confirm that a slaughter of our battalion has occurred, a squad of enemy tanks moves across the horizon. We kneel in the sand as the tanks head slowly north, and there is nothing for us to do but watch.

I imagine a possible horror—as we took turns sleeping and watching the empty desert, our unit was slaughtered by a renegade enemy force, and Johnny and I will arrive to a mass of fatalities, the only two marines living from a battalion of a thousand men. Who will carry the standard now? Johnny looks afraid, as he did just a few nights prior, as we crawled the rise, ready to engage the enemy who'd shot at us with rockets.

He says, "Swoffie, I don't like this. I've never not had a pickup. Dunn wouldn't allow it. He'd run out here and carry us back on his skinny fucking shoulders."

"Maybe they gave Cortes the map and compass."

"Even Cortes would find us. It's nearly a straight shot. Lock and load. Let's go find out what the fuck."

Johnny assembles his M203 and me my M16 and we fasten our sniper rifles to our bodies with slings.

We patrol tactically the entire route to the assumed battalion coordinates. We speak only in hand signals—Halt, Eyes Right, Decrease Speed, Increase Speed, Shift Right, Shift Left, I Do Not Understand. We are once again undergunned and out of support, two flabby, worthless tits left to jiggle in the wind, most alone in this widest and darkest of lands. I imagine the scene back at battalion, all of my mates dead and dying. I imagine the dubious fame that will come to Johnny and me, the last bearers of the standard: 2/7 is dead. Tell it to the commandant. After such atrocities units are disbanded and marines are banned from mentioning the ghost battalions.

It takes us about three hours to move within two hundred meters of the draw where the battalion should be bivouacked. By 1000 they're supposed to be en route to the next fight or at least packed and ready to roll. But we don't encounter them during the patrol, we don't come upon anyone. We dump our packs and sniper rifles at the bottom of the rise and low-crawl up it. All I can see ahead of me is sand and sky, still some smoke from the oil fires, but more blue than I've seen in weeks. The sand is warm against my body. Johnny pauses and loads a grenade into his breech. I've been on burst the entire patrol, and my finger is still on the trigger, sweating against the trigger.

Nearer the top of the rise we hear music and screaming, and Johnny thinks it must be a trick, a ploy, and we continue slowly, prepared for the worst, prepared for an assault or to witness the results of a great atrocity. We crawl to the top of the rise, and on the other side we see

Headquarters & Support Company 2/7 behaving as if they're on liberty. Men are lying naked on sleeping pads, soaking up the sun that bursts between the gray smoke clouds. Weapons and rucks and uniforms are strewn about the camp. Two men throw a football back and forth. A poker game is full of players, and a crowd of bettors surrounds the makeshift card table, the losers arguing as each hand ends. Two gas masks, impaled upon metal fence posts, face us—oh, dreadful but magical skulls!

Johnny and I sit and watch the company live what two days ago, two hours ago, two minutes ago, would've been our wild and dangerous fantasy. We're unable to move, our legs stuck beneath us as under a great weight. We must continue our last bit of war—we know what the commotion means, why First Sergeant Martinez is handing out cigars and dancing shirtless and playing a kazoo when he isn't smoking his cigar, and we know why he's allowing Jimi Hendrix to pipe through the comm towers. But Johnny and I stay on the rise, we sit for an hour or ten minutes or half an hour or all day, watching men we know and love celebrate the end of our little war.

Eventually, I put my rifle on safe, and Johnny removes the grenade from his weapon—he shuts the breech and the sound is like an iron door closing on history. We descend the rise, and the first sergeant is the first to greet us, smiling broadly, and in his face I see his family and the happiness of a family man, this from a marine I've never seen happy except while insulting or degrading a subordinate, and he says to us, "Oh, fuck, you guys got stuck out there, didn't you? I had Siek drive the colonel up north for a look-see. Sorry, guys, you crazy snipers, you crazy bastards, but the war is over, the motherfucker is over." And he slaps us both upon the back and shoves cigars in our faces.

We make our way to the STA area, where everyone apologizes for leaving us out there, but they really did run short of vehicles because of the mad rush of staff officers up to Kuwait City to view the victory. And they are so happy on peace that Johnny and I don't care, we call them bastards and sons of bitches for making us run a tactical patrol for eight klicks without communication while the goddamn war was over, but we really don't care.

The music plays throughout the day, Hendrix, the Stones, the Who, music from a different war. Ours is barely over but we begin to tell stories already. Remember that time. Remember when. Can you believe?

I wonder if we're being fooled. I want to read the news in a newspaper, or hear it on the radio. So much information is bad information.

But by nightfall, after I've heard Siek tell us about the happy civilians he saw on the outskirts of Kuwait City, I begin to believe. Siek has acquired a stack of wooden pallets from an ammunition dump. We douse the pallets with diesel and light a fire, and we gather in a circle around the flames. We have nothing special to cook and only water to drink, but we have our stories, and these go on for some time. The stories will never end.

Because we don't have liquor, my platoon mates celebrate by chewing tobacco, perhaps the only marine vice I haven't acquired. Atticus swears to me I'll get a buzz, and I realize that I want a buzz, or anything to fill the onset of a nameless emptiness. I try a mouthful of the dark, musty leaves. I chew and suck on the leaves, forming them into a tight ball. My lips and gums go numb. I spit into the fire a few times, just as my mates, and I do feel a good buzz. I swallow some of my spit. I close my eyes, the world spins, and I fall slowly backward off my ammunition box, onto my back. I roll over onto my hands and knees. No one notices me. Their war stories march through my brain like a parade of epileptics. My stomach turns. I vomit. It feels as though I'm regurgitating the last seven months of my life. This is how I welcome the peace.

We spend a few weeks in Kuwait, clearing bunkers, and this is where I will become intimate with the detritus and almost kill myself.

STA 2/7 is ordered to clear three large enemy positions, one artillery and two entrenched infantry. Our mission is to empty the bunkers and trenches of weapons and equipment and especially to look for chemical weapons and any intelligence that might be considered relevant to the debriefing. We know that the only things relevant to the debriefing are the corpses.

The count of the dead: many of them, many fewer of us. This is a good count, these are good numbers. Let's go home.

The cleanup mission is a freelance operation. We gear up in our three Humvees and head out each morning from the battalion bivouac, and the captain only wants to hear from us if something goes wrong, if we engage a sleepy enemy platoon, a group of men who missed the great assault, or if a munitions cache explodes or someone steps on a mine.

We gleefully run through the enemy positions, noting the hundreds of different ways a man might die when five-hundred-pound bombs are dropped on his weakly fortified position or when his tank or troop carrier is blown nearly inside out. Some of the corpses in the bunkers are hunched over, hands covering their ears, as though they'd been patiently waiting. Maggots and whatever other insects enjoy a corpse are busy with the decaying remains. Near some positions shallow graves have been dug. I hope that at the end of the day the casualties were gathered and buried with honor or at least respect. In some positions corpses are stacked on one another, and bottom to top one can tell the stage of decay, a reeking calendar of death. In one bunker I see three different stages of decay on three different corpses, which leads me to believe that the men died at different times, and that the last man alive in the bunker spent a few or many days waiting to die near his two death-bloated friends. I can't understand why he didn't bury the men or at least move them from his bunker, but maybe they were a comfort, a cold comfort—helping him to know his end so intimately, sleeping next to it and smelling it and waiting. Many of the men in the bunkers seem to have died not from shrapnel but concussion, and dried, discolored blood gathers around their eyes and ears and nose and mouth, no obvious trauma to their bodies. A few weeks into the air campaign the United States began employing the daisy-cutter bomb, a weapon originally used in Vietnam to clear helicopter landing zones. Three feet above the ground the daisy cutter detonates its 12,600-pound charge of aluminum-powder blasting slurry. If you were within two acres of the explosion and above ground or even in a barricaded bunker, you were sure to die. The infantry positions look like daisy-cutter test areas. The mouths of the dead men remain open in agony, a death scream halted. Can you hear?

I enjoy sitting in the bunkers and sifting through the dead men's effects. The Iraqis had been in these positions for months, and they made the bunkers comfortable if not formidable, with colorful blankets on the decks and nailed to the plywood roofs, pictures of family propped in shelves dug from the sand. I thumb through their letters, in Arabic, so I can't read them, but I don't need to read the script to know what it says: Please come home alive. We love you. The cause is just.

Near our bivouac, Crocket has found a corpse he particularly disagrees with. He says the look on the dead man's face, his mocking gesture, is insulting, and that the man deserved to die and now that he's dead the man's corpse deserves to be fucked with. And Crocket goes to the corpse again and again, day after day, and with his E-tool he punctures the skull and with his fixed bayonet he hacks into the torso. And he takes pictures. Johnny Rotten orders Crocket to stay away from the corpse, but he doesn't, Crocket is being driven mad by that corpse. I understand what drives Crocket to desecrate the dead soldier—fear, anger, a sense of entitlement, cowardice, stupidity, ignorance. The months of training and deployment, the loneliness, the boredom, the fatigue, the rounds fired at fake, static targets, the nights of firewatch, and finally the letdown, the easy victory that just scraped the surface of a war—all of these are frustrating and nearly unendurable facets of our war, our conflict. Did we fight? Was that combat? When compared to what we've heard from fathers and uncles and brothers about Vietnam, our entire ground war lasted as long as a long-range jungle patrol, and we've lost as many men, theater-wide, as you might need to fill two companies of grunts. Crocket—hacking at the dead Iraqi soldier and taking pictures of the waste—is fighting against our lack of satisfaction.

One morning before Crocket starts his work on the corpse—the body by now a hacked-up, rotting pile of flesh—I bury it. I use my E-tool to cover the dead man with sand. I start at his feet and build a mound that rises six or so inches above his body, and I finish at his mutilated face, the thing no longer a face, his body no longer a corpse but a monument to infinite kinds of loss.

Crocket discovers that I've buried his man, and he calls me a coward and a bitch and an Iraqi-lover. I tell him I've done everyone a favor by burying the corpse, even him, and that someday he'll be grateful I've stopped him.

He says, "Look around, the dead motherfuckers are everywhere. I'll find another one." And maybe he does.

Crocket isn't the only marine desecrating corpses, though. At company formation First Sergeant Martinez says, "Because we are U.S. marines, and honorable, we do not shoot dead men, we do not carve their skulls open with our E-tools, we do not throw grenades into a pit of corpses, and after we don't do these things, we don't take pictures of the resultant damage. If we do take pictures, and the pictures are discovered, we will be punished under the Uniform Code of Military Justice. And if we steal weapons or articles of identification or other battlefield trophies from the corpses, we will also be punished under the UCMJ. Carry on."

One morning we receive a call over the radio that our battalion is in queue for the victory lap through Kuwait City, and that if we want to join the convoy, we should meet the five-tons at such and such coordinates at 1100.

Our convoy rambles through the outskirts of the city, through the poor neighborhoods, where olive-skinned and overweight mothers clutch babies to their large breasts and with one hand wave Kuwaiti and American flags. Their homes are made of stone and held together, it seems, through the creative manipulation of plywood and nails. The only Kuwaitis we see are these women and young children. They chant, "USA, USA," and we wave, and occasionally a jarhead jumps from his truck and hugs a woman or a child while one of his buddies snaps a picture. These must also have been the neighborhoods of the expatriate workers, the workers from the PI and Malaysia and India and Egypt working for cheap with limited human rights, the people whose population, before the invasion, had nearly matched that of the nationals. These Kuwaiti women with their children aren't the ones we fought for: we fought for the oil-landed families living in the palaces deep with gold, shaded by tall and courtly palm trees. These flag-waving women are just like us, these women are our mothers, and those children dirty at the mouth with skinned and bloody knees, they are us and our sisters and our neighborhood friends.

Our convoy is not allowed to drive farther than this ghetto. We're turned around by MPs, stationed at checkpoints preventing us from entering the actual city, from driving through the neighborhoods where in the homes, the palaces, I imagine women and men are busy making lists of the assets and property stolen or vandalized during the Iraqi occupation, while they lived in five-star hotels in Cairo and London and Riyadh.

We turn around and pass the same women and children from earlier, and I assume they've been placed there by the Kuwaiti and U.S. governments, handed the flags, and told to stand in their gravel yards at certain hours while the U.S. troops pass, *and smile and wave your flags and act happy for your freedom.* Maybe I'm wrong, maybe during the occupation they stowed the U.S. flags in their kitchen cupboards, waiting for this glorious day.

One of the hero medals we'll rate will be the Kuwaiti Liberation Medal, a handsome gold medal with what looks to be palm fronds jutting from it. While most medals arrive wrapped in cardboard and plastic, the KLM will be presented in its own collectible box with hinges and a clasp. The rumors will say that the Kuwaiti government offered to pay each American service member who'd served in the region ten thousand American dollars, but the U.S. government refused, claiming the troops weren't for sale. Other rumors will surround the medal: if you pay your way to Kuwait and present your medal upon landing at the airport, untold pleasures await you, pleasures of the flesh delivered by Kuwaiti women—grapes from the vine, wine spit into your mouth from her mouth, her sisters and friends, entering all of the holes like the ancients talked about, the whole sexy deal. Also, the medal is said to be made from pure gold, with a market value of $1,000. None or all of this will be true but I will never know and never care.

After the victory lap we return to the artillery position. I've become comfortable darting in and out of the enemy bunkers, the absent presence of the enemy surrounding me—their colorful blankets and weapons and the Swedish and Russian rations they left behind, the Russian and British munitions, and the pictures of their families and their letters—I've even become comfortable with their corpses bloodied and decayed.

I enter a command position at the southern edge of the perimeter, and as I duck into the bunker, staring at the gun plan affixed to a piece of plywood—the plan drawn on green construction paper with a red felt pen so that it resembles the dark fantasy of a five-year-old boy—I feel a faint tug at my ankle, and my first thought is that someone in his final moments of death, here all these days and finally dying, has reached for me, but I realize that it is a booby trap installed by retreating soldiers. If I continue my forward motion I will trip the trap and die horribly. I realize all of this not in the length of that sentence, but in the length of my life, my life strung out thin along the wire. I stop, back away, and I stare at the goddamn trap and my stupidity and carelessness that hang from the trip wire like a bag of cheap bones. The fragmentation grenade I would've detonated is at head level, tucked into a sand pocket the size of a ripe pear, I can see in the damp sand the finger marks of the man who dug the pocket and carefully rigged the grenade. Of course, I'm familiar with grenades—intimate, even, as I have a few of my own hanging from my body—but this is the first grenade I've heard before it explodes, as though it beats like a heart. I loosely fasten a length of nylon rip cord around the trip wire. I remove the gun plan from the plywood and shove it into my cargo pocket. I back up forty feet from the embrasure, kneel in the sand, as in supplication, and yank the cord as though I'm extracting a life from out of the hole, and the bunker blows, and I own my life again.

I don't enter another bunker, and I tell the rest of the platoon they're insane if they continue the mission, that we've all been insane for ten straight days, and lucky. They seem to think it's natural that I nearly killed myself on a booby trap, but that I detected it and am now safe. No one even asks me, "Are you all right?"

The treasures in the bunkers—correspondence, a bayonet, a beret, a helmet, homemade Iraqi dog tags with the information scrawled by hand with an awl—the worthless treasures call. The platoon continues collecting relics for the same reasons Crocket puts the damage to the corpses—in order to own a part of the Desert, to further scar this landscape already littered with despair and death, and to claim and define themselves, define their histories, to confirm that they are marines, combatants, jarheads, to infuse the last seven months of their young lives with value, and to steal history from the dead Iraqi soldiers who now have nothing to remember.

For this complete absence of memory the dead men are envied their deaths, that perpetual state where they are required only to go on being dead. No other consequences exist for the corpse. The corpse suffers violence and contempt, the corpse is shot and knifed and cursed and burned, but the corpse will not suffer loneliness and despair and rage.

The captain from S-3 suggests STA get together with him and the few enlisted marines from his shop and that we all fire the weapons that STA has gathered from the enemy positions. This means the AK-47s and RPGs. We accept the captain's offer because without his support we won't be allowed to fire the weapons in the psychotic and frenzied fashion the situation requires.

Our cache holds four to five hundred AKs and three dozen RPGs.

Our targets, the disabled Iraqi weapons and vehicles, are plentiful. The captain even attempts to get one of the Iraqi tanks running so we can fire it. He spends an hour poking in and around the T-62, but he has neither the knowledge nor the tools to enable the weapon.

The Iraqi soldiers took poor care of their rifles. We've pried the weapons from the hands of dead men who hadn't performed rifle maintenance for days or weeks, but the pitiful state of the weapons— the rust, the filthy barrels, and sand-filled trigger mechanisms— encourages us to curse the men and their poor discipline. Such sloppy soldiering further decreases their stature as our former enemies.

Kuehn says, "These bastards would've gotten about two magazines off before their weapons failed. Jesus, this wasn't an army, it was a pack of assholes with some rifles."

"I haven't seen one set of cleaning gear," Martinez says. "I bet they weren't issued cleaning gear. They probably had to supply their own. This is crazy. Frontline troops with dirty weapons."

I say, "It's as though they wanted their weapons to fail."

"Their weapons didn't fail," Johnny says. "They failed their weapons."

We throw the AKs into a pile, a metal confusion of barrels and stocks and bolts. The RPGs we handle more delicately, placing them in an orderly line. The captain doesn't want us to waste our time attempting to clear failed weapons or changing magazines, and he suggests that when a weapon malfunctions or runs out of ammunition, we throw it in a discard pile. The fire will be a free-for-all; as long as you're safe and remain behind the firing line, you may shoot at anything on the other side of the firing line.

I've studied the AK for years, know its capabilities by heart, and had often assumed that the weapon would kill me in battle. But the battle is over. Now the dirty AKs look like children's toys, and I feel as though I've been fooled again, by myself and propaganda. Also, I feel like a bit of a traitor, holding the enemy's weapon, now firing the enemy's weapon, the *snap snap snap* of the firing pin piercing the shell, the projectiles screaming downrange. I don't care what I hit, in front of me there is desert, and tanks and bunkers and troop carriers and still in some of the carriers, corpses, but I fire, as next to me my platoon mates fire, from the hip, with no precision, as though we are famous and immortal and it doesn't matter that we'll likely hit nothing firing from such an absurd and unstable position, but we burn through the magazines, and when the dead click sounds, meaning the magazine has ended, or a mangle of metal occurs—bolt action stuck in the chamber, like a key stuck in a lock—because the weapon has failed, we throw the rifles aside, watching them leave our hands and land in a tumble, as though throwing aside a disturbing memory that will someday resurface. The RPGs explode with a pop. No one hits a target with an RPG, rather the rounds bounce and flail, exploding finally for nothing. We fire and fire the AKs, a factory of firepower, the fierce scream of metal downrange and discharged cartridges and sand flying everywhere, now all of us shooting in the air, shooting straight up and dancing in circles, dancing on one foot, with the mad, desperate hope that the rounds will never descend, screaming, screaming at ourselves and each other and the dead Iraqis surrounding us, screaming at ourselves and the dead world surrounding us, screaming at ourselves, at the corpses surrounding us and the dead world.

I throw my rifle onto the discard pile and run toward the Humvee, and I dive under the vehicle as the fire line continues to send a wall of metal into the air, and I weep, and I hear my screaming friends, those men I love, and I know we'll soon carry that mad scream home with us, but that no one will listen because they'll want to hear the crowd-roar of victory.

To be a marine, a true marine, you must kill. With all of your training, all of your expertise, if you don't kill, you're not a combatant, even if you've been fired at, and so you are not yet a marine: receiving fire is easy—you've either made a mistake or the enemy is better than you, and now you are either lucky or dead but not a combatant. You will receive a Combat Action Ribbon, and if unlucky enough to have been hit but not fatally, a Purple Heart, or if you're hit fatally, your mother will receive your Purple Heart, but whether you are dead or not, you haven't, with your own hands, killed a hostile enemy soldier. This means everything.

Sometimes you wish you'd killed an Iraqi soldier. Or many Iraqi soldiers, in a series of fierce firefights while on patrol, with dozens of well-placed shots from your M40A1, through countless calls for fire. During the darkest nights you'd even offer your life to go back in time, back to the Desert for the chance to kill. You consider yourself less of a marine and even less of a man for not having killed while at combat. There is a wreck in your head, part of the aftermath, and you must dismantle the wreck.

But after many years you discover that you cannot dismantle the wreck, so you move it around and bury it.

It took years for you to understand that the most complex and dangerous conflicts, the most harrowing operations, and the most deadly wars, occur in the head.

You are certain you'd be no better or worse a man if you'd killed one or all of the men you sometimes fantasize about killing. Probably, you are incorrect, and you would be insane or dead by your own hand if you'd killed one or all of those men. You would've been a great killer. You would've been a terrible killer.

If you'd killed those men, you would've told your mother, "No, I never killed anyone," and even though you have indeed killed no one and have told your mother this, still she has said, numerous times, while weeping, "I lost my baby boy when you went to war. You were once so sweet and gentle and now you are an angry and unhappy man."

Acknowledgments

Many people made this anthology.

At Thunder's Mouth Press and Avalon Publishing Group:
Thanks to Tracy Armstead, Will Balliett, Sue Canavan, Kristen Couse, Maria Fernandez, Linda Kosarin, Shona McCarthy, Dan O'Connor, Neil Ortenberg, Paul Paddock, Susan Reich, David Riedy, Simon Sullivan and Mike Walters for their support, dedication and hard work.

At The Writing Company:
Taylor Smith oversaw editorial and rights research. Nate Hardcastle and Nathaniel May took up slack on other projects.

At the Portland Public Library in Portland, Maine:
The librarians helped collect books from around the country.

Finally, I am grateful to the writers whose work appears in this book.

P e r m i s s i o n s

We gratefully acknowledge everyone who gave permission for written material to appear in this book. We have made every effort to trace and contact copyright holders. If an error or omission is brought to our notice we will be pleased to correct the situation in future editions of this book. For further information, please contact the publisher.

Excerpt from *Making the Corps* by Thomas E. Ricks. Copyright © 1997 by Thomas E. Ricks. Reprinted by permission of Scribner, an imprint of Simon & Schuster Adult Publishing Group. ❖ Excerpt from *Over There: A Marine in the Great War* by Carl Andrew Brannen. Copyright © 1996 by C.A. Brannen Estate in the United States. Used by permission of Texas A&M University Press. ❖ Excerpt from *Helmet for My Pillow* by Robert Leckie. Copyright © 1957 by Robert Hugh Leckie. Used by permission of Bantam Books, a division of Random House, Inc. ❖ Excerpt from *Semper Fi, Mac* by Henry Berry. Copyright © 1982 by Henry Berry. Reprinted by permission of HarperCollins Publishers, Inc. ❖ Excerpt from *The Good War* by Studs Terkel. Copyright © 1984 by Studs Terkel. Reprinted by permission of Donadio & Olson, Inc. ❖ Excerpt from *Flags of Our Fathers* by James Bradley with Ron Powers. Copyright © 2000 by James Bradley and Ron Powers. Used by permission of Bantam Books, a division of Random House, Inc. ❖ Excerpt from *The Long Road of War: A Marine's Story of Pacific Combat* by James W. Johnston. Copyright © 1998 by the University of Nebraska Press. Reprinted by permission of the University of Nebraska Press. ❖ Excerpt from *Goodbye, Darkness* by William Manchester. Copyright © 1979, 1980 by William Manchester. Reprinted by permission of Don Congdon Associates. ❖ Excerpt from *The Greatest Generation* by Tom Brokaw. Copyright © 1998 by Tom Brokaw. Used by permission of Random House, Inc. ❖ Excerpt from *The Coldest War* by James Brady. Copyright © 2000 by James Brady. Reprinted by permission of St. Martin's Press, LLC. ❖ Excerpt from *The Proud Bastards* by E. Michael

Bibliography

The selections used in this anthology were taken from the editions listed below. In some cases, other editions may be easier to find. Hard-to-find or out-of-print titles often are available through inter-library loan services or through Internet booksellers.

Berry, Henry. *Semper Fi, Mac: Living Memories of the U.S. Marines in World War II.* New York: Arbor House, 1982.

Bradley, James, with Ron Powers. *Flags of Our Fathers.* New York: Bantam Books, 2000.

Brady, James. *The Coldest War: A Memoir of Korea.* New York: Thomas Dunne Books, 1990.

Brannen, Carl Andrew. *Over There: A Marine in the Great War.* College Station, Texas: Texas A&M University Press, 1996.

Brokaw, Tom. *The Greatest Generation.* New York: Random House, 1998.

Helms, E. Michael. *The Proud Bastards.* New York: Zebra Books, 1990.

Johnston, James W. *The Long Road of War: A Marine's Story of Pacific Combat.* Lincoln, Nebraska: University of Nebraska Press, 1998.

Leckie, Robert. *Helmet for My Pillow.* New York: Random House, 1957.

Manchester, William. *Goodbye, Darkness: A Memoir of the Pacific War.* Boston: Little, Brown and Company, 1980.

Puller, Lewis B., Jr. *Fortunate Son.* New York: Grove Weidenfeld, 1991.

Ricks, Thomas E. *Making the Corps.* New York: Scribner, 1997.

Sager, Mike. "The Marine." Originally appeared in *Esquire,* December 2001.

Schaeffer, Frank, and John Schaeffer. *Keeping Faith: A Father-Son Story About Love and the United States Marine Corps.* New York: Carroll & Graf, 2002.

Schwartz-Nobel, Loretta. *Growing Up Empty: The Hunger Epidemic in America.* New York: HarperCollins, 2002.

Swofford, Anthony. *Jarhead.* New York: Scribner, 2003.

Sympson, Kenneth P. *Images from the Otherland.* Jefferson, North Carolina: McFarland & Company, 1995.

Terkel, Studs. *The Good War: An Oral History of World War II.* New York: Pantheon Books, 1984.

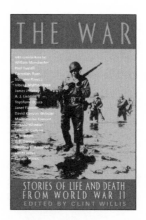
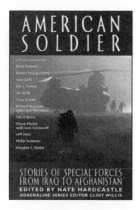
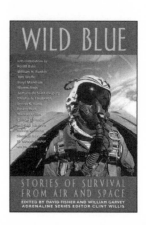

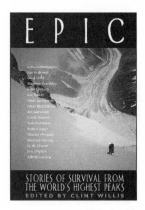

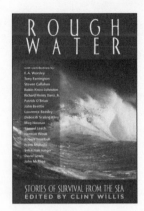
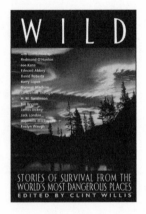